MINIDICTIONARY OF COMPUTING

MINIDICTIONARY OF COMPUTING

OXFORD UNIVERSITY PRESS
1986

Oxford University Press, Walton Street, Oxford OX2 6DP

Oxford New York Toronto
Delhi Bombay Calcutta Madras Karachi
Petaling Jaya Singapore Hong Kong Tokyo
Nairobi Dar es Salaam Cape Town
Melbourne Auckland

and associated companies in
Beirut Berlin Ibadan Nicosia

Oxford is a trade mark of Oxford University Press

British Library Cataloguing in Publication Data

Minidictionary of computing.
1. Electronic digital computers—
Dictionaries
I. Illingworth, Valerie
004'.03'21 QA76.15

ISBN 0–19–211656–8

Text prepared by
Market House Books Ltd., Aylesbury
Printed in Great Britain
at the University Printing House, Oxford
by David Stanford
Printer to the University

PREFACE

THERE has been a tremendous growth in the uses to which computers can be put and in the number of people using them. Modern life has been affected in a variety of ways, arousing a range of emotions from excitement and fascination to fear and hostility. There is, therefore, a real need and a growing desire to know more about computers and computing, about new uses, new techniques, and new equipment.

The *Minidictionary of Computing* defines and describes over 1000 terms used in computing. The entries are intended to be as informative as possible, yet easy to understand. The dictionary should thus prove valuable to those studying and teaching computing at school and college and to those who use computers at work or at home.

VALERIE ILLINGWORTH

November 1985

Compiler

Valerie Illingworth B.SC. M.PHIL.

Consultant Editor

John Illingworth B.SC. M.SC.

Head of User Services
Computing Service
University of York

GUIDE TO THE DICTIONARY

The terms defined in the dictionary are arranged in strict alphabetical order, with abbreviations and synonyms given in brackets after the headword.

Within the entries, asterisks (*) before a word or group of words indicate additional entries that the reader could consult for further information.

Words in *italics* are terms closely associated with the subject of the entry in which they appear and are therefore described here, rather than in an entry of their own.

When a term is an abbreviation, synonym, or is defined within another entry, a brief cross reference (*Abbrev. for, Another name for, See* . . .) is made to the appropriate entry.

A

abort To halt a processing activity in a computer before some planned conclusion has been reached. The activity is halted, by the *operating system or by human intervention, because a point has been reached beyond which processing cannot continue. The process may have tried to obey an undefined instruction or may have failed to obey some operating condition of the computer. It is also possible for the processing activity to bring itself to a halt when it 'realizes' that it cannot reach a successful conclusion. A human monitoring the progress of a program may terminate it because it has gone on too long, or is producing meaningless output.

ABS *See* Basic.

absolute address 1. An *address in a programming language, high-level or low-level, that identifies a storage location (or a device) without the use of any intermediate reference. *See also* relative address.

2. An address permanently assigned by the machine designer to a storage location.

3. *Another name for* machine address.

absolute addressing An *addressing mode in which an *absolute address is used in a *machine instruction in order to identify a location or device to be accessed.

access 1. To gain entry to data in a *storage device.

2. To gain entry to a computer system, e.g. by *logging on from a terminal.

3. The act or process of reading or writing data. *See also* random access; serial access.

access methods *See* file; database.

access time The time taken to retrieve a particular item of data from a storage location. This is equivalent to the time interval between an item of data being called from store and being ready to use. The access time depends on the method by which the data is accessed and on the type of storage.

There is *random access to data in *main store, and the data is available for use almost immediately: the access time of the *semiconductor memory now used for main store is typically 0.5 microsecond.

There is also random access to data on *magnetic disk *backing store, but the access time is considerably longer than for main store – typically tens of milliseconds. The access time for disk storage has two components: the time taken for the read/write head to get to a particular *track is called the *seek time*; the delay allowing an item of data in that track to become available under the read/write head is known as the *latency*, and on average is equal to half the time for a complete revolution of the disk. The time required to transfer data between disk and main store also forms part of the access time.

In the case of *magnetic tape, data is retrieved by *serial access and it may take several minutes to reach a particular storage location.

accumulator An electronic device – a *register – that acts as a temporary store in the *arithmetic and logic unit (ALU) and in which the result of an arithmetic or logic operation is formed. For example, a number (held in main store) can be added to the existing contents of the accumulator and the total would then appear in the accumulator; the addition is performed by the ALU. If, say, the number 5 is held in the accumulator and the number 12 is to be added, then the contents (which are in binary form) will change

from 00000101 to 00010001

In this case the accumulator holds 8 bits. The number of bits stored is normally equal to the *word length. In some processors there is only one accumulator. In others there are a number of general-purpose registers, any one of which can act as an accumulator.

The existing contents in an accumulator may be the result of a previous operation by the ALU, or they may have been copied into the accumulator from main store or cleared to zero. When data is copied from main store it is said to be *loaded* into the accumulator. A 'load accumulator' instruction would be required for this. Data can also be taken from an accumulator and put into a specified location in main store, this time using a 'store accumulator' instruction.

acknowledgment A means by which a device receiving transmitted data can indicate to the sending device whether the data has been correctly received or not. The receiving device returns a confirming message, known as a *positive acknowledgment*, for each block of data received correctly. When an *error is detected in a block of data, the receiver returns a *negative acknowledgment* to indicate that this block should be retransmitted by the sending device.

A failure on the part of the receiver to send an acknowledgment of either kind within a set time, or the failure of the sender to respond to an acknowledgment by sending another block in a set time, is called a *timeout, and normally results in retransmission of the last block or another acknowledgment.

acoustic coupler A device enabling binary data from, say, a portable terminal or a microcomputer to be converted into a form that can be transmitted along a telephone line. (Telephones cannot at present accept binary signals.) An ordinary telephone handset is placed in a depression in the acoustic coupler to make the connection between coupler and telephone system. The resulting telephone signal is a sequence of low- and high-pitched sounds that represent the binary 0s and 1s making up the data. An acoustic coupler also accepts such a signal from a telephone line, converting it into the corresponding data that can then be fed to a computer. The binary data is fed into and out of the acoustic coupler by cable.

Ada *Trademark* A *programming language named after Ada, Lady Lovelace, the mathematician and sometime assistant to Charles Babbage. Ada was developed as a result of a competition for a new programming language organized by the US Department of Defense in the late 1970s. It was designed to be used in *embedded systems, i.e. in situations where a computer forms part of a specialized system such as a cruise missile or a manufacturing plant. Ada is a large high-level language embodying concepts developed in earlier languages such as *Pascal, but carrying them much further. There is now an international standard for Ada.

ADC *Abbrev. for* analog to digital converter. *See* A/D converter.

A/D converter (ADC) *Short for* analog to digital converter. A device for sampling an *analog signal and converting it into an equivalent *digital signal, i.e. for converting a continuously varying signal, such as a voltage, into a series of binary values that are suitable for use by a computer. *See also* D/A converter.

adder An electronic device – a *logic circuit – that adds together two numbers. It can also subtract two numbers using two's complement arithmetic (*see* complement). The numbers are represented as binary signals that are fed into the device (*see* digital signal). The binary output represents the sum of the numbers.

A	0110
B	0100
S	1010
C	0100

Binary addition

When two binary (or decimal) numbers are added, each step of the addition generates a *sum digit*, which forms part of the answer, and a *carry digit*, which is passed to the next step. In the table, S is the sum and C the carry resulting from the addition of two binary numbers A and B, equal to 0110 (i.e. 6) and 0100 (i.e. 4). This is a type of *truth table.

Within the adder, addition is performed electronically on corresponding pairs of bits (the two least significant (leftmost) bits, the two next least significant bits, etc.). The circuitry involved in this must be able not only to add a particular pair of bits to produce a sum bit but must also be able to add the carry bit from the previous step in the addition. The sum bits together form the final answer that is output from the device. The final carry bit is discarded or is used to detect *overflow.

add-in card (add-in board) *Another name for* expansion card.

address 1. A number used to specify a *location within computer memory, usually to allow storage or retrieval of an item of information at this location. The words address and location are actually used as synonyms, as in ordinary speech. In backing store an address identifies a specific *sector on a magnetic disk or a specific *block on a magnetic tape. In main store an address identifies a particular location holding a *word or a *byte. When a location is specified it is said to be *addressed.* In some computers, processor *registers and/or *input/output devices can also be addressed.

The reference to an address appears in a *machine instruction. An instruction is normally made up of a combination of an *operation code and some way of specifying the *operand (or operands) upon which the operation is to be performed. This is commonly done by specifying the address of the operand in its actual form as determined by the computer hardware, i.e. by specifying the *machine address. Use of the machine address in an instruction allows a storage location to be accessed directly. The process is known as *direct addressing.*

Direct addressing is one of a variety of processes by

which the storage location to be accessed is determined from the machine instruction. Alternative *addressing modes are used in cases where the machine address is too large to be comfortably included in a machine instruction, or where it is not necessary or not possible to assign an explicit address.

2. The means used to specify the location of a participant in a computer *network. When a piece of information is to be carried on the network, the address is indicated by the sender and forms part of the transmitted signal.

address bus *See* bus.

addressing mode Any of various methods by which an *address can be specified in the address part of a *machine instruction. The methods include *direct addressing, *immediate addressing, *indirect addressing, and *indexed addressing, all of which are commonly available in a modern computer. Examples of these addressing modes are given in the table for a fictitious processor. The instructions all place a value into register 1; next to each instruction is a description of where the value is obtained.

address part A part of a *machine instruction that usually contains only an *address, or information on where to find or how to construct an address. There may be more than one address part in an instruction. In a *jump instruction one of the addresses may specify the location of the next instruction to be executed.

address register A *register (i.e. a temporary location) in which an *address is stored. *See also* instruction address register; memory address register.

address space *See* machine address.

AI *Abbrev. for* artificial intelligence.

Algol-60 A high-level *programming language whose name is derived from **algo**rithmic **l**anguage. It was the result of the deliberations of an international committee in the late 1950s, which culminated in the Algol-60

Report in 1960. Algol-60 was a turning point in language development since it was designed to reflect mathematical *algorithms rather than the architecture of computers. It has strongly influenced many succeeding languages such as *Pascal and *Ada. Algol-60 has always been more popular in Europe than the USA but its popularity has waned recently. The language stabilized with the issue of the Revised Algol-60 Report in 1972.

instruction	source of value
move 1, 1	the contents of location 1
move immediate 1, 1	the value 1, given in the instruction
move indirect 1, 1	the value found at the address stored at location 1
move indexed 1, 1 (2)	the value found at the address formed by adding 1 to contents of register 2
move 1, TABLE +3	the value found at the address formed by adding 3 to the value of the symbol 'TABLE'

Addressing modes

algorithm A set of simple and clearly defined instructions or steps that when followed precisely enables some operation to be performed. No personal judgments have to be made. The operation could involve, say, baking a cake, constructing a cupboard, building a house, producing business accounts, and so on. It may involve a mathematical calculation – e.g. addition, multiplication, taking a square root – or a selection process. Algorithms can be devised for a great variety of operations, ranging widely in complexity. As the complexity increases, the number of steps to be taken increases. The same operation can often be performed by different algorithms.

Algorithms are used for the solution of problems. Since they involve no personal judgment, they are suitable subjects for computers to handle. When a computer is to perform some specific task, an appropriate algorithm is selected or is specially written. It is expressed in a formal notation – a *programming language – and as such forms a major part of a computer *program. Much that is said about programs applies to algorithms, and vice versa.

The length and complexity of algorithms has been greatly extended by the advent of computers. It is necessary to verify that algorithms will perform satisfactorily the operation required of them, especially with the longer and more complicated ones. Because of the difficulty of formally proving the correctness of algorithms, this is often done by thorough *testing.

allocation *See* resource allocation; storage allocation.

alphanumeric character Any of the 26 letters of the alphabet, capital or lower case (i.e. A–Z, a–z), or any of the digits 0–9. An *alphanumeric character set* is a *character set that contains the alphanumeric characters and may in addition include some *special characters and the *space character.

ALU *Abbrev. for* arithmetic and logic unit.

amplitude *See* signal.

analog computer A computer that accepts and processes data in the form of a continuously variable quantity whose magnitude is made proportional to the value of the data. An analog computer solves problems by physical analogy, usually electrical. Each quantity (e.g. temperature, speed, displacement) that occurs in the problem is represented in the computer by a continuously variable quantity such as voltage. Circuit elements in the computer are interconnected in such a way that the voltages fed to them interact in the same way as the quantities in the real-life problem interact. The output voltage then represents the numerical solution of the problem.

Analog computers are used in situations where a continuous representation of data is more convenient or more useful than the discrete representation that is required by a *digital computer. Their major application is in *simulation, i.e. in imitating the behaviour of some existing or intended system, or some aspect of that behaviour, for purposes of design, research, etc. Another important application is *process control in industry or manufacturing, where data has to be continuously monitored.

An analog computer can be used in conjunction with a digital computer, forming what is known as a *hybrid computer*. A hybrid computer, which can process both analog and discrete data, often has advantages over an analog computer in, say, process control.

analog signal A continuously varying value of voltage or current. *Compare* digital signal.

analog to digital converter *See* A/D converter.

analogue *UK spelling of* analog, sometimes preferred in UK computer literature.

AND gate A *logic gate whose output is high only when all (two or more) inputs are high, otherwise the output is low. It thus performs the *AND operation on its inputs and has the same *truth table. The truth table for a gate with two inputs (A, B) is shown, where 0 represents a low signal level and 1 a high level.

AND operation A *logic operation combining two

A	B	output/outcome
0	0	0
0	1	0
1	0	0
1	1	1

Truth table for AND gate and AND operation

statements or formulae, A and B, in such a way that the outcome is true only if A and B are both true; otherwise the outcome is false. The *truth table is shown in the diagram, where the two truth values are represented by 0 (false) and 1 (true). The operation can be written in several ways, including

A AND B   A & B   A.B

A and B are known as the *operands and the symbol between them (AND, &, .) is a *logic operator for the AND operation.

In a computer the AND operation is used in *high-level languages to combine two logical expressions according to the rules stated above. It is used in *low-level languages to combine two *bytes or *words, producing a result by performing the AND operation on each corresponding pair of bits in turn. If 8-bit words are used, then for example with operands

01010001
11110000

the outcome of the AND operation is

01010000

See also AND gate.

annotation Explanation added to a program to assist the reader. It may take the form of handwritten additions to the program *listing, but more often is in the form of *comments included in the program text.

ANSI The American National Standards Institute, the organization that determines US industrial standards, including some used in computing, and ensures that these correspond to those set by the International Organization for Standardization, ISO.

APL A high-level *programming language whose name is derived from the words **a p**rogramming **l**anguage. It was developed by Kenneth Iverson in the early 1960s for *interactive computing, which was a new concept at the time. The advent of the microcomputer has brought it new popularity. Its main feature is its unusual *syntax, in which single character operators perform complex tasks. Unfortunately the APL *character set is quite different to other programming languages and requires special *keyboards and *hardware character generators. There is a draft international standard.

application package (software package) A set of programs directed at some application in general, such as *computer graphics, *word processing, *CAD (computer-aided design), or statistics. Application packages are often driven by a series of commands. These commands make the packages perform the specific items of their repertoires that are required in a particular situation. The commands may be quite complex and may form a *command language*, a type of specialized *high-level language.

applications-orientated language *See* high-level language.

applications program A computer *program that is written for or by the end-user or end-users of a computer system. A given computer system performs a particular role within an organization, and an applications program makes a direct contribution to performing that role and meeting the needs of the users. For example, where a computer system handles a company's finances, a payroll program would be an applications program. An applications program does not contribute to the effective use of the computer system. *Compare* systems software.

applications programmer A person who specializes in writing, developing, or maintaining *applications programs.

architecture The description of a computer system at a somewhat general level, including details of the *instruction set and *user interface, *input/output operation and control, the organization of *memory and the available *addressing modes, and the interconnection of the major units. A particular architecture may be implemented by a computer manufacturer in the form of several different machines with different performance and cost.

archive *See* file archive.

argument (actual parameter) A value or address that is passed to a *procedure, *subroutine, or *function at the time it is *called. For example, in the Basic statement

```
100    Y = SQR(X)
```

X is the argument of the SQR (square root) function. *See also* parameter.

arithmetic and logic unit (ALU) The part of the processing unit of a computer in which *arithmetic operations, *logic operations, and related operations are performed. The ALU is thus able, for example, to add or subtract two numbers, negate a number, compare two numbers, or do AND, OR, or NOT operations. The choice of operations that can be carried out by an ALU depends on the type (and cost) of the computer. The ALU is wholly electronic.

The operations are performed on items of data transferred from *main store into *registers – temporary stores – within the ALU. In some processors all arithmetic and logic *operands have to be placed in a special register called the *accumulator, while in other processors any register may be used. The result of the operation is subsequently transferred back to the main store. The movement of data between main store and ALU is under the direction of the *control unit. The arithmetic or logic operations to be performed in the ALU are specified in the operation part of *machine instructions. The control unit interprets each instruction as it is fetched from main store and directs the ALU as to which operation (if any) is required.

arithmetic instruction A *machine instruction specifying an *arithmetic operation and the *operand or operands on which the arithmetic operation is to be performed. An example, expressed in *assembly language, might be

ADDI 3,4

This is an instruction to add 4 to contents of register 3, placing the result in register 3 and setting the carry bit if the result is too big to fit.

See also logic instruction.

arithmetic/logic unit *See* arithmetic and logic unit.

arithmetic operation An operation that follows the rules of arithmetic, the most commonly occurring examples being addition, subtraction, multiplication, and division. In computing, arithmetic operations may be carried out on signed or unsigned *integers or *real numbers. They are normally performed in the *arithmetic and logic unit of a computer. *See also* arithmetic operator; operand.

arithmetic operator A symbol representing a simple arithmetic operation (e.g. addition or multiplication) that is to be performed on numerical data, quantities, etc. The operators used in a particular programming language may differ from those in general use, as shown in the table. The operations

7 multiplied by 2

6 divided by 3

would thus be written as 7*2 and 6/3 in most high-level languages including Basic. Some languages have sepa-

operation	operators	
	in general use	in Basic
addition	+	+
subtraction	–	–
multiplication	× or .	*
division	÷ or /	/
exponentiation	5^2	5 ↑ 2

Arithmetic operators

rate operators for integer division and remaindering (*see* integer arithmetic). Some languages do not have an operator for *exponentiation. Implied multiplication, as in $a(b + c)$, is not allowed in most languages.

An example of how arithmetic operators are used, in Basic, is as follows:

```
10    D = SQR((X(1) – X(0)) ↑ 2 + X(2)*3)
```

This is equivalent to

$$D = \sqrt{((X_1 - X_0)^2 + 3X_2)}$$

arithmetic shift *See* shift.

arithmetic unit *Usually, another name for* arithmetic and logic unit.

array One form in which a collection of data items can be stored in computer memory. The data items are arranged in a particular order or pattern. They are all of the same type, for example all integers or all real numbers. This collection of data items is referred to as an array. More usually, however, the word array refers to the set of storage *locations in which the data items are placed, keeping their original arrangement.

The set of locations forming an array is referenced by a single *identifier, chosen by the programmer. Each element in an array (i.e. a location or its contents) can be specified by combining one or more *subscript* values with the identifier. Subscripts are usually integers and are generally placed in brackets after the identifier. The number of subscripts required to specify an element gives the *dimension* of the array.

The simplest array is a single sequence of elements. This is a *one-dimensional array*, only one subscript being necessary to select a particular element. For example, a list of peoples' ages could form an array named AGE; the age of the eighth person in the list is found by specifying AGE(8). The subscript may be a *variable. A one-dimensional array is also known as a *vector*.

In a *two-dimensional array* (also called a *matrix*), the elements are arranged in the form of a table with a fixed number of *rows* and a fixed number of *columns*. Each element is distinguished by a pair of subscripts; the first subscript gives the row number, the second gives the column number. For example, A(3,7) refers to the element in row three and column seven of the array A. Again, the subscripts may be variables.

The values of a subscript range from a lower limit (usually 1 or 0 unless otherwise specified) to an upper limit. These limits specify the total number of elements in an array, and are called *bounds*. The bounds of an array can be declared in various ways, depending on the programming language. In Basic, for example, a DIMENSION statement is used:

```
110     DIM X(4,10)
```

This is a declaration of a two-dimensional array, X, with 5 rows and 11 columns, since the default lower bound in Basic is zero.

arrow keys Four keys on a *keyboard that are labelled with up, down, left, and right arrow symbols and can be used for control of the *cursor on a display screen.

artificial intelligence (AI) The concept or area of study concerned with the production of computer programs that perform tasks that, when done by people, require intelligence. These tasks are usually intellectual, e.g. the playing of chess and other games, the solving of problems, the formation of plans, the proving of theorems. Tasks such as seeing and hearing present greater problems. The programs can have applications in science and technology and in computer-assisted learning, and may assist in the study of the workings of the human brain. *See also* expert system; robot.

ASCII (pronounced ass-key) American National Standard Code for Information Interchange, a standard code for the interchange of information between computer systems, data communication systems, and associated equipment. Since it is a standard code (rather than one developed by a particular manufacturer), it allows equipment of different manufacturers to exchange information. It is thus widely used. ASCII encoding produces coded characters of 7 bits, and hence provides 2^7, i.e. 128, distinct bit patterns. (An 8th bit is included for a *parity check.) These 128 characters make up the ASCII *character set: they consist of *alphanumeric characters, the *space character, *special characters, and *control characters. The character set is shown in table 1, while the control characters are explained in table 2. The binary encodings shown in table 1 are for the character

$$b_7 b_6 b_5 b_4 b_3 b_2 b_1$$

Thus the encoding for G is 1000111 and the encoding for g is 1100111. *See also* ISO-7.

assembler A program that takes as input a program written in *assembly language and translates it into *machine code. Each instruction in assembly language is usually converted into one machine instruction. The input to the assembler is called the *source program*; the output is called the *object program*. The translation process is known as *assembly* and the program that is translated is said to have been *assembled*. The entire

b_4	b_3	b_2	b_1	$b_7 b_6 b_5$ = 0 0 0	0 0 1	0 1 0	0 1 1	1 0 0	1 0 1	1 1 0	1 1 1
0	0	0	0	NUL	DLE	space	0	@	P	`	p
0	0	0	1	SOH	DC1	!	1	A	Q	a	q
0	0	1	0	STX	DC2	"	2	B	R	b	r
0	0	1	1	ETX	DC3	#	3	C	S	c	s
0	1	0	0	EOT	DC4	$	4	D	T	d	t
0	1	0	1	ENQ	NAK	%	5	E	U	e	u
0	1	1	0	ACK	SYN	&	6	F	V	f	v
0	1	1	1	BEL	ETB	'	7	G	W	g	w
1	0	0	0	BS	CAN	(	8	H	X	h	x
1	0	0	1	HT	EM	)	9	I	Y	i	y
1	0	1	0	LF	SUB	*	:	J	Z	j	z
1	0	1	1	VT	ESC	+	;	K	[	k	{
1	1	0	0	FF	FS	,	<	L	\	l	|
1	1	0	1	CR	GS	–	=	M	]	m	}
1	1	1	0	SO	RS	.	>	N	^	n	~
1	1	1	1	SI	US	/	?	O	—	o	DEL

ASCII character set

NUL	null character	DLE	data link escape
SOH	start of header	DC1	device control 1
STX	start of text	DC2	device control 2
ETX	end of text	DC3	device control 3
EOT	end of transmission	DC4	device control 4
ENQ	enquiry	NAK	negative acknowledge
ACK	acknowledge	SYN	synchronous idle
BEL	bell	ETB	end of transmission block
BS	backspace	CAN	cancel
HT	horiz. tabulation	EM	end of medium
LF	line feed	SUB	substitute
VT	vert. tabulation	ESC	escape
FF	form feed	FS	file separator
CR	carriage return	GS	group separator
SO	shift out	RS	record separator
SI	shift in	US	unit separator
		DEL	delete

ASCII control characters

program must be assembled before it can be executed. *See also* compiler; interpreter.

assembly language A type of *programming language that is a readable and convenient notation (in human terms) for representing programs in *machine code. Assembly language was originally devised to alleviate the tedious and time-consuming task of writing programs actually in machine code. It may be used nowadays, in preference to a *high-level language, for reasons of speed or compactness.

Assembly language is the most commonly used *low-level language. Different forms are developed for different computers, usually by the computer manufacturers. The features of a particular assembly language thus reflect the facilities of the machine on which it is employed.

Each instruction in assembly language corresponds to a *machine instruction. The programmer can use alphabetic *operation codes with mnemonic significance (e.g. LDA is commonly used for 'load accumulator'), and can use symbolic names, personally chosen, for *addresses of storage locations or registers (*see* symbolic addressing). *Addressing modes can also be expressed in a convenient way. In addition assembly language allows the use of various number systems (e.g. *decimal, *octal, *hexadecimal notation) for numerical constants, and allows the programmer to attach *labels to lines of the program.

A program known as an *assembler translates the assembly language program into machine code. It can then be executed by the computer.

assignment statement A program *statement that assigns a new value to a *variable. Each variable is associated with a particular *location or group of locations in memory. An assignment statement will thus cause a new value to be placed at the appropriate storage location(s). The assignment statement is fundamental to most programming languages. It is indicated by a special symbol, such as = or :=. This is called the *assignment operator*. The symbol used depends on the language.

The expression on the right of the assignment operator is given to the variable whose name appears on the left. If, say, the value of a variable C is to be increased by one, this is expressed in Basic and Fortran as

C = C + 1

and in Pascal and Algol as

C := C + 1;

and is read as C becomes C + 1. In a program *flowchart the symbol ← is often used to indicate an assignment, as in

C ← C + 1

associative store (content-addressable store) A storage device in which a *location is identified by what is in it rather than by its position. The location contains a particular item of data – a *search word* – for which a search can be conducted by the storage device. This can be achieved in various ways. The desired data in the location is in close association or proximity to the search word. Associative stores are used, for example, as part of a *virtual storage facility.

asynchronous Involving or requiring a form of timing control in which a specific operation is begun on receipt of a signal to indicate that the preceding operation has been completed. Operations do not therefore occur at regular or predictable times. *Compare* synchronous.

asynchronous transmission A form of transmission in which data is sent as it becomes available. The time at which the start of transmission occurs is arbitrary, although the rate at which the bits comprising the data are subsequently transmitted is fixed.

Atlas *See* second generation computers.

audit trail A record showing the occurrence of specified events relevant to the *security of a computer system. For example, an entry might be made in an audit trail whenever a user logs on or accesses a file. Examination of the audit trail may detect attempts at violating the security of the system – by, say, unauthorized reading or writing of data in a file – and help to identify the culprit.

availability The actual *available time expressed as a percentage of planned available time. Any shortfall will be due to faults or breakdowns. In a modern computer system an availability that is not in the high nineties (say less than 98%) is cause for concern.

available time The amount of time in a given period that a computer system can be used by its normal users. During this period the system must be functioning correctly, have power supplied to it, and not be undergoing repair or maintenance.

B

backend A program that is used to convert output from a general-purpose program into a specific form. For example, a graphics program might produce picture information in a quite general form, which is then processed by a backend specific to the sort of output device required. There would be a different backend for each device – plotter, VDU, graphics printer, etc.

background processing The processing of computer programs with a low priority at times when programs with a high priority are not using the computer. The low-priority programs are called *background programs* while the high-priority programs are known as *foreground programs*. Background programs are submitted by users from terminals but are not processed immediately. They are placed in a *background queue* and are executed when resources – main store, processor, etc. – become available. During background processing there is no opportunity for interaction between user and computer. Background processing is similar to and often referred to as *batch processing. Background processing together with *foreground processing takes place in many *multiaccess systems.

backing store (backing storage) Storage devices in which programs and data are kept when not required by the *processor (or processors) of a computer. Programs can only be executed, however, when they are in the computer's *main store. A program plus associated data is therefore copied from backing store into main store when required. The storage *capacity of main store is much smaller than the capacity available as backing store. Only the program that is currently being executed is (or needs to be) in main store. The use of backing store means that a computer has access to a large repertoire of programs and to large amounts of data, and can call on these as and when it needs them.

The time taken to retrieve a particular item from backing store and transfer it directly into main store must be brief. *Random access to these items is thus necessary rather than *serial access. *Magnetic disks – *hard and *floppy – provide random access and are extensively used for on-line backing storage. *Magnetic tapes are serial-access devices and are therefore used as off-line backing store. Programs and data can be transferred from tape to disk for processing, or can be copied from disks to tape.

backup A file, device, or system that can be used as a substitute in the event of a loss of data, development of a fault, etc. A backup file, for example, is a copy of a file that is taken in case the original is unintentionally altered or destroyed and the data lost. It is not stored *on-line. A floppy disk may be copied for the same reason. When a copy is made it is said to *back up* the original version. *See also* dump.

Backus-Naur form *See* BNF.

band printer *See* line printer.

bar code A pattern of parallel lines of variable width and spacing that provides coded information about the item on which it appears. The codes are read by relatively simple equipment, known as *bar-code readers*, using optical or magnetic sensing techniques. Bar codes are found, for example, on goods sold in supermarkets, where they are used to identify the product and its cost at the checkout point and to update stock and sales records. They are also used in library books for identification purposes.

barrel printer (drum printer) *See* line printer.

base (radix) The number of distinct digits (and possibly letters) used in a particular *number system. *Decimal notation has base 10, *binary notation has base 2, *octal notation has base 8; the digits used in these three systems are 0–9, 0 and 1, and 0–7 respectively. *Hexadecimal notation has base 16 and uses the digits 0–9 and the six letters A–F. The base of a number can be indicated by means of a subscript, as in

101_{10}, i.e. 101 in decimal notation
101_2, i.e. 101 in binary notation, i.e. 5_{10}

base address, base address register *See* relative address.

Basic A group of similar high-level *programming languages whose name is derived from the words **b**eginners **a**ll-purpose **s**ymbolic **i**nstruction **c**ode. The original Basic was developed in the mid-1960s for *interactive computing, which was a new concept at the time. Since then many computer manufacturers have developed their own dialects, and the emergence of the microcomputer has increased the diversification to the point where Basic is now often extremely difficult to move from one computer to another. An ANSI standard defines a minimal subset of Basic; a more complete standard is in preparation.

Basic is a simple language, is easy to learn, and is of particular importance to beginners. It allows easy modification of programs since the program text is kept in main store during execution. Basic is normally interpreted although it may also be compiled (*see* interpreter, compiler).

All dialects of Basic should include the following components:

REM introduces a *comment line;
INPUT performs input from the keyboard or a file;
READ performs input from a DATA statement elsewhere in the program;
DATA introduces a line of data values;
PRINT performs output to the screen or a file;
IF introduces an *if then else statement;
FOR introduces a *loop;
NEXT terminates a *loop;
LET introduces an *assignment statement – may usually be omitted;
DIM declares *arrays;
GOSUB calls a *subroutine;
RETURN returns from a *subroutine to the statement after the GOSUB;
STOP halts execution of the program;
END indicates the end of the program text;
SQR square root function;
INT function truncating real numbers to integers – the fraction is discarded;
ABS function returning the absolute value of a number, i.e. without a sign;
SGN function returning –1 for negative numbers and 1 for positive numbers.

Apart from these components there are many statements and commands that occur in some dialects and not in others, and some that mean entirely different things in different dialects.

batch processing A method of organizing work for a computer in which items of work are queued up, and the *operating system takes one job at a time from the queue and processes it. Each job must be entirely self-contained – it must not require any intervention from the person who submitted it. This is because the order in which the jobs are run is at the discretion of the operating system, which will take into account the estimated time to run the job and its demands on resources such as main store or tape drives. If a job is particularly large it may not be run until the middle of the night.

Originally batch processing involved feeding *punched cards into the computer's card reader, where the cards comprising one or more separate jobs were called a *batch*. Nowadays work is submitted to the *batch queue* by creating on backing store a file containing the commands necessary to perform the desired task. The operating system puts the file into the batch queue and eventually retrieves it and obeys the commands. *See also* background processing.

baud A unit for measuring the speed at which *signals travel in a computer or in a communication system such as a telephone link. One baud is normally assumed to be equal to one *bit per second, the signal being a sequence of the binary digits 0 and 1. One baud may however be equal to one symbol per second or one digit per second. In general the baud is equal to the number of times per second that the signalling system changes state. Signalling speeds can vary from a few thousand baud (for say the link between a terminal and a computer) up to tens or hundreds of millions of baud (for, say, data transmission by satellite).

BCD *Abbrev. for* binary coded decimal.

benchmark A way in which the performance of computer systems – hardware and software – can be compared. It is normally in the form of a specially designed test or problem. For example, a system may be subjected to a known workload and the time taken to complete it is measured; this time can then be compared with the times achieved by other systems. The systems are said to have been *benchmarked*. A *multiuser system may be benchmarked by another computer simulating the action of tens or hundreds of individual users all going through a predetermined sequence of actions.

When using a benchmark to evaluate two or more computer systems, it is important that a prospective purchaser uses a benchmark that reflects the sort of use to which the system will be put.

bidirectional printer *See* character printer.

binary code A rule for transforming data, program instructions, or other information into a symbolic form in which only the two binary digits 0 and 1 are used. Once encoded there is no way of distinguishing an instruction from a piece of data. The process of transforming letters, digits, and other characters into sequences of binary digits is called *binary encoding*, and the representation used or produced is called a *binary encoding*. The *binary notation used to represent numbers in a computer is a binary encoding. The representation of characters using, for example, the *ASCII scheme is another example. *See also* code.

binary coded decimal (BCD) A *code by which each decimal digit, 0, 1, 2, . . ., 9 is transformed into a

decimal digit	0	1	2	3	4
BCD code	0000	0001	0010	0011	0100
decimal digit	5	6	7	8	9
BCD code	0101	0110	0111	1000	1001

Binary coded decimal

particular group of 4 binary digits (or bits). In the standard form of BCD, each decimal digit is represented by the group of 4 bits whose value is equivalent to the decimal digit, as shown in the table. The decimal number 58.271 would thus be coded

0101 1000.0010 0111 0001

The form of a decimal number in BCD is usually different from its representation in *binary notation.

binary digit Either of the two digits 0 and 1. *See* bit.

binary encoding *See* binary code.

binary fractions Binary fractions are usually handled in *floating-point notation. They can however be represented in *fixed-point notation, e.g. .0101 or 11.101,

.6875		.3750		.7500		.5000
2		2		2		2
——	→	——	→	——	→	——
1.3750		0.7500		1.5000		1.0000
↓		↓		↓		↓
leftmost bit						rightmost bit

Conversion of decimal fraction .6875 to binary equivalent, .1011

where the positional value decreases from left to right by powers of 2: the leftmost bit after the point has the value 2^{-1} (i.e. ½ or 0.5), the next bit to the right having the value 2^{-2} (i.e. ¼ or 0.25), and so on. The fraction .011 therefore has the value

$$(0 \times 2^{-1}) + (1 \times 2^{-2}) + (1 \times 2^{-3})$$

The decimal conversion is thus

$$.25 + .0625 = .3125$$

Conversion of a decimal fraction to binary is shown

in the table. It is done by repeated multiplication by 2, the bit resulting before the point being removed to form the bits of the binary fraction. The process is continued until a zero fraction is obtained or the required accuracy is obtained. *See also* binary notation.

binary logic 1. The electronic components used in a computer system to carry out *logic operations on binary variables (i.e. quantities that can take either of two values). The components consist of *logic gates and *logic circuits.

2. The methods and principles underlying this implementation of logic operations.

binary notation (binary system) The number system employed in computing to represent numbers internally. It uses the two digits 0 and 1 and thus has a *base 2. These digits are known as *binary digits* (or *bits*), and a *binary number* is composed of a sequence of bits, e.g. 1001. Like decimal notation the binary system is a positional notation: the value of a binary number depends not only on the bits it contains but also on their position in the number. The positional value increases from right to left by powers of 2. For example, the binary number 10100 has the value

$$1 \times 2^4 + 0 \times 2^3 + 1 \times 2^2 + 0 \times 2^1 + 0 \times 2^0$$

Conversion from binary to decimal can thus be achieved by multiplying each bit in the number by the relevant power of 2 (the least significant (rightmost) bit having a positional value of 2^0, i.e. 1), and adding them together. The above binary number, 10100, is thus equivalent to the decimal number 20.

Conversion from decimal to binary is achieved by repeated division of the decimal number by 2. The sequence of remainders forms the bits of the binary number, the first remainder being the least significant bit, and so on. Division stops when the quotient becomes 0. The table shows the steps in such a conversion. *See also* binary fractions; floating-point notation.

binary number *See* binary notation.

$23 \div 2 = 11$	remainder 1 (rightmost bit)
$11 \div 2 = 5$	remainder 1
$5 \div 2 = 2$	remainder 1
$2 \div 2 = 1$	remainder 0
$1 \div 2 = 0$	remainder 1 (leftmost bit)

Conversion of decimal 23 to binary equivalent, 10111

binary operator (dyadic operator) *See* operator.

binary representation (bit representation) The representation used within a computer for numbers, *characters, and *machine instructions, and having the form of distinctive sequences of the two *bits 0 and 1. *See also* binary code; binary notation; complement; floating-point notation; character set.

binary search *See* searching.

binary signal *See* digital signal.

binary system Any system involving just two possible values, two alternatives, or two items. One example is the binary number system, i.e. *binary notation, in which numbers are represented by means of the two digits 0 and 1. These two digits are known as *bits. They are used in computing not only in binary notation but to represent the two possible values, alternatives, etc., of any binary system or situation, including the two possible directions of magnetization of a spot on a magnetic disk or tape, the presence or absence of a hole in a paper tape, or a low or high signal fed to a logic gate. A bit represents the smallest unit of storage and hence of information in the binary system.

binary tree *See* tree.

bind 1. To assign values to the *parameters used in a procedure, subroutine, or function at the time that the procedure, subroutine, or function is *called; this binding remains in force throughout the call.

2. To associate the *variables used in a program in a *high-level language, or the symbolic addresses or labels used in a program in *assembly language, with particular *addresses in computer memory.

bipolar technology *See* integrated circuit.

bistable *Another name for* flip-flop.

bit *Short for* binary digit. Either of the two digits 0 and 1 used in computing for the internal representation of numbers, *characters, and *machine instructions. The bit is the smallest unit of information and of storage in any *binary system within a computer. *See also* binary notation.

bit density *See* density.

bit rate The number of *bits transmitted or transferred per unit of time. The unit of time is usually the second; the bit rate is then the number of bits per second, or *bps* in abbreviated form.

bit representation *Another name for* binary representation.

bit string A *string of *bits, e.g. 0111.

black box A self-contained unit in, for example, a computer system or a communications system, whose function can be understood without any knowledge or reference to its electronic components or circuitry. The notion of a black box is useful to someone with little or no electronics training who is trying to find out, say, what a particular peripheral device does.

block A group of *records that a computer can treat as a single unit during transfers of data to or from *backing store. This unit of transfer is sometimes called a *physical record*. The data records in the block are then called *logical records*. The number of data records, i.e. logical records, in a block is called the *blocking factor*. Blocks have either a fixed length or a variable length.

A stream of data to be recorded on magnetic tape is

divided into blocks, and is subsequently read block by block (*see* tape unit). Successive blocks are separated by *interblock gaps (IBGs)* in which nothing is recorded. Recording in blocks is used for convenience in handling the tape and for error management: any errors occurring in the recording and reading of data are dealt with block by block. The equivalent recording subdivision on a magnetic disk is a *sector.

block diagram A diagram that represents graphically the interconnection between elements of a computer system. The elements may range from electric circuits to major units of hardware. They are shown as labelled rectangles or other geometric figures, and are connected by lines. The whole diagram can represent any level of description, from an electric circuit to an overall computer system.

blocking factor *See* block.

BNF *Abbrev. for* Backus-Naur form. A symbolic notation in which the *syntax of a programming language can be expressed.

board *Short for* circuit board or printed circuit board.

Boolean algebra An extension of the principles of algebra into the field of logic. It was first put forward in 1847 by the English mathematician George Boole and is now of particular importance in computing. Boole applied the methods of algebra to problems in logic involving statements and conclusions that can be given a truth value – either *true* or *false* – and thus have a binary nature. These true or false expressions can be combined by the logical operations *and* and *or* and negated by the operation *not* to give a conclusion whose truth or falsity can be determined from the rules of Boolean algebra.

Boolean algebra is basic to many aspects of computing. For example it is used in high-level languages in conditional statements:

IF NOT(a < b) AND (x = 0) THEN . . .

or logical assignments and expressions:

answer := (char = 'Y') OR (char = 'y')

It is also used in the design of the electronic circuits – *logic gates and *logic circuits – that control the flow of signals. *See also* truth table; Boolean expression.

Boolean expression (logical expression) An expression that is formed according to the laws of *Boolean algebra. It contains variables that take the values *true* or *false* and that are linked by *logic operators. An example is

a AND (b OR NOT c)

a, b, and c are variables or expressions (such as x > 1) that return the values *true* or *false*; AND, OR, and NOT are operators. A Boolean expression can be used to form a *function whose value is either *true* or *false* depending on the combination of values assigned to the variables. This function is known as a *Boolean function* or *logical function*. A Boolean function can be represented in a *truth table. It can also be transformed into a *logic diagram of logic gates.

Boolean function *See* Boolean expression.

boot (boot up) *See* bootstrap.

bootstrap In general, a means or technique enabling a system to bring itself into some desired state. The word is used in several ways in computing. Most commonly, a bootstrap is a short program whose function is to load another longer program into a computer. For example, when a computer is first switched on its *main store will be empty except for those parts fabricated in *ROM (read-only memory). A bootstrap stored in ROM is capable of reading from backing store (which is *non-volatile) the *operating system, or some part of it, without which the computer cannot operate. The computer is then said to be *booted up* or *booted*, and a program can then be loaded into the machine.

bounds of an array. *See* array.

bpi *Abbrev. for* bits per inch. *See* density.

bps *Abbrev. for* bits per second. *See* bit rate.

branch 1. *Another name for* jump.

2. A set of instructions that are executed between two *branch instructions.

branch instruction A *machine instruction that controls the selection of one set of instructions from a number of alternative sets during the execution of a program. A branch instruction is usually regarded as being the same thing as a jump instruction. *See* jump.

breadboard A *circuit board on which experimental arrangements of electronic components can be built and tried out. The arrangements can be easily modified.

breakpoint A point in a program at which execution is halted temporarily. An examination can then be made of the values of program *variables at that point. Breakpoints may sometimes be conditional – execution only pauses if certain conditions are true. There may be a count involved so that the breakpoint only operates after it has been passed a certain number of times. *See also* debugging.

bubble memory A type of memory in which data in binary form is represented by the presence or absence of minute magnetized regions (*bubbles*) within an oppositely magnetized magnetic material. Magnetic fields are used to form the bubbles and to move them along a path through the surface of the stationary magnetic medium. Bubble memory is a form of *serial-access memory but the data path is constructed so that the *access time to a particular data item is very short. It is usually *nonvolatile and can store a huge number of bits (typically one million) in a very small area. Having no moving parts it is more rugged than magnetic disk. As yet, however, it has only found limited application.

bubble sort *See* sorting.

buffer 1. A temporary store for data in transfer, normally used to compensate for the difference in the rates at which two devices can handle data during a transfer. It allows the two devices to operate independently, without the faster device being delayed by the slower device. Buffers generally form part of the *main store of a computer, holding data that is awaiting processing or is awaiting transfer to a magnetic disk or an output device such as a printer or a VDU. A buffer may also be built into a peripheral device: many printers have a buffer to compensate for the relatively slow speed of printing compared with the speed with which the information to be printed is received.

2. Any device, circuit, etc., that is inserted between two other devices to compensate for differences in operating speeds, in timing, in voltage levels, etc. For example, in a tape unit a short but varying length of magnetic tape is maintained as a buffer between the tape reels and the capstan driving the tape past the read and write heads. It compensates for differences in acceleration at the reels and at the capstan.

bug An *error in a program or a system. It is usually a localized error occurring when a working version of the program or system is being produced, rather than an error introduced during design. *See also* debugging.

bulletin board A general facility on a computer *network allowing any user of the network to leave messages that can be read by all the other users. This can be contrasted with *electronic mail messages, which are read only by the addressees. Bulletin boards are popular among amateur computer enthusiasts and may be found on public data networks such as *Prestel.

bureau An independent agency providing computer services to the public. It offers both software and hardware facilities. The user usually simply supplies the input data for a specified job, such as payroll or bookkeeping, and pays for the results.

burster A device that separates into sheets *continuous stationery produced as output from a *printer. The paper is split at the perforations across its width. With multipart stationery a burster frequently also acts as a *decollator, separating the copies and possibly sorting them into stacks and removing the interleaved carbon paper. A burster may also trim the edges of the stationery, removing the ragged edges left by the perforations and the sprocket holes down each side.

bus A set of conducting wires – a pathway – connecting several components of a computer and allowing the components to send *signals

C

C A *programming language developed in the early 1970s by Denis Ritchie at Bell Laboratories in the USA for systems development, and in particular for writing the operating system *UNIX in order to make it *portable. C has the *control structures usually found in *high-level languages but has features that make it suitable for writing *systems software. Its popularity is increasing with the spread of the UNIX operating system, but it is by no means confined to UNIX machines.

cache memory (cache) Extremely fast *semiconductor memory that is used in high-performance computer systems in association with *main store. Its *access time is much shorter than that of main store and it is therefore used to increase the accessibility to data required by the processor. It is a temporary store, i.e. a *buffer, that is continually updated so that it contains the most recently accessed contents of main store.

When the processor requires an instruction not currently in the cache, then a whole block of memory (size depends on the particular system) is copied from main store into the cache; the next instructions for execution are then likely to be in the cache as well as the one currently required. This is a very successful strategy and significantly increases execution speeds. The contents of a cache may be modified by the program, so it will be necessary to copy them back into main store before refilling the cache with another block.

CAD (computer-aided design) The application of computer technology to the design of a product. CAD is used especially in architecture and electronic, electrical, mechanical, and aeronautical engineering. Designs can be created by computer using information fed in by experts and also acquired from other sources, for example specifications of component sizes or building regulations. During the design process the design itself is displayed on a screen and can be tested and modified by the technical designer. Dialogue between designer and computer is displayed on a separate screen. The computer can analyse various characteristics of the design, the results being fed back to the designer. The final design is normally drawn by a flatbed *plotter, with design specifications, etc., listed on printout.

The CAD output, the design of, say, a *printed circuit board, may then be passed to other systems for computer-aided manufacture (CAM) and computer-aided testing (CAT). The combined process of computer-aided design and manufacture is known as *CAD-CAM*. The whole procedure – computer-aided design, manufacture, and testing – is often referred to as *CADMAT*.

CADCAM *See* CAD.

CADMAT *See* CAD.

CAI *Abbrev. for* computer-aided or -assisted instruction. *See* CAL.

CAL *Abbrev. for* computer-assisted learning. Any use of computers to aid or support the education and training of people. CAL can test attainment at any point, provide faster or slower routes through the material for people of different aptitudes, and can maintain a progress record for the instructor.

This application is also known as *CBL (computer-*

based learning), *CAI (computer-aided* or *-assisted instruction)*, and *CMI (computer-managed instruction)*.

calculator An electronic device that can perform simple arithmetic, and often other operations, on numbers entered from a keyboard. Final solutions and intermediate numbers are generally presented on *LCD or *LED displays. Present-day calculators range from very cheap devices that can add, subtract, multiply, and divide numbers to those that can perform complex mathematical and statistical operations and may be programmed. Add-on memory modules containing specialist programs – for navigation, say – can be used with the more expensive calculators, as can small printers. The dividing line between sophisticated calculators and small microcomputers is no longer clear-cut.

call An action whereby a program or a section of a program – a *procedure, *subroutine, or *function – is brought into effect. Control is transferred to the *entry point of this program or program section, causing the program or program section to be immediately executed by the computer. The program or program section is said to have been *called*. The program that issued the call is the *calling program*.

A piece of code, known as the *calling sequence*, is required to perform a call. The calling sequence includes some means of passing the necessary data to the program or program section (*see* parameter), and of returning control to the calling program following execution of the program or program section. When a whole program is to be called this is done by the *operating system, to which control is returned after execution together with an indication of the success or failure of the program.

calling program *See* call.

calling sequence *See* call.

capacity (storage capacity) The amount of information that can be held in a storage device. It is usually measured in *bytes or in *bits. For example, the capacity of a *floppy disk can be more than one million bytes, i.e. one megabyte (1 M byte), while the capacity of a *Winchester disk used on a large mainframe computer can be over one thousand million bytes, i.e. over one gigabyte (1 G byte). Again, the capacity of *main store may be up to one megabyte in smaller computers and up to 64 megabytes on larger systems.

card 1. A *printed circuit board, often of a fairly small size.

2. *See* punched card.

card punch A device that encodes data by punching holes in cards. It can be operated by hand using a keyboard – and is then known as a *keypunch* – or it can be operated by signals from a computer. *See* punched card.

card reader A device that reads data encoded on cards and converts it into binary code for processing by a computer. The data is represented by magnetic patterns in, say, a *magnetic stripe on a plastic card or by patterns of holes in a *punched card.

cartridge A removable module containing a magnetic tape, magnetic disk, integrated circuitry, printer ink ribbon, or some other computer-related device. It is usually designed so that the contents remain permanently inside the cartridge (or attached to it) and are not handled by the operator. The modular form thus protects and facilitates the use of the contents. *See also* tape cartridge; disk cartridge; ROM cartridge.

case statement A conditional *control structure that appears in many programming languages and allows a selection to be made between several choices; the choice is dependent on the value of some expression. For example, Pascal has

```
case expression of
   selector 1: choice 1
   selector 2: choice 2
```

selector 3: choice 3

...

end

If the expression evaluates to one of the selector values, then that choice is executed. Standard Pascal does not define what happens if the expression matches no selector.

The case statement is a more general structure than the *if then else statement, which allows a choice between only two alternatives. It can in fact be written in the form of a *nested if:

if ... then ...
else if ... then ...
    else if ... then ... (and so on)

A case statement could be used in selecting, say, a month in the year or one age group out of six age groups. It is often employed in programming *menus. A similar control structure appears in some other languages as a *switch statement.

cassette A container holding *magnetic tape and from which the tape is not normally removed. The casing protects the tape and makes it easier to handle. The tape is 4 mm (0.15 inches) wide and of various lengths, and is wound between two small reels. The cassettes used in computing are either standard audio cassettes or cassettes usually of similar dimensions to audio cassettes but made with greater precision.

Cassettes are used in the cheaper versions of domestic computers, and are employed for data storage in, say, *point-of-sale terminals. Information is recorded on and retrieved from the tape by means of a type of *tape unit similar to an ordinary domestic cassette player; the read and write heads protrude through slots in the cassette to make contact with the tape. Cassettes are cheaper than *floppy disks but transfer data very much slower and have lower storage capacities. *See also* tape cartridge.

cathode-ray tube (CRT) *See* display.

CBL *Abbrev. for* computer-based learning. *See* CAL.

CCD memory A type of *semiconductor memory that is particularly suited to applications where data is accessed in a serial manner. It is composed of tiny electronic elements called *charge-coupled devices (CCDs)*, each of which acts essentially like a *shift register that can store several hundred bits of data. CCD memory is slower than comparable *RAM but faster than magnetic *backing store.

Ceefax *Trademark* The British Broadcasting Corporation's *teletext service.

cell A *location in memory or a *register. It is usually capable of holding a single item of information in binary form such as an integer or instruction, but may hold only a single bit.

central processor (central processing unit, CPU) The principal operating part of a computer. It consists of the *arithmetic and logic unit and the *control unit, i.e. the units in which program instructions are interpreted and executed. Sometimes *main store is considered a component of the central processor.

Over the past decade, the functions in the larger or more complex computers have become distributed among various units, each able to handle one or more tasks quite independently. In these systems the term central processor (or central processing unit) is inappropriate, and the word *processor (or processing unit) is used.

chad The piece of paper, plastic, etc., that is removed when a hole is punched in a data medium. For example, the punching of sprocket holes along the edges of continuous stationery produces chad. Large quantities of chad were produced when punching cards and paper tape.

chaining 1. An arrangement whereby one item in a sequence contains the means for locating the next item. For example, a *file may be organized such that each entry contains the *address of the next entry in a sequence. The entries can then be dispersed randomly within a storage device. One particular entry may belong to more than one sequence.

2. A technique whereby the final action of a program is to load its successor into main store. For example, a suite of demonstration programs could be chained together with the last one chaining to the first, thus providing a continuous demonstration.

chain printer *See* line printer.

channel A route along which information can be sent. It may for instance be a telephone link between two computers or a cable connecting a terminal to a computer. It may also be the route followed by data between a user's program and a file on backing store.

character A symbol used in representing data and in organizing and possibly controlling data. A character may be one of the 26 letters of the alphabet, one of the digits 0–9, a punctuation mark, bracket, plus sign, etc. Note that **A** and **a** are different characters, and that a computer distinguishes between the capital letter **O** and zero, **0**, and between the lower case letter **l** and one, **1**. *See also* character set; byte.

character encoding 1. The process of transforming letters, digits, and other characters into an encoded form. *See* code.

2. The symbolic representation used for the characters in a given *character set when encoding them. The symbols are usually the two binary digits 0 and 1. *ASCII and *EBCDIC are two widely used character encoding schemes.

character printer A *printer that produces a single character at a time, printing them in the order in which they appear in a line. Printing rates of 200 characters per second (cps) can be attained. Most printers are now *bidirectional*: the printing mechanism – known as the *print head* – prints as it moves from left to right along one line and then prints on the following line as it returns from right to left; this increases printing speed. *Logic seeking* is used in many designs; this increases productivity when printing other than full lines by making the head move at high speed over areas that are to remain blank.

Character printers can be either impact or nonimpact printers (*see* printer), the *daisywheel printer being an example of the former and the *thermal printer an example of the latter. In addition, printers can be either matrix or solid-font printers (*see* printer).

character recognition *See* OCR; MICR. *See also* OMR; document reader.

, ; : . ? !

( ) [ ] { }

" ' # % & | \

+ − * / > < =

Typical special characters used in a character set

character set A collection of different *characters that can be used for some purpose. A very simple example is the letters of the alphabet. The characters that are valid within a given programming language also form a set. Yet another example is the collection of characters that a computer can handle. This latter set would have to include the characters of the one or more programming languages used on the computer.

The character set handled by a particular computer usually includes the *alphanumeric characters (letters and digits), together with the *space character, *special characters, and *control characters. Typical special characters are shown in the table; they include punctuation marks, brackets, and the symbols used in *arithmetic and *logic operations. The alphanumeric, space, and special characters are known as graphic or printable characters, i.e. they are symbols that can be produced by printing, writing, etc. In contrast the control characters each produce a particular effect, such as a new line or backspace.

Within a computer all these characters must be represented in binary form. There are two widely used encoding schemes for characters; these are *EBCDIC, used on IBM machines, and *ASCII, which is in more general use. The 128 different bit patterns used in ASCII and the 256 used in EBCDIC are themselves character sets.

character string *See* string.

check A process for validating the accuracy of an item of information, which may be a piece of data or part of a program. It is thus a means of detecting *errors. A check is performed, for example, following the transfer of the item to or from a magnetic disk or tape, following its transmission across a computer network, or following its computation.

A single *check digit* may be used in performing the check. This digit is added to one end of the item of information when it is encoded, and is derived arithmetically from the digits making up the item. It can be used subsequently to determine whether the item contains an error (or errors). In some cases a group of characters may be used to perform a check rather than a single digit. *See also* parity check; modulo-*n* check.

check digit *See* check; modulo-*n* check.

checkpoint A point in some processing activity, or a place in a program, at which a *dump – a copy – is taken of data associated with the active program. It is hence the point or place from which the program can subsequently be *restarted. The use of checkpoints guards against system failure during very long program executions: if anything goes wrong, the execution can be continued from the last checkpoint once repairs have been made. The frequency of checkpoints depends on the reliability of the system.

checksum *Another name for* modulo-*n* check.

chip 1. A small section of a single crystal of semiconductor, usually silicon, that forms the substrate (i.e. base) on which an *integrated circuit is fabricated.

2. *Informal name for* integrated circuit.

chip socket A device to allow easy replacement of chips (*integrated circuits) on a *printed circuit board. The chip socket is soldered to the circuit board and the chip is pushed into the socket, which has a small hole for each of the chip's legs. With larger chips care is needed to avoid bending the legs of the chip on insertion.

cipher, ciphertext *See* cryptography.

CIR *Abbrev. for* current instruction register.

circuit board A rigid board of insulating material on which an electric circuit has been or can be built. The term is commonly used to refer to a *printed circuit board. Circuit boards come in a variety of sizes, some of which are standardized.

circular shift *See* shift.

clear 1. To set the contents of a register, counter, or storage location to zero.

2. To erase all the characters from a VDU screen, leaving it blank.

clock An electronic device (normally a quartz oscillator) that provides a series of pulses at extremely regular intervals of time. The interval between successive pulses, i.e. their rate of repetition, is known as the *clock rate*. In computers the clock rate is measured in megahertz, i.e. there are at least one million pulses per second.

Because of its constant rate, the signal from a clock is used to synchronize related pieces of computer equipment. Their operations can therefore be controlled so that events take place in sequence at fixed times. For example, clock pulses can be fed to all the *flip-flops in a computer, causing them to change state at the beginning (or the end) of each clock pulse. The primary clock rate controls the fastest parts of the computer, while slower components are timed by numerous submultiples of this rate.

clock rate *See* clock.

cluster A group of terminals, magnetic tapes, etc., whose operations are under the control of a master device, known as a *cluster controller*. Data will be exchanged between the cluster controller and a (possibly distant) computer along a single pathway, the controller having the task of then directing the data to the correct member of the cluster.

CMI *Abbrev. for* computer-managed instruction. *See* CAL.

CMOS *Abbrev. for* complementary metal oxide semiconductors. A family of *logic circuits that are all fabricated with a similar structure by the same *integrated-circuit techniques. They are a type of MOS technology and are characterized by very low power requirements. Compared with *TTL and *ECL they have high *packing densities but low *switching speeds.

coaxial cable (coax) An electric cable having two or more conducting paths, one conducting path being surrounded by but insulated from another conducting path, which may in turn be surrounded by and insulated from a third conductor (and so on). The outermost cable is often earthed. Coaxial cable provides a continuous path along which electrical signals (usually of high frequency) can be conveyed from one point to another in a system.

Cobol A high-level *programming language whose name is derived from the words **co**mmon **b**usiness **o**riented **l**anguage. It was developed specifically for administrative and financial use in the late 1950s and early 1960s. It was adopted by the US Department of Defense, and is still the most widely used commercial data-processing language. There is an international standard.

code 1. A rule for transforming data or other information from one symbolic form into another. In the codes employed within a computer, the symbols used are generally restricted to the two *bits 0 and 1. The process of transformation is called *encoding*, and the symbolic representation used or achieved is known as an *encoding*. The process of reconverting the coded information into its original form is called *decoding*. Like encoding the decoding process follows a strict rule. Both processes are thus algorithmic in nature. They are carried out by an *encoder* or a *decoder*. These may be in the form of a piece of hardware or a piece of software.

Different kinds of codes are used in computing for different purposes. For example, when characters – letters, numbers, etc. – are fed into a computer they are transformed into a *character encoding, such as *ASCII, so that they can be manipulated by the computer equipment. Again, *error-detecting and *error-correcting codes are used to improve the reliability of data when it is transferred to or from disk or tape or when it is transmitted.

2. Any piece of program text written in a programming language.

3. The particular language in which a piece of program text is written, e.g. machine code or source code.

4. The encrypted form of a message. *See* cryptography.

5. To represent data or a program in a symbolic form.

cold start *See* restart.

collating sequence An ordering of characters in a character set used within a computer. It is employed, for example, in sorting into alphabetic or alphanumeric order.

COM *Short for* computer output on microfilm. Computer *output recorded in miniaturized form on microfilm, either on a reel of film or on card-sized sheets of film known as *microfiche*. The term COM also applies to the techniques used to produce this form of output. The information is usually output from magnetic tape and having been decoded is considerably reduced in size before the recording process, enabling a large amount of information to be stored. Special optical viewers must be used to enlarge the information on the microfilm so that people can read it. New film or fiche must be produced if additions or corrections are required.

COM is used, for example, in libraries to catalogue books by author and subject and in garages to list car components. Microfilm and microfiche also have applications in areas that do not require a computer, e.g. in the recording of books, newspapers, and other documents.

combinational circuit *See* combinational logic.

combinational logic A simplified form of *Boolean algebra that is used in the design of *logic circuits. The circuits in combinational logic are known as *combinational circuits*. They contain only *logic gates such as AND, OR, and NOT gates. The behaviour of these components are described by *truth tables. It is then possible to describe the whole circuit by drawing a truth table (as is done in the diagram at logic circuit). The output of the circuit at a particular time can thus be determined by the combination of inputs.

command *See* command language.

command language A kind of programming language by means of which a user can communicate with the *operating system of a computer. Statements in such a language are called *commands*. They are requests from someone using a terminal or a microcomputer for the performance of some operation or the execution of some program, examples being 'list', 'sort', 'delete', 'load', 'run'. *Job control languages are a type of command language. *See also* application package.

comment Part of the text of a program that is included for the benefit of the human reader and is ignored by the *compiler. The way in which a comment is constructed depends on the programming language. It might be contained in brackets of some sort, for example

{ ... } in Pascal
/* ... */ in PL/I

Some languages prefer end-of-line comments, which are introduced by a specified character (such as ; -- or !) and are automatically terminated at the end of a line. Other languages, including Fortran and some varieties of Basic, restrict comments to be whole lines starting with a special *label, such as C (Fortran) or REM (Basic).

communication card (communication board) *See* expansion card.

communication channel (transmission channel) A *channel, i.e. an information route, for data transfer. *See also* communication system.

communication line (transmission line) Any physical medium used to carry information between different locations. It may, for example, be a telephone line, an electric cable, an optical fibre, a radio beam, or a laser beam. *Compare* data link.

communication network *See* communication system; network.

communication system Any system by which information can be conveyed from one point – the *source* – to another point – the *destination* – with due regard to efficiency and reliability. There may be more than one source and/or more than one destination, in which case the system is called a *communication network*. The information is sent from source to destination via a *communication channel. In general the channel will distort the information (due to *noise) and will produce *errors in it. In order to reduce the effect of noise, the information is converted into an encoded form before transmission through the channel and is subsequently decoded at its destination. *See also* network.

compatibility 1. The ability of a computer to directly execute program code originally produced for another computer. This generally occurs for successive computers in a family of machines made by a particular manufacturer. Since later computers are almost always more capable (have a larger instruction set and/or more memory), a computer that is able to run a program of a less capable machine is said to be *upward compatible*.

2. The ability of a piece of hardware (e.g. a storage device or a terminal) to be used in place of the equipment originally specified or selected. If the equipment substituted is made by another manufacturer, and fits into the computer without any modifications and works straight away, it is said to be *plug compatible*.

compilation *See* compiler.

compilation error An error, generally a *syntax error, detected when a program is compiled. *See* error.

compilation time The time taken to perform the compilation of a program. *See* compiler; compile time.

compiler A program that takes as input a program written in a *high-level language, such as Pascal or Fortran, and translates it into *machine code. Each *statement in the high-level language is converted into many *machine instructions, sometimes hundreds. The input to the compiler is called the *source program* and the output is called the *object program*. The object program is usually stored separately from the source program. The translation process is known as *compilation*, and the program that has been translated is said to have been *compiled*. The entire program must be compiled before it can be *executed.

A compiler not only translates program statements but includes *links for *procedures and *functions from the system library and allocates areas in main store. It generates the object program on magnetic disk or tape. The object program can subsequently be loaded into and run by a computer. The compiler can also produce a *listing of the source program, if required, and reports the errors (mainly *syntax errors) found in the source program during compilation; it normally indicates the position and nature of these errors.

Each high-level language that can be run on a particular computer requires its own compiler or *interpreter. Program run times are much faster when a compiler is used rather than an interpreter. Once compiled, the same program can be run any number of times. In contrast, an interpreter must be used each time the program is run. *See also* assembler.

compile time The period of time during which a program in a high-level language is translated into *machine code, so that the program can subsequently be executed by a computer. It is at compile time that information about the program, such as a compiler listing or a *symbol table may be produced to aid later *debugging. *See also* compiler; run time.

complement of a digit, integer, truth value, proposition, or formula. The outcome of a *NOT operation on that entity. The complement of the binary digit 0 is 1 while the complement of the binary digit 1 is 0. The complement of the truth value *true* is *false* and vice versa. The complement of the proposition ‘this object is spherical’ is ‘this object is not spherical’.

In general, the complement of a digit, d, can be found from the formula

$$(B - 1 - d)$$

where B is the *base of the number system (equal to 10 in decimal notation, 2 in binary notation). The complement of the decimal digit 6 is thus 3.

The complement of a whole number, i.e. an integer, is obtained by replacing each digit in the integer by its complement. In binary notation this gives the *one's complement*. (In decimal notation it gives the *nine's complement*.) The one's complement of 0110 is thus 1001. In binary notation the *two's complement* is formed by the addition of 1 to the one's complement. The two's complement of 0110 is thus 1001 + 1, i.e. 1010. To determine the original integer from its one's or two's complement, the same process is repeated: the complement is taken (for the one's complement) or the complement is taken and 1 is added (for the two's complement).

One's complement and two's complement are both used in computing. A one's complement is produced by a NOT operation on the binary number concerned, converting 1s to 0s and 0s to 1s; a two's complement is produced by a further addition of 1. Two's complement arithmetic is simpler than one's complement arithmetic and is used both in the representation of negative numbers and in subtraction. Each positive number is represented in its usual form in binary notation except that it always has at least one leading 0. Each negative number is represented by its two's complement and always has at least one leading 1. For example, the decimals +34 and −34 are represented in 8-bit two's complement notation as

00100010
11011110

respectively. There is no need for a separate plus or minus sign. The leftmost (most significant) bit indicates the sign (0 for +, 1 for −) and is called the *sign bit*. The largest positive number in an *n*-bit word has the form

01111 . . . and is equal to $+(2^{n-1} - 1)$

The largest negative number has the form

10000 . . . and is equal to $-(2^{n-1})$

In the case of subtraction, one number can be subtracted from another by adding its two's complement.

For example, the subtraction 27 – 19 (decimal) is equivalent in binary to

11011 – 10011

and in two's complement arithmetic is achieved, using an 8-bit word, by the sum

00011011 + (11101100 + 1) = 00001000

The 'carry' drops off the end and is ignored. The leading zero indicates that the result is a positive number.

computed GOTO *See* GOTO statement.

computer A device by which data, represented in an appropriate form, can be manipulated in such a way as to produce a solution to some problem. It is able to perform a substantial amount of computation with little or no human assistance. In general when the word computer is used by itself it refers to a *digital computer.* The other basic form of computer is the *analog computer, which is far less versatile and thus finds far fewer applications.

A digital computer accepts and performs operations on *discrete data*, i.e. data represented in the form of combinations of *characters. Before being fed into the computer the characters consist of digits, letters, punctuation marks, etc. Inside the computer all these characters are in binary form, encoded as combinations of binary digits, or *bits (*see* binary representation). *Arithmetic and *logic operations are performed on these strings of bits following a set of instructions. The instructions form what is known as a *program, which is stored along with the data in the *memory of the computer.

The main components of a (digital) computer are:

(a) devices for the *input and *output of data and programs;

(b) memory (*main store and *backing store) in which to store the data and programs;

(c) a *control unit and an *arithmetic and logic unit (ALU) for processing the data following the sequence of program instructions; the control unit and ALU are generally combined into a *central processor.

The instructions of the stored program are executed one after another; a device in the control unit (the *instruction address register) indicates the *location in memory from which the next instruction is to be taken. The instructions indicate how items of data, specified by their locations in memory, are to be used, or what information is to be read from the input devices or written to the output devices.

Computers range widely in performance, size, and cost. They are often classified as *microcomputers, *minicomputers, or *mainframes. All three groups may be used as general-purpose machines, capable of solving a wide variety of problems. Alternatively they may be designed for a special purpose or for a limited range of problems.

computer-aided design *See* CAD.

computer architecture *See* architecture.

computer-assisted learning (computer-assisted instruction) *See* CAL.

computer-based learning *See* CAL.

computer graphics A mode of computer processing and output in which a large part of the output information is in pictorial form. The information may range from a simple graph to a highly complicated engineering design, molecular structure, etc. It may be in one or more colours, and may be labelled.

The output from a computer graphics system may be displayed on a *VDU screen or may be in the form of a permanent record produced by a *plotter. Information is input to the computer by various means such as a *digitizing pad, *mouse, or *light pen. The computer can be made to manipulate the information, for example to straighten lines, move or erase specified areas, expand or contract details. Images may be two-dimensional, i.e. flat, or in the case of designs, models, etc., may appear three-dimensional. It is sometimes possible to display or draw three-dimensional images from different viewpoints. It is also possible to simulate motion in a displayed image.

computer instruction *Another name for* machine instruction.

computer network *See* network.

computer-orientated language *See* low-level language.

computer system (computing system) A self-contained set of computing equipment consisting of a *computer, or possibly several computers, together with associated *software. Computer systems are designed to fulfil particular requirements.

computer word *See* word.

computing system *Another name for* computer system.

concatenation An operation by which two *strings are joined together in a specified order. The result is itself a string whose length equals the sum of the lengths of the two strings. If one string, A, is given by "com" and another string, B, by "puter", then the concatenation of A and B yields "computer". The concatenation of A and B is denoted by, for example,

A + B   A & B   A || B

depending on the programming language used.

conditional Taken in some but not all circumstances. *See* control structure; jump.

conditional jump (conditional branch) *See* jump.

conferencing *See* teleconferencing.

configuration The particular pieces of hardware making up a computer system, and the way in which they are interconnected. *See also* reconfiguration; configure.

configure To select various optional settings of a program so that it will run to best advantage on a particular computer. The program may need to know whether the display is monochrome or colour, what sort of printer is available, how many disks are available, and so on. Once the program has been configured, the initial settings will be stored and used the next time the program is run. All kinds of programs, from word processing programs on microcomputers to mainframe operating systems, need to be configured. *See also* reconfiguration.

console A part of a computer used by an operator or a maintenance engineer to communicate with the computer and monitor its operation. The operation of a computer is controlled largely by a set of programs known as the *operating system. As operating systems have become more advanced, consoles have become less complex. Nowadays a console is usually a desk-height surface supporting a *keyboard, one or more *VDUs, and relevant reference manuals; there may also be a number of switches and indicators mounted on a panel. Again, it is possible for a *terminal to be used as a console.

constant A value or an item of data that is fixed or that cannot change. It may, for example, be a numerical constant, like π, whose value must be specified, or it may be a *literal.

content-addressable store, content-addressed store *Other names for* associative store.

continuous stationery Paper that is perforated at regular intervals across its width enabling it to be fan-folded into a stack of 'pages'. It has a row of regularly spaced holes – known as *sprocket holes* or *tractor holes* – down each side so that it can be fed automatically through a *printer by means of *tractor feed. Before printing, the paper may be blank or may be pre-printed forms. It may be *multipart* stationery, consisting of two or more lots of paper with interleaved carbon paper and folded into a single stack.

control bus *See* bus.

control character A member of a *character set whose occurrence in a particular context produces a particular effect. It may start, stop, or modify the recording, processing, transmission, or interpretation of data. For example, there are control characters for 'delete', 'carriage return', 'horizontal tab', 'start of text', and 'end of text'. *Compare* graphic character.

control key *See* keyboard.

control store *See* microprogram.

control structure A structure in a high-level programming language used to express the flow of control in a program, i.e. the order in which instructions are executed. There are three basic ways in which control can flow. Instructions can be executed in strict order, giving a *sequential* flow; this is the normal flow of control and requires no special control structure. Use of a *conditional* control structure permits the execution of one of a specific number of possible instruction sequences; this is commonly achieved by an *if then else statement or by the more general *case or *switch statement. Use of an *iterative* control structure allows a sequence of instructions to be executed repeatedly; this is generally achieved by some form of *loop. For each of these three types of flow control there is one entry point and one exit point.

control total A number produced by adding together corresponding fields in all the *records in a file. It is used for checking purposes (*see* check). A control total may or may not have a sensible meaning in the outside world. A *hash total* is a meaningless control total. It is used solely for verifying the records in the file, and hence for checking the reliability of the associated program and computer.

control unit The part of a computer that supervises the execution of a *program. It is a component of the processing unit and is wholly electronic. Before a program can be executed it must be translated into a sequence of *machine instructions. The control unit receives the machine instructions in the order in which they are to be executed. It interprets each instruction and causes it to be executed by sending command signals to the *arithmetic and logic unit (ALU) and other appropriate parts of the computer. The data required for the execution is moved between *main store, ALU, and other portions of the machine in accordance with the sequence of instructions and under the direction of the control unit.

The control unit contains *registers, *counters, and other elements enabling it to perform its functions. In its simplest form it has an *instruction address register, an *instruction register, and a register to decode the operation part of the instruction. It can then operate in a two-step *fetch-execute cycle*. In the *fetch step* the instruction is obtained from main store and loaded in the instruction register; the decoder can then determine the nature of the instruction. In the *execute step* the indicated operation, or operations, are carried out, including the necessary references to main store to obtain or store data. In some cases no reference to memory is required, as when a *jump instruction occurs. In other cases an additional step is required, as in *indirect addressing when two (or more) memory references are needed.

Control units nowadays can be very much more complex than this, containing additional registers and other functional units that can, for instance, prepare the next instruction for execution before the current one is complete. The variations on this principle are known as *instruction overlap*, *instruction pre-fetch*, or *pipelining*. At present the functions of most control units are accomplished by means of *microprograms.

conversational mode *See* interactive.

coprocessor A microprocessing element designed to extend the capabilities of the main *microprocessor in a microcomputer. For example, it may have better mathematical processing capabilities, including high-speed floating-point arithmetic and calculation of trigonometric functions. Another design could provide database management facilities. A coprocessor extends the set of instructions available to the programmer. When the main processor receives an instruction that it does not support, it can transfer control to a coprocessor that does. More than one coprocessor can be used in a system if the main processor has been suitably designed.

copy To *read data from a source, leaving the source data unchanged, and to *write the same data elsewhere. The physical form of the data in this destination may differ from that in the source, as occurs when data is copied from paper tape to magnetic tape or from magnetic disk to main store.

core store A form of magnetic storage widely used for *main store in computers built between the mid-1950s and mid-1970s. It has been displaced in present-day machines by *semiconductor memory – *RAM and *ROM. Core store consists essentially of tiny rings of ferrite (the brown material used to coat magnetic tapes). The ferrite rings, called *cores*, are strung at the intersections on a grid of wires. Each core can be magnetized in either of two ways (clockwise or anticlockwise) by passing electric currents in particular directions through the grid wires. The two states of magnetization of a core are stable and can be distinguished, and can thus be used to store one *bit of information: one state is used to represent a binary 1, the other a binary 0. A group of cores can therefore be used to store a sequence of bits representing, say, a particular character (*see* binary representation). The state of magnetization can be sensed, again by means of electric currents, and thus the stored information can be read.

corrective maintenance *Maintenance that is performed after a fault has been found – in hardware or software – in order to correct that fault. *Compare* preventative maintenance.

corrupt To alter data stored in a computer system, usually accidently, and hence introduce errors. The process is known as *data corruption*. It results in a loss of data *integrity.

counter An electronic device whose 'state' represents a number, and that on receipt of an appropriate signal causes the number represented to be increased (or decreased) by unity. Only a fixed group of numbers can be represented. Once all these numbers have occurred, one after the other, the sequence starts again. The counter is usually able to bring the number represented to a specified value, such as zero. In a computer system a counter can be used as a *timer* if the signal received is a clock pulse (*see* clock), the counter normally counting down from a selected value and raising an *interrupt when it has finished.

CP/M *Trademark* An *operating system produced by Digital Research. It was intended for use on microcomputers with floppy disks and the 8-bit Intel 8080 microprocessor, or either of the later Intel 8085 or Zilog Z80 8-bit chips. A version of CP/M for use with the 16-bit microprocessor chips in the Intel 8086 family is called CP/M-86; the earlier version is now known as CP/M-80. Both versions are for use on microcomputers with a single user at any one time. MP/M is a multiuser version of CP/M, and is also produced by Digital Research.

cps *Abbrev. for* characters per second, used to describe the rate of output of say a printer or sometimes the rate at which data is processed or transferred.

CPU *Abbrev. for* central processing unit.

crash 1. (system crash) A system failure that requires at least operator intervention and often some maintenance before system running can resume. The system is said to have *crashed*.

2. *See* head crash.

cross assembler An *assembler that runs on one computer, producing an object program to run on a different computer. It is usually used to generate software for microcomputers whose memory is too small to support an assembler, or for *embedded systems such as the computers in washing machines or cruise missiles.

cross compiler A *compiler that runs on one computer, producing an object program to run on a different computer. It is usually used to generate software for microcomputers whose memory is too small to support a compiler, or for *embedded systems such as the computers in washing machines or cruise missiles.

CRT *Abbrev. for* cathode-ray tube. *See* display.

cryptography The protection of a message so as to make it unintelligible to anybody not authorized to receive it. The sender of a message renders it into an unintelligible form by processing it. This processing is known as *encryption*. Many techniques are known for the conversion of the original message, known as *plain text*, into its encrypted form, known as *cipher*, *ciphertext*, or *code*. The original message is recovered by processing the encrypted message. When this is done by an authorized recipient holding the secret key to the encryption, the processing is known as *decryption*. Recovery of the message is expected to be impossible without prior knowledge of the key.

current instruction register (CIR) *Another name for* instruction register.

cursor A symbol on a VDU screen that indicates the 'active' position, for example the position at which the next character to be entered will appear. The cursor may be a bright character-sized rectangle, possibly flashing on and off, or an underline, again possibly flashing.

cursor keys Keys on a *keyboard that can be used to move the *cursor to a new position on a display screen. They may be *arrow keys.

cut sheet feed A technique for feeding paper into a

printer, the mechanism used being called a *cut sheet feeder*. The feeder picks up a single sheet from a pile of sheets in a hopper and feeds it into the printer. In more sophisticated feeders there may be a number of hoppers, for example one for headed top sheets, one for plain second sheets, and one for envelopes. A multipage letter complete with envelope may thus be printed. *See also* tractor feed; friction feed.

cycle 1. A sequence of events that is repeated regularly and in the same order. A piece of hardware may operate in such a way, examples being the *storage cycle of a storage device and the fetch-execute cycle of a *control unit.

2. (cycle time) The minimum period of time required to complete such a sequence of events, i.e. the time between the start of one sequence and the start of the next. The term is often used specifically to mean *storage cycle, i.e. the minimum time required between successive accesses to a storage device.

cycle time *See* cycle.

cylinder *See* disk pack.

cypher *Variant of* cipher. *See* cryptography.

D

DAC *Abbrev. for* digital to analog converter. *See* D/A converter.

D/A converter (DAC) *Short for* digital to analog converter. A device for converting a *digital signal into an equivalent *analog signal, i.e. for converting the output from a computer (in the form of a series of binary values) into a continuous representation. *See also* A/D converter.

daisywheel printer A type of impact character printer, i.e. a *printer that prints a character at a time by

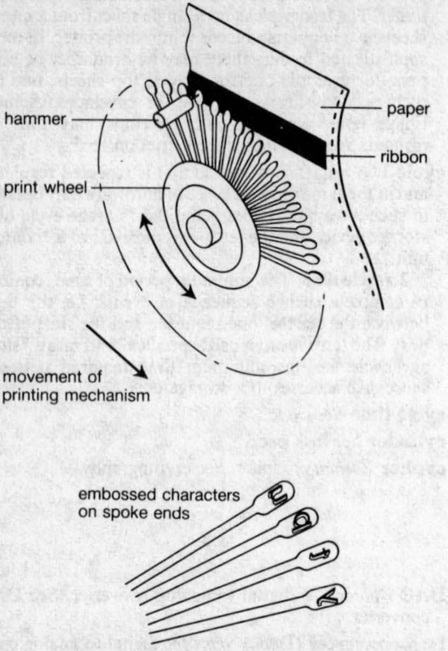

Print wheel of a daisywheel printer

mechanical impact. The printing mechanism involves a rimless 'wheel' consisting of 96 spokes that extend radially from a central hub; solid characters are embossed on the ends of the spokes (see diagram). This *print wheel* is rotated until the required character is opposite the printing position, and a hammer then strikes it against the inked ribbon and paper. The print wheel is interchangeable, enabling different character sets to be used. The quality of the print is high, and daisywheel printers are used for printing letters, documents, etc. A typical printing rate is 60 characters per second; developments are leading to higher speeds and also to slower but cheaper machines (speed and price are closely related).

data In computing, the basic facts – numbers, digits, words, characters – that are fed into a computer system (in the required form) to be stored and processed for some purpose. In this case data is regarded as the *input to a computer system as opposed to the *output of the system, i.e. the results obtained from processing. It is possible, however, for the results of one process to serve as the data – the input – to another process.

The word data is also used as distinct from program instructions. In this case data refers to all the *operands that a program handles, i.e. the numbers or quantities upon which *arithmetic and *logic operations are performed. Note that *statements in a high-level language can serve as data for a *compiler, and that the resulting *object program is data for a *link loader.

See also information.

DATA *See* Basic.

databank A system that offers facilities to a community of users for the deposit and withdrawal of data on a particular topic, such as trade statistics or share prices. The user community is usually widespread and the databank itself may be a public facility. Access to a databank may, for instance, be via *videotex or some other form of *network. The data to be accessed may be organized as a *database or as one or more *files.

database A set of *data files – i.e. an organized collection of related data – that is defined and accessed by a set of programs known as a *database management system (DBMS). The *records in a database are addressable and can be accessed in any order. Databases are thus stored on magnetic disk rather than magnetic tape. The organization of the records in a database, and the methods used to access the data, are more sophisticated than those of a data file with no associated DBMS.

Databases are usually more complex than data files, and are often collections of data previously held in many separate files. They are not necessarily large and complex however: DBMS software is available on small as well as large computers. Storing data as conventional files can limit the data's use to one particular application. A database provides data that is available to all users of the system, and may be shared by a number of different applications.

A database together with its DBMS and disks is often referred to as a *database system*. A data item in a database is typically associated with many other items, some of which may be in the same record. Data is usually retrieved by giving values of specified items in order that the database system should respond with the values of specified associated items. For example, a system might retrieve the registration numbers of all cars of a given colour, make, and year of registration. *See also* database language.

database language Any of a group of languages (nonprogramming) used for setting up and communicating with *databases. A particular database language will be associated with a particular database. Each language consists of at least one *data description language (DDL)* and at least one *data manipulation language (DML)*. The DDL is used to define the structure of the *records within the database files and the relationships between them. It can be used to specify what type of information is to be stored – numbers, characters, dates, etc. – as well as which values are to be used for indexing. The DML is then used to copy the data into the database files and manipulate and retrieve it in various ways. That part of the DML used for retrieving the data may be called the *query language.*

database management system (DBMS) A collection of programs that handle and control all accesses to a *database and that maintain the integrity of the database, i.e. the correctness of the stored data. It achieves this by carrying out instructions couched in the *database language associated with the database. A DBMS thus has features in common with *operating systems and *compilers. The DBMS allows access to the database by a number of users. A good DBMS is characterized by the ease and speed with which complex searches and retrievals are carried out and the flexibility and power of the way databases are specified.

database system 1. *Short for* database management system.

2. A *database together with its database management system (software) and storage devices (hardware).

data bus *See* bus.

data capture A process by which data can be extracted during some operation or activity and can then be fed into a computer. The equipment involved may be connected directly to a computer, allowing the incoming data to be monitored automatically. The use of *point-of-sale terminals in a supermarket involves data capture: although the prime objective of the operation is the sale to the customer, the type of product sold can be recorded and hence stock control can be improved.

data cleaning (data vetting) The process of checking *raw data for completeness, consistency, and validity. Any bad characters, out-of-range values, and inconsistencies are either removed or brought to the attention of someone for a decision.

data coding The use of standard abbreviations or simplified representations in the recording of data on documents, the input of data via a keyboard, etc. This reduces the work involved and the chance of error. For example, the letters Y and N can be used for 'yes' and 'no'.

data collection The process by which data from several locations is collected together before it is fed into a computer.

data compression *See* pack.

data corruption *See* corrupt.

data description language (DDL) *See* database language.

data dictionary A set of descriptions of the data components of some computer-based system. It is normally held in the form of a *file or *database. It gives information about the nature of the data – meaning, relationships with other data, format, etc. – and its use. A database, for example, will have a data dictionary. A data dictionary is an important tool in the effective planning of a computer-based system, and in the overall control, storage, and use of data in the operational system.

data entry The process by which an operator feeds data into a computer by means of an input device. *See also* direct data entry.

data file A *file containing data, i.e. the numbers, text, etc., upon which operations are performed by a computer. A data file is normally organized as a set of *records. *Compare* program file; database.

data flowchart (system flowchart) *See* flowchart.

data integrity *See* integrity.

data link The physical medium – telephone line, electric cable, etc. – by which two locations are connected for the purpose of transmitting and receiving data, together with the agreed procedures (i.e. the *protocol) by which the data is to be exchanged and any associated devices or programs.

data logging 1. The recording of all data passing

through a particular point in a computer system. The point chosen can, for example, be in a pathway to or from a VDU. The record – or *log* – that is produced can be used to reconstruct a situation when, say, a fault occurs in the system or an unexpected result is obtained.

2. The regular sampling of a number of quantities, such as temperature, flow rate, and pressure, by a device known as a *data logger*. The information is stored within the logger and periodically transmitted to a computer for analysis.

data manipulation language (DML) *See* database language.

data preparation The conversion of data into a coded form that can be read by a machine and hence fed into a computer. The operation of a keypunch to encode data on *punched cards is an example. The necessity for data preparation has been largely removed with the advent of *direct data entry.

data processing (DP) The operations conducted mainly in business, industrial, and government organizations whereby data is collected, stored, and *processed on a routine basis in order to produce information, regularly or on request. The operations almost always (but not necessarily) involve computers. A DP system usually handles large quantities of data organized in a complex way. Typical applications include production of payslips, accounting, market research and sales forecasting, stock control, and the handling of orders.

data protection The protection of data handled in a computer. The term is usually applied to confidential *personal data*, i.e. data concerning a living person who can be identified from that information, and possibly including some opinion expressed about that person. Credit ratings produced by banks, donations received by charities, transactions by mail-order firms, and personal records kept by government agencies and the police all involve data concerning the individual; for ease of access, ease of updating, saving of space, and other reasons, this kind of information is now usually stored in computers.

Legislation exists or is being introduced in many countries to protect personal data when it is stored in computers. The aim is to control the potential for misuse of such information. Personal data could, for example, be extracted from one stored record and correlated with data concerning the same person from another file. The combination of information that could result is considered an infringement of privacy.

The UK enacted the Data Protection Act in 1984 to comply with a convention signed by all member countries of the Council of Europe. The Act is concerned only with personal data. It comes into effect in stages over a three-year period. It establishes an independent public register: from November 1985 *data users* – people holding personal data – have been able to register their activities with the Data Protection Registrar. Data users have to declare the type of data held, the type of sources used for this data, and the type of person to whom the data could be disclosed. All data users must be registered by May 1986.

Since September 1984 *data subjects* – the subjects of personal data – have in effect a right of action for damages caused by inadequate *security in systems holding personal data. From November 1987 a data subject will be entitled to obtain a printout from a registered data user of any personal data concerning him or her. (The Act is not described here in full.)

data retrieval The process by which data is selected and extracted from a *file, a group of files, a *database, or some other area of memory. *See also* information retrieval.

data structure Any of several forms in which a collection of data items can be organized and held in a computer. Examples include *arrays, *records, *files, *strings, and *trees. Various operations can be performed on the data, the choice depending on the type of data structure and the programming language.

data tablet *Another name for* digitizing pad.

data transfer The movement of data from one point to another. These points may, for instance, be storage locations within a computer system or at either end of a long-distance *transmission line.

data transfer rate The rate at which data can be moved between two points, for example from a magnetic disk to main store, from a magnetic disk to magnetic tape, or from one location on a *network to another.

data transmission *See* transmission.

data type The kind of data (e.g. integers, real numbers, strings) that can be identified by a *variable, an *array, or some other more complex data object in a programming language, the set of values that the variable, etc., is allowed to take, and the operations that can be performed on it.

data vetting *Another name for* data cleaning.

DBMS *Abbrev. for* database management system.

DDE *Abbrev. for* direct data entry.

debugging The identification and removal of *bugs – i.e. localized errors – from a program or system. The bugs in a program may, for example, be *syntax errors uncovered by the compiler, *run-time errors detected during execution of the program, or logical *errors, which are more difficult to identify. There are various diagnostic aids that can be used in debugging a program, including *trace programs or possibly a *debug tool. Again, a *diagnostic routine may be entered as a result of some error condition having been detected – in either software or hardware. *See also* error-detecting code; error-correcting code.

debug tool (debugger) A special program – a *software tool – that assists in the *debugging of programs by allowing the internal behaviour of the programs to be investigated. Typically a debug tool offers facilities for producing *traces, allows the planting of *breakpoints in the program being debugged, and permits examination and perhaps modification of program *variables when a breakpoint is reached.

decimal notation (decimal system; denary notation) The familiar number system, using the 10 digits 0–9. It thus has a *base 10. The value of a number is determined not only by the digits it contains but also by their position in the number. The positional value increases from right to left by powers of 10. For example, in the decimal number 473, 3 is in the units place, 7 is in the tens place, and 4 is in the hundreds place.

rain	N	N	Y	–	–	–
snow	N	N	N	Y	–	–
fog	N	N	N	N	Y	Y
temp. (°C)	>8	<8	–	–	>0	<0
take bike	×					
take car		×	×			
take train				×	×	
stay home						×

Decision table for travelling to work

decision table A table that indicates all the conditions that could arise in the description of a problem, together with the actions to be taken for each set of conditions. It thus shows precisely what action is to be taken under a particular set of circumstances. Decision tables can be used in specifying what a program is to do (but not how it is to achieve this).

A decision table usually has four parts (see diagram). One part (top left) lists the possible conditions, while another part (bottom left) lists the possible actions. The remaining parts show the conditions under which each action is selected. The top right section specifies the conditions by means of a Y (yes), N (no), or – (don't care); the bottom right indicates, by means of a cross, the particular action to be taken for each set of circumstances. The diagram shows a decision table for deciding how to travel to work.

declaration An expression in a computer program that introduces an entity for part of the program, gives it a *name, and establishes its properties. The entities that can be named include *variables, *arrays, *procedures, and *files. The declaration is fundamental to most programming languages, the form it takes depending on the language.

decoder, decoding *See* code.

decollator A device that separates the copies of multipart *continuous stationery produced as output from a *printer. *See also* burster.

decryption *See* cryptography.

dedicated Committed entirely to a single purpose or application. For example, a computer can be dedicated to controlling a machine tool, creating charts and graphs for TV programs, or synthesizing musical sounds.

default option A predetermined action to be performed, or a value to be used, if no specific action or value has been indicated. For instance, a printer might assume a page length of 11 inches or a Fortran compiler might assume that the user did not want a compiler listing. Both these defaults could be overridden by specific instructions to the contrary.

deletion (erasure) Removal or obliteration of an item

of data or of a collection of data. Data that has been fed into a system by *keyboard and displayed on a screen can be deleted by operating a function key or cursor; this removes the necessary data and corrects the spacing. With magnetic tape or disk, deletion of data is achieved by overwriting with new data or *null characters.

delimiter A character or group of characters used to mark the beginning or end of a program *statement, *control structure, or some other item of data. Many languages use *begin* and *end* to delimit complex statements. Most languages use single or double quotation marks to delimit character *strings. *See also* separator; terminator.

demodulation, demodulator *See* modulation.

demountable disk *Another name for* exchangeable disk store.

denary notation (denary system) *Other names for* decimal notation.

density 1. A measure of the amount of data that can be stored per unit length or per unit area of a storage medium. It may be quoted in terms of *bit density*, i.e. the number of *bits per unit length or per unit area. The density of *magnetic tape is usually given as the maximum number of bits per inch (bpi) or bits per mm that can be recorded along a *track. The density of a *magnetic disk can be quoted as the maximum number of bits per *sector, the number of sectors per track, and the number of tracks per disk or per inch.

2. *See* packing density.

deposit To place a value in a *location in memory or in a *register in a processor, i.e. to store a value.

diagnostic routine Part of a program, or a sequence of instructions *called by a program, that is entered as a result of the detection of some condition causing an *error. A diagnostic routine may analyse the cause of the error, or provide information that can be used for this purpose. It might attempt to isolate the cause of the error to a particular piece of hardware or software.

dictionary *See* data dictionary.

digit Any of the numerals (or possibly letters) used in a particular *number system. Decimal notation uses 10 numerals:

0, 1, 2, 3, 4, 5, 6, 7, 8, 9

Binary notation uses the numerals 0 and 1. Octal notation uses the numerals 0 to 7. Hexadecimal notation uses 16 digits: 10 numerals (0–9) and 6 letters (A–F).

digital computer A computer that accepts and performs operations on *discrete data*, i.e. data represented in the form of combinations of digits, letters, or other *characters. Compared with an *analog computer, a digital computer is much more versatile and hence much more widely used. It is thus generally referred to simply as a computer. *See* computer.

digital logic **1.** The electronic components used in a computer system to carry out *logic operations on discrete variables. Usually only binary variables are involved (i.e. quantities that can take either of two values), and the term *binary logic* can then be used. The components consist of *logic gates and *logic circuits.
2. The methods and principles underlying this implementation of logic operations.

digital signal An electrical *signal whose voltage at any particular time will be at any one of a group of discrete (distinct) levels. The voltage therefore does not vary continuously (unlike an *analog signal). In general there are just two discrete levels: the voltage jumps back and forth between the two levels over a period of time; such a signal is often called a *binary signal.* (A digital signal is therefore usually but not necessarily a binary signal.) The *logic gates and *logic circuits used in computers handle two levels of voltage, and thus their inputs and outputs are binary signals; the high level of voltage is usually used to represent binary 1, with the low level representing binary 0.

digital to analog converter *See* D/A converter.

digitized signal The representation of a continuously varying signal in a digital form. The digitized signal has values that are identical to those of the continuously varying (i.e. analog) signal but only at discrete (separate) instants of time. As a result, the voltage or current changes in steps between discrete (distinct) values. For example, if the voltage of an analog signal is measured at discrete intervals, then the sequence of measured values is a digitized signal; the analog signal is said to have been *sampled* so as to produce the digitized signal.

digitizing pad (digitizing tablet) A flat surface that can be placed on a desk and is used together with a penlike device for the input of data to a computer graphics system. (Larger surfaces are also available and are known as *digitizing tables* or *boards*.) The position of the pen on the digitizing pad can be accurately and rapidly located by any of a variety of methods; it is measured in terms of the x and y coordinates of the point of contact, i.e. the horizontal and vertical distances of the pen from one corner of the digitizing pad. The position is thus in a digital form that can be fed into the computer. When the pen is moved by hand over the surface, closely spaced positions can be measured. A *digitized signal representing the path of the pen is thus generated. The digitizing process is activated by one or more switches or buttons on the pen.

The main use of a digitizing pad plus pen is to convert an existing picture, such as a map or engineering design, into a digital form; the picture is placed or projected on the pad and the pen is moved along the outlines, etc.

DIL *Short for* dual in-line. *See* DIP; DIL switch.

DIL switch A device similar in form to a *DIP, but instead of an integrated circuit the package contains a row of small switches making or breaking the circuit between opposite pairs of legs. DIL switches are commonly used for setting the default state of printers, terminals, etc.

DIM *See* Basic.

dimension of an array. *See* array.

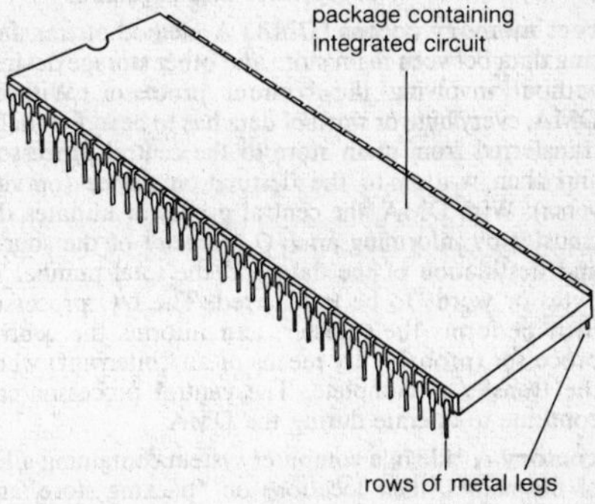

DIP

DIP *Short for* dual in-line package. An *integrated circuit contained in a rectangular plastic or ceramic package with a row of metal legs down each of the long sides (see diagram). The legs can either be soldered into holes in a *printed circuit board or inserted into a *chip socket.

direct access *Random access to a storage device, at present almost always a magnetic disk.

direct-access file *See* file.

direct addressing An *addressing mode in which the address specified in a *machine instruction is the actual address to be used, i.e. the location to be accessed is given explicitly. The address specified is then called a *direct address*. *See also* address.

direct data entry (DDE) Any process by which data is fed directly into a computer and is written in the computer's *on-line *files stored on disk. The data is usually entered by an operator at a keyboard.

direct memory access (DMA) A method of transferring data between main store and other storage devices without involving the *central processor. Without DMA, every byte or word of data has to be individually transferred from main store to the central processor, and then written to the destination device (or vice versa). With DMA, the central processor initiates the transfer by informing an *I/O processor* of the source and destination of the data and the total number of bytes or words to be transferred. The I/O processor then performs the transfer, and informs the central processor (probably by means of an *interrupt) when the transfer is complete. The central processor can continue to operate during the DMA.

directory A *file in a computer system containing a list of file names, their locations on *backing store, and their size, as well as other information such as creation date, author, date of last access, and *file protection code. A computer system may have many directories. On a *multiaccess system each user has a directory and the *operating system also has one or more. On a microcomputer system each *floppy disk has its own directory. Directories are used by the operating system to locate files when given their names, and by computer users to keep track of what files are available.

disable To switch off a device or prevent the operation of a particular function of a device or a particular feature of a program. *Compare* enable.

disassembler A program that attempts to translate machine code back into *assembly language, i.e. it performs the reverse function of an *assembler. It is used as an aid to *debugging. It is only the one-to-one relationship between machine instructions and assembly language instructions that makes this process possible. It would not work with high-level languages.

disc *UK spelling of* disk, sometimes preferred in UK computer literature. *See* magnetic disk.

discrete data *See* computer.

disk *Usually short for* magnetic disk. *See also* optical disk.

disk cartridge A module consisting of a single hard *magnetic disk permanently housed inside a protective plastic cover. The disk is typically 3 to 14 inches in diameter (76 to 356 mm). A disk cartridge is used in a specially designed *disk drive, from which it can be removed and replaced by another cartridge. It is thus an *exchangeable disk store. Once the cartridge is clamped to the rotation mechanism in the disk drive, the disk can rotate freely. The read/write heads are positioned by being inserted automatically through a window in the cover or by the cover being lifted automatically. Disk cartridges can have a storage *capacity of up to 25 megabytes.

disk crash *Another name for* head crash.

disk drive (disk unit) A peripheral device that has a mechanism for rotating one or more *magnetic disks at constant high speed, and devices known as *read/write heads* (plus associated electronics) for writing and reading data on the spinning disk(s). Data is recorded on one or (more usually) both sides of a disk, along concentric tracks in the magnetic coating. Items of data are stored and retrieved by the process of *random access.

Two basic types of disk drive are available. One type uses *hard disks and is designed for high performance and large storage *capacities. The other type is designed for low purchase price and uses inexpensive storage media in the form of *floppy disks.

In disk drives using hard disks, the disks are either *fixed* in position or are *exchangeable*, i.e. removable and replaceable. Hard disks must always be carefully protected from the slightest physical damage. In fixed disk drives the disks and read/write heads are hermetically sealed inside the device. A fixed disk has a higher storage capacity than a similar-sized removable disk. Exchangeable disk store is either in the form of *disk packs, each containing several disks, or *disk cartridges, each containing a single disk. Both forms have protective covers that remain in place until the device is inside the disk drive. *See also* Winchester disk drive.

In floppy disk drives the disks are always removable and do not require such careful protection. Disk plus protective envelope is fed into the disk drive by hand through a slot, and is automatically mounted on the rotation mechanism. Rotation speeds (typically 360 revolutions per minute) are considerably lower than for hard disk drives. The read/write head or heads operate through slots in the envelope. Floppy disk drives are extensively used in small computers.

In a disk drive there is usually one read/write head per recording surface, either touching it (in the case of a floppy disk) or very close to it (in the case of a hard disk). The head is normally mounted on an arm that moves radially (i.e. towards and away from the disk centre). To read or write data, the head is accurately positioned by the disk drive over the required track, and then waits until the right sector rotates into place underneath it. In some hard disk drives the heads are fixed in position over each track of the recording surface; these *fixed heads* decrease the *access time but increase the cost of the unit.

When the head is to write data, it receives an electrical signal coded with the data and converts it into magnetized patterns along the specified sector of a specified track. (The head is an electromagnetic device.) The data is encoded in one of the appropriate disk *formats. For reading data, the head senses the magnetized patterns in the specified sector and produces a corresponding electrical signal.

A large disk will probably be used by many people for many purposes. The allocation of storage space on the disk is therefore handled automatically by a complex program held permanently in the computer.

diskette *Another name for* floppy disk.

disk format *See* format; magnetic disk.

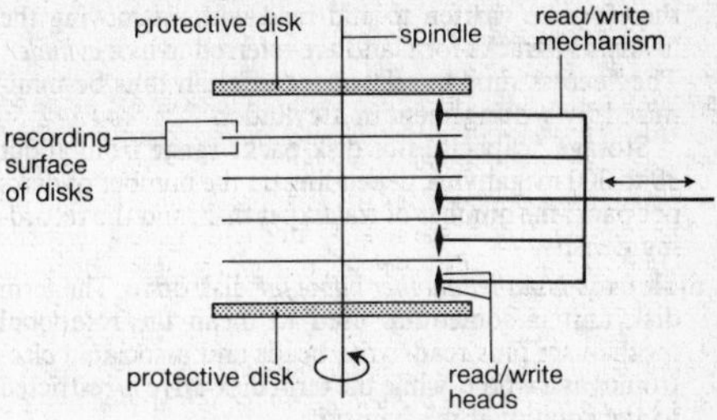

Disk pack with six disks

disk pack A form of disk storage used in a specially designed *disk drive, from which it can be removed and replaced by another pack of the same type. It is thus an *exchangeable disk store. It is an assembly of identical *magnetic disks permanently mounted on a single spindle (see diagram). The disks are 14 inch (350 mm) hard disks. Their number varies from 5 to 12 per pack. A similar-sized disk used for protective rather than recording purposes is fitted to the top and bottom of the assembly; in a 6-disk pack there are thus 10 recording surfaces. When not mounted on a disk drive the assembly is kept in plastic covers to protect it from damage and dust. The bottom cover is removed just before mounting the pack; the top cover can only be removed when the pack is mounted.

Once the pack is mounted, the read/write mechanism moves automatically into position and the pack is set into rotation. A read/write head is provided for each recording surface. The heads are carried on a single comb-like mechanism that is moved radially between the disks. The heads thus all move together, and can be positioned over the same track number on each of the recording surfaces. This set of tracks can therefore be written to and read without moving the heads; the tracks form and are referred to as a *cylinder*. The *access time to related records can thus be minimized by writing them in a cylinder.

Storage *capacities of disk packs range from about 30 to 300 megabytes, depending on the number of disks per pack, the number of tracks per disk, and the recording density.

disk unit *Usually, another name for* disk drive. The term disk unit is sometimes used to mean the rotational mechanism plus read/write heads and associated electronics as a whole, while the term disk drive is restricted to the rotational mechanism.

display 1. To make information visible on a screen.

2. The device that enables information – textual or pictorial – to be seen but not permanently recorded. The most widely used technology involves a *cathode-ray tube (CRT)*: in most cases the image is formed and changed as a beam of electrons continually traces a pattern of horizontal lines (a *raster*) on the screen, as occurs in a domestic TV; in some CRT devices the image is formed by 'drawing' individual lines on the screen, of any length and at any angle.

Another technology, gaining in popularity, is the *plasma panel display*: in this device electrical discharges through a gas lead to the production of characters or pictorial information on the panel, which is flat and is smaller and more rugged than CRT display devices. *See also* LCD; LED display.

distributed processing The processing of data in a system in which a number of independent but interconnected computers can cooperate. The system itself is known as a *distributed system*, an example of which is a *local area network. The processors involved may be situated at different places and are connected by communication lines. They normally have their own peripherals – terminals, disks, printers – so that 'local' data can be processed and 'local' decisions made. Data with a wider application can be exchanged over the communication lines.

distributed system *See* distributed processing.

DMA *Abbrev. for* direct memory access.

documentation The written information describing the operation, structure, and use of hardware or software. It may be in the form of manuals, often in loose-leaf format to make amendments and additions simple. Alternatively it may be held on *backing store and be accessible from a computer *terminal; this is called *online documentation*. Software documentation normally includes a tutorial guide to new users, a reference section, an explanation of error messages, an installation guide, and perhaps a small detachable summary card. Hardware documentation is similar but includes a technical specification and a trouble-shooting and maintenance-engineers manual.

Good documentation is crucial to the success of any computer system. Although it has had a deservedly poor reputation in the past, the situation is improving as more manufacturers employ specialist documentation writers.

document reader An *input device that reads data directly from a document and feeds it, in coded form, into a computer. The document reader has to recognize characters on the document, or to sense marks on it. It operates by *OCR (optical character recognition), *MICR (magnetic ink character recognition), or *OMR (optical mark reading). The documents can generally be read not only by the input device but also by people, and may involve more than one reading process, for instance OCR and OMR.

do loop *See* loop.

do-nothing operation *Another name for* no-op instruction.

dot matrix printer A *printer that creates each character as an array or matrix of dots. The dots are usually formed by transferring ink by mechanical impact. The device is almost always a *character printer, i.e. it prints a character at a time. It typically has a print head containing 7 or 9 thin rods, known as *needles*. The needles are selectively operated as the head moves along the line, thus building up each character as required; characters are usually 4 or 5 dots wide. In many printers the number of characters per inch (cpi) can be varied (see diagram). Generally between 100–400 characters per second can be printed. Better quality print is produced by increasing the number of needles, but this reduces the printing rate.

Dot matrix printers can print a large selection of shapes and styles of letters and digits, and may also print Arabic characters or the idiograms of oriental languages. In addition to characters it is possible to produce diagrams, graphs, etc.

double-density disk *See* floppy disk.

double-length word *See* precision.

double precision *See* precision.

double-sided disk *See* floppy disk.

download To send programs or data from a central or controlling computer to a remote terminal or to a microcomputer.

downtime The time, or the percentage of time, during which a computer is not available for use. If the com-dot_matrix_printing,_12cpi

characters in bold type

characters in italic type

digits 0,1,2,3,4,5,6,7,8,9

Dot_matrix
printing_at
6_cpi

**CAPITALS IN
BOLD TYPE**

*CAPITALS IN
ITALIC TYPE*

DIGITS 0,1,2,
3,4,5,6,7,8,9

Examples of dot matrix printing

puter has been taken out of service for regular *preventative maintenance, then this is *scheduled downtime*. If the computer breaks down and has to be taken out of service for repairs, then this is *unscheduled downtime*.

DP *Abbrev. for* data processing.

drum *See* magnetic drum.

drum plotter *See* plotter.

drum printer *Another name for* barrel printer, used especially in the USA. *See* line printer.

dry run Execution of a program for purposes of checking that the program is behaving correctly rather than for producing useful results. The results of execution are compared with the expected results. Any discrepancies indicate an error of some sort, which must be removed before the program is put into productive use.

dual in-line package *See* DIP.

dumb terminal *See* terminal.

dump To copy or make a copy of some or all of the contents of a storage device at a particular instant in order to safeguard against loss of data, to check for errors in a program, or for some other purpose. The data copied is called a *dump*. For example, in a system handling large numbers of users' files stored on magnetic disks, the contents of the disks are dumped periodically on magnetic tape. This provides a reference copy of the data in the event of, say, accidental overwriting or damage of the disks. Again, when a system *crash occurs, a printed version of the contents of main store and possibly backing store is produced. This can be studied to try and determine the immediate cause of the crash. Dumping can also be performed at some selected point in the execution of a computer program, usually during *testing or *debugging of the program, or may occur when a program is brought to an unplanned halt, i.e. is *aborted.

duplex transmission (full-duplex transmission, FDX) Transmission of data between two endpoints, the data being able to travel in both directions simultaneously. Duplex transmission is used over telephone networks and terminal communication lines, and any other situation in which it is desirable that both ends be allowed to transmit at once. *Compare* half-duplex transmission; simplex transmission.

dyadic operator (binary operator) *See* operator.

dynamic 1. Changing or capable of being changed over a period of time, usually while a system or device is in operation or a program is running. For example, a *dynamic allocation* of a resource can be made while the system is running, and *dynamic RAM* is a type of semiconductor memory that requires its contents to be rewritten periodically since they degrade with time.
2. Taking place during the execution of a program, as happens with a *dynamic dump*.
Compare static.

E

EBCDIC (pronounced eb-see-dic) *Abbrev. for* extended binary coded decimal interchange code. A *code developed by IBM and used for the interchange of data between equipment manufactured by or associated with IBM. EBCDIC encoding produces coded characters of 8 bits, and hence provides 2^8, i.e. 256, different bit patterns. These 256 characters form a *character set, consisting of letters, digits, special characters such as punctuation marks, and control characters.

echo To reflect transmitted data back to its point of origin. (As in ordinary speech the word is also used as a noun.) For example, characters typed on the keyboard of a *terminal will not appear on the display of the terminal unless they are echoed. The echo may be produced within the terminal itself, by the computer to which the terminal is attached, or by an intervening *modem. *See also* echo check.

echo check A way of establishing the accuracy achieved during the transfer of data between, say, devices in a computer system or computers in a *network. When the data is received it is stored and is also sent back – *echoed – to its point of origin. The returned data is compared with the original data and errors can then be detected. *See also* check.

ECL *Abbrev. for* emitter-coupled logic. A family of *logic circuits that are all fabricated with a similar structure by the same *integrated-circuit techniques. The circuits are bipolar in nature and are all characterized by very high *switching speeds, but have high power requirements and a low *packing density compared with *CMOS. *See also* TTL.

edge connector Part of a *printed circuit board (PCB) where a number of the metallic conducting tracks meet the edge of the board, at right angles, to form the male half of a plug and socket. The tracks are broadened, thickened, and usually gold-plated to provide a good electrical contact; the PCB itself provides the necessary strength and rigidity. A single edge connector may have a hundred or more individual connections, half on each side of the board. The female half of the connector, the socket, consists of a number of sprung metal contacts, embedded in plastic, which make contact with the corresponding pads on the PCB when the two halves are pressed together.

editor *See* text editor; link editor.

EDSAC *Abbrev. for* Electronic Delay Storage Automatic Calculator. *See* first generation computers.

EDVAC *Abbrev. for* Electronic Discrete Variable Automatic Computer. *See* first generation computers.

electric cable *See* coaxial cable; twisted pair; ribbon cable.

electronic filing A computer-based system for the storage, cataloguing, and retrieval of documents. It plays a major role in an *electronic office. The 'objects' in an electronic filing system are usually stored on magnetic disk or tape and can be organized using a variety of methods. They may be letters, complex reports, charts, graphs, pictures, etc., which are created, manipulated, or deleted as required.

electronic funds transfer The use of computers to bring about payments between individuals and/or organizations such as banks or companies.

electronic mail Messages sent between users of computer systems, the computer systems being used to transport and hold the messages. Sender and recipient(s) need not be on the same computer to communicate or *on-line at the same time. The mail-handling program will have facilities for typing in messages, selecting one or more recipients, and checking for incoming mail. It may also be able to forward copies of incoming messages to other people, provide *teleconferencing facilities, or delay messages until a given time or date. A single message may possibly combine text, graphics, and other forms of information.

electronic office A computer-based system designed for office tasks. This may involve the use of *electronic filing, *word processing, *databases, *computer graphics, *electronic mail, and *teleconferencing.

embedded computer system Any system that uses a computer as a component dedicated to a particular task. Examples are programmable washing machines, arcade video games, and satellite navigation systems. It is not possible for the operator of a washing machine to reprogram it to play games, whereas a general-purpose computer system can perform a series of unrelated tasks under the control of the operator.

empty string (null string) A *string with no characters. Not all programming languages cater for empty strings, and the concept, although useful, should be treated with care.

emulation The imitation of all or part of one computer system by another computer system such that the imitating system executes the same programs, accepting the identical data and producing the identical results (but not necessarily in the same way), as the system imitated. A device or program used in producing an emulation is called an *emulator*. A particular emulation could be used as a replacement for all or part of the system being emulated, and furthermore could be an improved version. For example, a new computer may emulate an obsolete one so that programs written for the old one will run without modification.

In contrast with a *simulation, an emulation is usually a realistic imitation; a simulation may be no more than an abstract model.

enable To switch on a device or to select and activate a particular function of a device or a particular feature of a program. *Compare* disable.

encoder A means by which data is converted into a coded form. It may be a hardware device, such as a *keyboard, or a piece of software. *See also* code.

encoding *See* code.

encryption *See* cryptography.

END *See* Basic.

ENIAC *Abbrev. for* Electronic Numerical Integrator and Calculator. *See* first generation computers.

enter key *Another name for* return key.

entry point (entry) The point to which control is passed when a program or a section of a program – a *procedure, *subroutine, or *function – is *called. The entry point is the first instruction in the program or program section to be executed (or more specifically is the *address or *label of this instruction). There may be more than one entry point in a program or program section.

EPROM *Abbrev. for* erasable programmable read-only memory, i.e. erasable PROM. A type of *semiconductor memory that is fabricated in a similar way to *ROM. The contents, however, are added after rather than during manufacture and then if necessary can be erased and rewritten, possibly several times. In the nonprogrammed state the contents are all usually set at binary 1. The desired contents are obtained electronically by a device known as a *PROM programmer*, which sets selected elements to binary 0. The contents are erased (i.e. reset to binary 1) normally by exposure to ultraviolet radiation, and can then be reprogrammed. It is only outside a computer that an EPROM can be programmed. Within a computer the contents cannot be changed; they can only be read. *See also* PROM.

EQ gate *Short for* equivalence gate.

equivalence A *logic operation combining two statements or formulae, A and B, in such a way that the outcome is false when either A or B is true but not both; otherwise the outcome is true. The *truth table is shown in the diagram, where the two truth values are represented by 0 (false) and 1 (true). The operation can be written as A ≡ B.

equivalence gate (EQ gate) A *logic gate whose output is low only when one of its (two or more) inputs is high and the rest are low; otherwise the output is high. It thus performs the operation of *equivalence on its inputs and has the same *truth table. The truth table

A	B	output/outcome
0	0	1
0	1	0
1	0	0
1	1	1

Truth table for equivalence gate and equivalence

for a gate with two inputs (A, B) is shown, where 0 represents a low signal level and 1 a high level. *See also* nonequivalence gate.

erasable PROM *See* EPROM.

erasure *Another word for* deletion.

error A discrepancy between the value or condition that is calculated, observed, or measured and the value or condition that is known to be accurate or correct, or that has been specified as being accurate or correct, or that was simply expected. In computing, errors can be caused by some failure in the hardware of the system or by some condition occurring in the software.

Errors may arise, for example, as data is being transferred to or from magnetic disk or magnetic tape, i.e. as data is being written or read. They may also arise during the transfer of data between a terminal and a computer or between two computers. Errors may be caused by a flaw in the storage medium, by a fault in a device, or by *noise in a communication channel. A binary 1 may then be incorrectly written, read, or transmitted as a binary 0, or a binary 0 as a binary 1, producing an error in the data. The detection, handling, and possible correction of such errors is an important aspect in computing. *See also* error-detecting code; error-correcting code.

In programming, errors may arise because the program fails to obey the *syntax of the programming language, i.e. the program breaks one of the rules defining how characters and sequences of characters can be combined. These are known as *syntax errors and are normally detected when the program is compiled. Other programming errors may not become apparent until the program is executed. These are called *run-time (or execution) errors, and may arise from, say, attempted division by zero or from *overflow. *Logical errors* are another type, occurring because the logic or design of the program is incorrect; a *jump to the wrong instruction is an example. Logical errors can arise if the problem that the program is designed to solve is not fully understood, so that the wrong *algorithm is selected or written. Yet again, errors may arise from the *rounding or *truncation of numbers, producing *rounding* or *truncation errors.*

error-correcting code Any of a variety of *codes used to correct *errors that occur, for example, during the transfer of data. The data is sent along a channel as a coded signal, with each element of the code constructed by an encoder using a specific rule. A decoder at the other end of the channel detects any departure from this construction, i.e. any errors, and automatically corrects them – with a high probability of success. It is possible for errors to be corrected by an *error-detecting code, by a request for the retransmission of the affected data. Error-correcting codes are more complex and hence more costly to implement than error-detecting codes but reduce the necessity for retransmission.

error-detecting code Any of a variety of *codes used to check data for certain kinds of *errors that may have occurred, say, during transfer of the data or due to a writing or reading process. The information is encoded in such a way that a decoder can subsequently detect – with a high probability of success – whether an error has arisen. A fixed number of bits, k, is normally taken into the encoder at a time, and then output as a codeword consisting of a greater number of bits, n. Each codeword in a particular code is constructed following a specific rule. The decoder will subsequently take in n bits at a time and output k bits. On each codeword the decoder performs a *check for errors. If an error is detected then generally the sending device is requested to retransmit the affected set of bits. *See also* acknowledgment; error-correcting code.

error diagnostics Information that is presented following the detection of some condition causing an *error, for example after an attempt to execute instructions in a program that are invalid or that operate on illegal data. The information is mainly to assist in identifying the cause of the error. Error diagnostics can be produced, for instance, by the *compiler, and the information would then generally concern *syntax errors. Other kinds of errors are detected at run time. In this case the error diagnostics may be produced by a *run-time system. *See also* debugging.

error message A message that reports the occurrence of an *error. There may be some attempt to diagnose the cause of the error. The message appears on a VDU screen or on a printout, or is stored in an *error file.*

error rate A measure of the proportion of *errors occurring in data transfers to or from a magnetic disk or magnetic tape or in data transmissions along a communication line. The error rate of, say, a magnetic tape system is usually given as the number of bits or bytes of data transferred per error, e.g. 1 error in 10^9 bytes (often expressed as an error rate of 10^{-9}). The error rate of a communication line may be expressed as the number of bits transmitted per error, e.g. 1 error per 10^5 bits. Since errors tend to come in bursts during transmission, the error rate is sometimes given as the percentage of error-free seconds.

ETX/ACK *See* flow control.

even parity *See* parity check.

exchangeable disk store (demountable disk) A disk storage medium – either a *disk pack or a *disk cartridge – that can be removed from a *disk drive and replaced by another of the same type. The store can be mounted on other disk drives of appropriate design. The use of exchangeable disk store produces a 'library' of disks and greatly increases the amount of data that can be stored.

exclusive-OR gate (XOR gate) *See* nonequivalence gate.

execute To carry out a *machine instruction or a computer *program. The process is described as *execution.* A program executes from the time that it is started until either it completes its task and returns control to the *operating system or it encounters an error whose severity prevents it from continuing. *See also* fetch-execute cycle; control unit.

execution *See* execute.

execution error *Another name for* run-time error.

executive *Another name for* supervisor.

exit An instruction in a program or *program unit whose execution by a computer causes control to be transferred away from that program or program unit. It follows that to *exit* from a program or program unit is to transfer control away from that program or program unit. A *return instruction* is an exit that returns control to a specified instruction in the program that originally *called the program or program unit.

expansion card (expansion board; add-in card) A *printed circuit board that can be plugged into an existing printed circuit board within a microcomputer in order to improve the performance and capability of the computer. An expansion card is inserted into a special *expansion slot*; several slots are provided. The cards are made either by the computer manufacturer or by specialist manufacturers, and may supply a particular need or offer a range of functions.

Memory cards provide additional memory (up to the maximum a computer can handle). *Graphics cards* enable monochrome graphics to be displayed on a monochrome screen lacking this facility, or colour graphics on a colour monitor, at various resolutions. *Communication cards* allow computers of different types and sizes to communicate – a micro could talk to another micro or to a minicomputer or a mainframe; *interface cards* are used for communications involving *modems, telex, or *local area networks. The popular *multifunction card* provides a range of functions on one circuit board. These typically include extra memory, a connection point for a printer, a connection point for communications, and a built-in digital clock.

expert system A computer program or system for commercial application, based on knowledge acquired from experts and used, for example, in medical diagnosis, mineral prospecting, and fault finding. The programs are produced by means of techniques developed in the field of *artificial intelligence for problem solving, etc.

exponent *See* exponentiation; floating-point notation.

exponentiation The operation of raising a number or algebraic expression to a power, i.e. of multiplying that number or expression by itself a given number of times. The common arithmetic notation for exponentiation is A^n, where the superscript n indicates the number of times A is multiplied by itself. The symbol n is the *exponent* of A, and A is said to be raised to the *power n*. For example,

$$2^4 = 2 \times 2 \times 2 \times 2 = 16$$

The value of 2^1 is 2; the value of 2^0 is taken to be 1. Exponents are not restricted to integers but may be fractional or negative.

Exponentiation is supplied in some form in most programming languages (although not in Pascal). It is represented by means of an *arithmetic operator. The most common representations are ↑ (used for example in Basic) and ** (used for example in Fortran). 2^4 can thus be written as 2↑4 or 2**4. In *order of precedence, exponentiation is performed before multiplication, division, addition, and subtraction. Thus

$$3 \uparrow 2 + 5 = 3^2 + 5 = 14$$

To indicate 3^{2+5} it would be necessary to use brackets, i.e.

$$3 \uparrow (2 + 5)$$

extended precision *See* precision.

F

failure Termination of the normal operation of some portion of a computer system, or of the whole system. A failure is the result of a *fault. The *mean time between failures (MTBF)* is often used as a measure of the *reliability of a computer system (*see* mean).

father file *See* master file.

fault An accidental condition that prevents some portion of a computer system from performing its prescribed function. It usually causes a *failure, although it is possible for a system to be *fault-tolerant.

fault-tolerant system A computer system that is capable of providing either a full or a reduced level of service in the event of a fault. In a fault-tolerant system if a disk were to develop a faulty track, then one of a number of spare tracks would automatically be brought into use in its place with minimum impact on the overall performance of the system.

FDX *Short for* full duplex. *See* duplex transmission.

feasibility study A study carried out before development of a proposed computer system in order to establish that the proposed system is possible, practical, and can serve a useful purpose. It may be a purely paper exercise or may involve the construction of an experimental or prototype version. It may concentrate on specific areas or decisions where the feasibility is questionable or the potential risk is greatest.

Ferranti Mark I *See* first generation computers.

fetch To locate and load a *machine instruction or item of data from main store. *See also* fetch-execute cycle; control unit.

fetch-execute cycle (instruction cycle) The two steps of obtaining a *machine instruction from main store and carrying it out. The fetch-execute cycle is under the direction of the *control unit and is repeated for every instruction.

fibre optics transmission *Transmission of data using special glass (or plastic) fibres, known as *optical fibres*. An optical fibre is very thin, flexible, and is made of very pure material that absorbs only a tiny proportion of the light passing through it. It is constructed in such a way that light can travel down the length of the fibre (which can exceed several kilometres) with very little loss through the walls. This is achieved by making the refractive index of the optical fibre vary across its diameter: it is lowest on the outside of the fibre and increases either smoothly or in one or more steps towards the centre. (The refractive index of a medium is a measure of how much light bends on entering that medium.) The light is thus made to snake or to zigzag down the centre of the fibre.

A simple fibre optics transmission system consists of a transmitter with a light source (such as a laser), a receiver with a light detector, and an intervening optical fibre. An electrical signal carrying the data to be transmitted is fed to the transmitter, and causes the light emitted by the source to be modulated, i.e. encoded with the data in some way (*see* modulation); normally the light is emitted as a sequence of pulses. The light signal enters and travels along the optical fibre, and at the other end is detected and converted back into the original electrical signal.

In fibre optics transmission a sheaf of optical fibres is used so that many signals can be carried at the same time. Optical fibres have become cost-competitive with *coaxial cable, with the advantages of having a much greater data-carrying capacity, much lower signal loss, immunity to electrical interference, and no signal interaction between the fibres.

fiche *Short for* microfiche. *See* COM.

field 1. A portion of a *record. It contains a fixed or variable number of letters, digits, or other characters.

2. A portion of a *machine instruction. It contains a

coded representation of, say, the operation to be performed or the address of the operand or operands.

FIFO *Abbrev. for* first in first out. *See* queue.

fifth generation computers The types of computer currently under development in a number of countries, and predicted as becoming available in the 1990s. The features are still conjectural but point towards the 'intelligent' machine. *See also* first, second, third, fourth generation computers.

file A named collection of information held temporarily or permanently on *backing store – magnetic disk or tape. The file name is stored in a *directory and is used to identify the file to the *operating system of the computer. Files may hold data, programs, text, or any other information, and can therefore be described as *data files, *program files, etc. They can also be broadly classified as *master files, *transaction files, or *reference files. Some files are *work files and have only a very brief existence.

Data files are normally organized as sets of related *records. The type of organization used for the records is designed to support one or more *access methods*. These are the methods used for the storage and retrieval of records. There are two basic types.

A file is *sequentially accessed* if the records are read or written one after another starting at the beginning. A file organized to support sequential access is known as a *sequential file*. Files held on magnetic tape are always sequentially accessed. The files are written in units known as *blocks, and are read in blocks. Sequential organization can also be used on magnetic disk for any files for which there is no requirement to access a particular record directly, but that are normally accessed by starting at the first record and moving through the file one record at a time. This is the case for many data files and also for program files and document files.

A file is *randomly accessed* if any record can be

accessed directly without having to pass over previous records in the file. A file organized to support random access is known as a *random-access file* (or *direct-access file*). Files can be randomly accessed only on magnetic disk. (Disks can thus hold randomly and sequentially organized files.) The two most common random-access methods are indexed sequential (*see* indexed sequential file) and *hashing. Random organization is used when the order of access of records is not known in advance and varies from one use of the file to the next.

file archive A collection of magnetic disks or tapes on which are held rarely used *files, which can be restored to the computer system if required. Files may be explicitly placed in the archive, or may be automatically moved there after they have remained unused for a given period.

file maintenance The maintenance of both the integrity of *files, i.e. the correctness of all the data values, and an efficient internal organization of files. It is performed by software. *See also* file management.

file management The overall management of *files, including their allocation to space on *backing store, control over file *access, the writing of *backup copies, the movement of files to the *file archive, and the maintenance of *directories. It is performed by software, basic file management being done by the *operating system of the computer. *See also* file maintenance.

file protection The protection of *files from mistaken or unauthorized *access of information or, in the case of *program files, from mistaken or unauthorized *execution. File protection may be concerned with the security of the contents of files, or with the protection of the disks or tapes on which files are held. The former is implemented by software, the latter by operating procedures.

filestore The portion of disk *backing store used for storing permanent *files, programs, data, etc.

file transfer The movement of entire *files from one computer system to another, typically across a *network. In order to transfer a file successfully there must be cooperating programs running on each system: the sender has to be able to specify the file name, ultimate destination, and authorization for the transfer to the receiver, and the receiver must agree to the transfer and inform the sender of its eventual success or failure. In *multiprocessing systems file transfer is normally achieved by *background processing.

file updating Inserting, deleting, or amending values in a file – usually a *data file – without changing the organization of the contents. File updating can be achieved in two ways. In one, commonly used in *data processing, the updating process is carried out by *batch processing. In the other, a file is displayed on an *interactive device and the operator can then see to amend it, using a special file editing program.

firmware Programs that do not have to be loaded into a computer but are permanently available in main store. They are held in *ROM (read-only memory) and thus are fixed in content even when the power supply is removed.

first generation computers The earliest computers to be produced, in the 1940s and early 1950s, based on the technology of the time. Electronic valves were used in the circuitry and storage devices were usually delay lines, electrostatic devices, or rotating *magnetic drums. Input/output was achieved mainly with *punched cards, punched *paper tape, and later on with *magnetic tape; simple *printers were available. The use of valves meant that first generation computers were very large in size, generated considerable heat and thus required cooling, and did not operate very fast or very reliably. They were still able to perform impressive computations. Most of them embodied the concept of the *stored program.

The following are important first generation computers.

ENIAC: design begun 1943 by J. W. Mauchley and J. P. Eckert at the University of Pennsylvania; operational 1946, but did not use a stored program and was regarded as a general-purpose electronic calculator.

EDVAC: design begun 1945 by J. von Neumann at the University of Pennsylvania, the proposal being the first written documentation of a computer with a stored program; not operational until 1952.

Manchester Mark I: design begun 1946 by T. Kilburn and F. C. Williams at the University of Manchester; regarded as the first operational stored program computer, with realistic problem-solving first achieved in April 1949.

EDSAC: design begun 1946 by M. V. Wilkes at Cambridge University; started operating in May 1949 as the first complete operational stored program computer.

Ferranti Mark I: commercial version of the Manchester Mark I, produced by Ferranti Ltd., Manchester, and delivered in 1951; it was the world's first commercially available computer. Ferranti's computer interests were sold, 1963, to ICT, which merged, 1968, with English Electric Leo Marconi to form ICL (International Computers Ltd.).

UNIVAC I: product of the American company Eckert-Mauchley Corp. and commercially available in 1951, shortly after the Ferranti Mark I. Eckert-Mauchley was formed in 1947 following development of ENIAC and later became Sperry-Univac.

LEO I: design begun 1947 by T. R. Thompson and J. Pinkerton for J. Lyons & Co. (a large UK catering firm) and operational by 1953; enhanced version (LEO II) marketed by Leo Computers Ltd., formed 1954. Leo Computers merged with English Electric, 1963, and is now part of ICL.

See also second, third, fourth, fifth generation computers.

fixed disk, fixed disk drive *See* disk drive.

1	2	3	4	5	6	7	8	9	10
J	O	N	E	S			1	0	3
S	M	I	T	H				8	7
B	R	O	W	N			1	2	3

Fixed format

fixed format Data arranged so that particular items always occur in particular positions. In the example shown in the diagram, the name always starts in the first position, while the numbers are in positions 8, 9, and 10. Because the whereabouts of each item of information is strictly defined, there is no need for gaps between the items. The format of the example could be 'A name in columns 1 to 5, an age in positions 8 and 9, and the number in the family in position 10.' *Compare* free format.

fixed head *See* disk drive.

fixed-point notation A representation of *real numbers that is in everyday use and in which a number is expressed in the form of a set of digits with the *radix point fixed in position so that the digits have their correct positional value (*see* number system). Examples of fixed-point notation in decimal and binary are

4927.54, 101011.11, 0.0000001

Fixed-point notation is used in computing in situations, such as commercial data processing, where huge quantities of numbers are handled, and the values are neither very large nor very small. The range of values that a computer can handle efficiently is limited by *word length: each item of information must fit into a word containing a fixed number of bits. A 16-bit word, for example, can have 2^{16} possible values, which can be used, say, to represent whole unsigned numbers from 0 to 65 535. Although more than one word can be used to represent a number and hence give a wider range of values, this increases processing time. Where a wide range is needed, *floating-point notation is used.

flag A device, item of data, etc., that can be set to a particular value to indicate that some condition or state has been attained by a piece of equipment or by a program. For example, an *overflow flag* is a single bit that is set to 1 when *overflow occurs in a register during an arithmetic operation; an *interrupt flag* is set when an *interrupt occurs.

The word *sentinel* is used as a synonym for flag but is usually used in the context of input and output. For example, an *end-of-data sentinel* indicates that all the data has been read. A flag or sentinel, once set, is subsequently used as a basis for a conditional *jump and similar decision processes.

flatbed plotter *See* plotter.

flat screen A type of *screen in the form of a thin flat panel rather than the protruding surface usually associated with the cathode-ray tube used in many display devices. Plasma panel *displays and *LCDs have flat screens.

flexidisk *Another name for* floppy disk.

flip-flop (bistable) An electronic circuit that has two stable states, either of which can be maintained until the circuit is made to switch or 'flip' to the other state. A change in output state requires a suitable combination of input signal(s) and existing output state; in effect, the receipt of a pulse will reverse the state. The two states are used in computer circuits to represent binary 1 and binary 0. Flip-flops can therefore store one *bit of information, and are widely used as storage elements, e.g. in *ROM and *RAM and in *registers. Various types have been developed, differing slightly in function.

floating-point notation A representation of *real numbers that allows both very large and very small numbers, and both positive and negative numbers, to be expressed in a convenient form. Examples are

$$1.3 \times 10^6, -2.5 \times 10^3, 0.65 \times 10^{-3}$$

Such numbers are encountered in science, maths, and engineering and cannot be handled efficiently in a computer in *fixed-point notation.

A floating-point number is represented by a pair of quantities called the *mantissa* and the *exponent*, and has the general form

$$m \times b^e$$

b is the base of the number system, equal to 10 in decimal notation; the mantissa, m, can be positive or negative; the exponent, e, is the power to which the base is raised, and is a positive or negative integer. In programming languages, whose character sets do not include superscripts, different conventions are used. A common one is to use an 'E' to stand for '10 to the power of', e.g.

$$2.7 \times 10^{-3} \text{ is written } 2.7\,\text{E} -3$$

Inside a computer a floating-point number is stored and manipulated as a sequence of bits. Typically, the first bit is a *sign bit*, indicating whether the mantissa is positive or negative; this is followed by a fixed number of bits giving the sign and magnitude of the exponent; this in turn is followed by a fixed number of bits representing the magnitude of the mantissa. The radix point of the mantissa is usually taken to be before the leftmost bit, i.e. the mantissa is a fraction. There may be, say, 7 bits for the exponent and 40 for the mantissa. This gives a wide range of numbers but means that on small machines each floating-point number needs several *words of store.

floating-point number A number expressed in *floating-point notation.

floppy disk (diskette; flexidisk) A relatively small

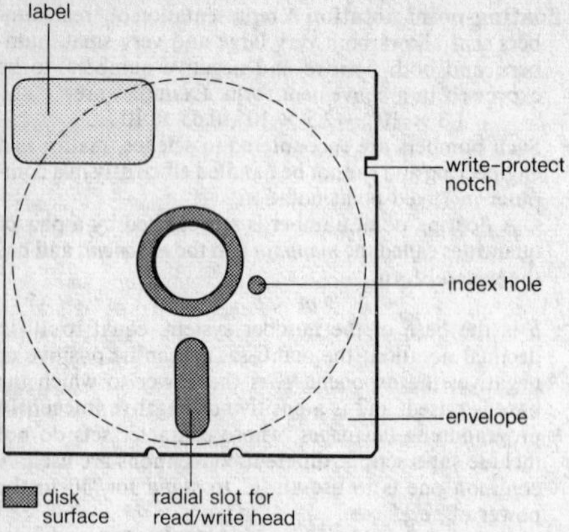

Floppy disk and envelope

flexible *magnetic disk, enclosed within a stiff protective envelope (see diagram). Floppy disks are extensively used in small computers as on-line *backing store and off-line storage devices. They have much smaller storage *capacities and much longer *access times than *hard disks, but are considerably cheaper and need less careful handling. Unfortunately floppy disks are frequently incompatible: a floppy disk recorded on one type of microcomputer cannot normally be used on a machine of a different make or sometimes even on another machine of the same make.

The most common size of floppy disk is the 5¼ inch diameter disk, often referred to as the *minifloppy*, while the newer size, or *microfloppy*, is usually $3\frac{1}{2}$ inches in diameter; the older 8 inch disk is now rarely seen. As with other magnetic disks, data is recorded in concentric tracks in the magnetic coating. The tracks themselves are divided into *sectors. *Single-sided* disks use only one surface for recording data; *double-sided* disks use both sides. There are recording techniques whereby the storage capacity of each track can be doubled; this gives *double density* as opposed to *single density*. Storage *capacities are increasing rapidly as the technology advances, and can exceed a megabyte.

The floppy disk remains inside its envelope when it is fed into a *disk drive for reading and writing purposes. A hole through the centre of the disk and envelope allows the disk to be positioned on the rotation mechanism and clamped in place. The disk rotates inside the envelope, becoming rigid as it spins. Radial slots in the envelope allow the read/write head (or heads in a double-sided disk) to make contact with the disk surface. A small *index hole* through envelope and disk is used for timing purposes. The disk drive can be prevented from writing to the disk by means of the *write-protect notch* in one edge of the envelope.

flops *Abbrev. for* floating-point operations per second. A commonly used measure of computer performance for very powerful computers, made in terms of the number of arithmetic operations that can be performed on *floating-point numbers in a period of one second. It is usually expressed in *megaflops* (*see* mega-).

flowchart 1. (program flowchart) A diagrammatic representation of the structure of a program, showing the actions performed by the program and the flow of control. It consists of a set of *boxes* of various standard shapes, interconnected by a set of *flow lines*. For clarity the lines may have arrows to indicate the flow of control. The different shapes of the boxes indicate either different kinds of activity or a decision to be made. The activity or decision is described within the boxes, typi-

symbol	use
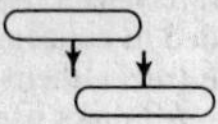	for indicating start or finish of a flowchart
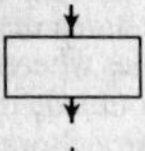	for any kind of processing activity, excluding decisions
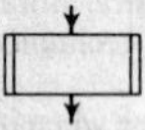	for a processing activity dealt with elsewhere, e.g. subroutine, procedure
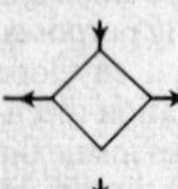	where a decision to be made, the two (or more) exits being labelled, e.g. 'yes' or 'no', in accordance with the possible choices
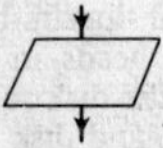	for any input or output operation
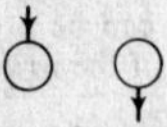	for indicating continuation on or from another part of flowchart
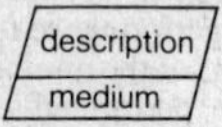 description / medium	for any input or output of data, however achieved
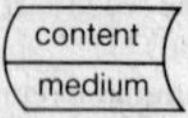 content / medium	for data held in any on-line file, the medium usually being disk or tape
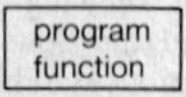 program function	for processing of data
	for indicating continuation elsewhere

Symbols in program flowcharts (top) and system flowcharts (bottom)

cally in natural language (e.g. English). In addition there are circular connector symbols that connect flow lines and are used, for example, when a flowchart continues on another page. Typical program flowchart symbols are given in the upper section of the table.

2. (system flowchart; data flowchart) A diagrammatic representation of a complete computer system, showing both the operations involved and the flow of data in the system. It does not indicate how the processing operations are carried out – this information would appear in a program flowchart. The number of flow lines entering and exiting each symbol depends on the situation. Typical system flowchart symbols are given in the lower section of the table.

flow control Procedures used to control the *data transfer rate, i.e. to limit the rate at which data is transferred to the rate at which it can be received – either at its final destination or at a series of points along its route.

There are three flow-control methods in common use. With *XON/XOFF* the receiver can temporarily halt the sender by transmitting an XOFF (transmitter off, *ASCII code 19), and an XON (transmitter on, ASCII code 17) when once more ready to receive; this method requires full *duplex transmission. With *ETX/ACK* the sender terminates a block of data with an ETX (end transmission, ASCII code 3), and the receiver responds with an ACK (acknowledge, ASCII code 6) only when it is ready for more data; this method can be used in *half-duplex communications but relies on the sender not sending too much at a time. Thirdly there is the use of *control signals*, where the receiver uses a separate wire to indicate to the sender whether it is ready for data.

footprint The area of floor or desk space occupied by a device, or the shape and size of panel opening into which it would fit.

FOR *See* Basic.

foreground processing The processing of a computer program that has been granted a high priority and can thus preempt the resources – main store, processor, etc. – of the computer from programs with a low priority. High-priority programs are called *foreground programs* while the low-priority programs are known as *background programs*. During foreground processing there is usually the opportunity for interaction between user and computer. Foreground processing together with *background processing takes place in many *multiaccess systems.

for loop *See* loop.

form A page of printer paper. It may be a single sheet or may be sheets joined together in the form of *continuous stationery. In either case it may be multipart so that copies can be produced. Individual sheets may be preprinted with headings or other information, possibly with lines or boxes.

format 1. The structure that is used in the arrangement of data. It is determined before use, and in some cases is set by industrial or international standards. There are various kinds. *Instruction format* defines the arrangement of the parts of a *machine instruction. *Printer format* defines the layout on paper of the output from a *printer, for example the areas of a page where printing will occur and the spacing between words and between lines. *Tape format* and *disk format* define the arrangements in which data can be recorded on *magnetic tape or *magnetic disk.

2. To prepare a blank storage medium, such as a disk, to accept data, or to put data into a predetermined structure. Such processes are known as *formatting*.

forms tractor *See* tractor feed.

Forth A *programming language designed originally for the control of scientific instruments from microcomputers with very small memories. It is a *low-level language that makes great use of the *stack, and is very compact. Although the current memory sizes of microcomputers have made the small size of Forth largely irrelevant, it is still popular as a substitute for *assembler language among microcomputer users.

Fortran A *programming language whose name is derived from **for**mula **tran**slation. It was first released by IBM in the mid-1950s. Fortran was one of the earliest *high-level languages generally available for scientific and technical applications, and has been under continuous development. The current international standard, Fortran 77, is due to be replaced by Fortran 8x in the late 1980s. Fortran is still probably the most widely used language for scientific work, even though its *control structures are relatively crude compared with more modern languages. Each new release has more sophisticated features, however, so Fortran may well remain the preferred scientific language.

fourth generation computers Computers currently in use and designed in the period from about 1970. Since the design of computers is a continuous process by different groups in several countries, it is difficult to establish when a generation of computers starts and finishes. Conceptually the most important criterion that can be used to separate fourth generation from *third generation computers is that they have been designed to work efficiently with the current generation of *high-level languages and are intended to be easier to program by their end-user. From a hardware point of view they are characterized by being constructed largely from *integrated circuits and have very large (multi-megabyte) main store fabricated from *semiconductor memory.

The availability of an ever-increasing range of integrated circuits has produced a rapid fall in the cost of hardware while software costs have continuously increased. This has led to the existence of many computers designed for special tasks such as communications, automatic control, and military systems, which in the past would have been general-purpose machines adapted to their task by software.

See also first, second, fifth generation computers.

fragmentation The breaking up of disk *files into a number of different sections scattered across a disk. It occurs when files of different sizes are frequently deleted and written. Each new file is written in the first available gap left by the deletion of a previous file; if the new file is too big for the gap then the rest is written in the next gap, and so on. The result is that a number of movements of the read/write heads of the *disk drive might be required to access each fragmented file, thus reducing the efficiency of the disk system. To get rid of the fragmentation, all the files are copied onto an empty disk, one at a time, thus ensuring that each file is in one piece.

free format Data arranged so that, although the items are in a specified order, the actual positions of the items are not defined. In free format it is necessary to have a separator such as some spaces and/or a comma between the items so that it is possible to tell when one ends and the next begins, for example

JONES,10,3
SMITH,8,7
BROWN,12,3
ROBINSON, 25, 1

The format here could be 'A name followed by an age followed by the number in the family.' *Compare* fixed format.

frequency division multiplexing (FDM) *See* multiplexer.

friction feed A technique for feeding paper into a *printer. Each sheet is fed in by hand and is gripped by a rotating roller, as in a typewriter. The paper cannot be positioned as accurately as it is with *tractor feed. *See also* cut sheet feed.

front-end processor A small computer, often a mini,

that is used to relieve a mainframe computer of some of the tasks associated with input/output. It receives data from a number of input/output devices (such as the terminals in a *multiaccess system), organizes it, and transmits it to the more powerful computer for processing. It also handles the output from the mainframe to the terminals. In a *network, a front-end processor may handle the control of communication lines, code conversion, error control, etc. It is more powerful than a *multiplexer in that it can perform simple editing, echoing, routing, etc.

full-duplex transmission *Another name for* duplex transmission. *See also* half-duplex transmission.

function A section of a program whose main purpose is to calculate a single value, such as the square root of a number, the sine or cosine of a number, or the length of a character *string. The item of data on which the calculation is performed, or its address in memory, is known as the *argument; the calculation may be performed on more than one item of data and hence there may be more than one argument. To perform the calculation the function must be *called.

A collection of different functions are provided as part of a programming language, and any of these can be used by the programmer without an understanding of the details of its internal working. Most languages also permit user-defined functions. *See also* procedure; parameter.

function key *See* keyboard.

function part *Another name for* operation part. *See* machine instruction.

G

G The symbol used for *giga-, or sometimes for gigabyte.

garbage Stored data that is no longer valid or no longer wanted. Removal of this superfluous data from store is known as *garbage collection*. *See also* GIGO.

gas panel display *Another name for* plasma panel display. *See* display.

gate *Short for* logic gate.

general-purpose computer A computer that can be used for any function for which it can be conveniently programmed and can thus perform a series of unrelated tasks.

generations of computers. An informal way of classifying computer systems on the basis of advances in technology, especially electronic technology, and latterly also on advances in software. The generation of computers currently in use is the *fourth generation (which succeeded the *third, *second, and *first generations), with *fifth generation computers currently under development. Since the design of computers has been a continuous process for decades – by a wide variety of people in different countries, faced with different problems – it is difficult (and not very profitable) to establish when generations start and finish.

generator A program that accepts the definition of an operation that is to be accomplished and automatically constructs a program for the purpose. An example is the *report generator*, which can be used in commercial data processing to extract information from files. The input to such a program is a description of the file structure and a specification of the information required and the way in which it should be presented to the user. The report generator can then construct a program to read the file, extract the desired information, and output it in the desired format.

giga- A prefix indicating a multiple of a thousand million (i.e. 10^9) or, loosely, a multiple of 2^{30} (i.e.

1 073 741 824

In science and technology decimal notation is usually used, and powers of 10 are thus encountered – 10^3 10^6,

10^9, etc. The symbol G is used for giga-, as in GV for gigavolt. Binary notation is generally used in computing, and so the power of 2 nearest to 10^9 has assumed the meaning of giga-.

The prefix is most frequently encountered in computing in the context of storage *capacity. With magnetic disks, magnetic tape, and main store, the capacity is normally reckoned in terms of the number of *bytes that can be stored, and the *gigabyte* is used to mean 2^{30} bytes; gigabyte is usually abbreviated to G byte or just to G, thus a 1.2 G byte Winchester disk can hold 1.2885 $\times$ 10^9 bytes.

Giga- is part of a sequence

kilo-, mega-, giga-, tera-, . . .

of increasing powers of 10^3 (or of 2^{10}).

GIGO *Abbrev. for* garbage in garbage out, signifying that a program working on incorrect data produces incorrect results.

global variable *See* scope.

golfball printer A type of impact character *printer whose printing mechanism was first used in electric typewriters. The characters are moulded on a spherical print head. The head is rotated (in two directions) in order to bring the required character opposite the printing position, and is then struck against the inked ribbon and paper. The head is interchangeable, enabling different character sets to be used. The golfball printer is slower than the *daisywheel printer.

GOSUB *See* Basic.

GOTO statement An unconditional *jump instruction in a high-level language. It causes the normal flow of control to be broken by specifying explicitly the next statement to be executed, usually by means of the statement number, as in

GOTO 99

Use of GOTOs can make programs difficult to follow and is thus no longer recommended. An extended form, the *computed GOTO*, appears in Fortran and is used to go to one of several statements, the choice dependent on the value of an integer variable. Many versions of Basic have a similar facility.

grandfather file *See* master file.

graphic character A symbol that can be produced by printing, typing, or handwriting. It may be an *alphanumeric character, a *space character, or a *special character, or it may be an underline character, a T-shaped symbol, an inverted T-shaped symbol, etc., used to create a simple box, table, and so on. *Compare* control character.

graphics *See* computer graphics.

graphics card (graphics board) *See* expansion card.

graphics display A *VDU with graphics capability, i.e. one that can display pictures, graphs, and charts as well as text.

graphics tablet *Another name for* digitizing pad.

graph plotter *See* plotter.

H

hacker A person who tinkers with *systems software, usually without authorization. A hacker may be a skilled programmer who produces useful additional features, but these features tend to be badly documented and have unfortunate side effects. With the growth of computer *networks there are now hackers whose aim is to breach the *security of remote computer systems, such as those owned by banks or government agencies. The motive is often merely personal satisfaction but occasionally malicious damage or fraud occurs. The hacker's equipment need only be a personal computer and a telephone *modem.

half-duplex transmission (HDX) Transmission of

data between two endpoints, the data travelling in either direction but only in one direction at a time. It cannot flow simultaneously in both directions. Only one signal wire is therefore required in half-duplex working. The time taken to reverse the direction of transmission from send to receive or from receive to send is called the *turnaround time*. Half-duplex transmission can be used for terminals that perform their own *echoing, and for any situation in which it is unnecessary for both ends to transmit simultaneously. *Compare* duplex transmission; simplex transmission.

halt instruction A *machine instruction that in a simple computer causes the processor to idle until an *interrupt is received, and in a more sophisticated computer will return control to the *operating system.

handshake An exchange of signals that establishes communication between two or more devices (by synchronizing them) and allows data to be transferred. The signals have various meanings such as

'I am waiting to transmit.'
'I am ready to receive.'
'I am not ready to receive.'
'I am switched on.'
'The data is available.'
'Data has been read successfully.'

hands on A method of operating a system in which a person is in control. This operator literally has hands on a keyboard and other switches to control the processes to be carried out by the system. The dependence on the capability of a person to run a medium-size or large computer has been reduced by the introduction of *supervisor programs or *operating systems.

hard copy A permanent copy, printed on paper for example, of information from a computer.

hard disk A rigid *magnetic disk. Hard disks must be carefully protected from damage and dust. They are used in the more expensive *disk drives, where they are either permanently mounted or are removable and replaceable as *disk packs or *disk cartridges. A higher recording *density can normally be achieved than with a flexible disk, i.e. a *floppy disk. The highest densities are attained on the hard disks used in *Winchester disk drives.

hard-sectored disk *See* sector.

hardware The actual equipment used in a computer system, including not only the major devices – such as VDUs, disk drives, and printers – and the electronic circuitry making up semiconductor memory, logic circuits, etc., but also cables, cabinets, and so on. *Compare* software.

hardware character generation A technique whereby a *VDU or *plotter can be directed (by receipt of a particular signal from a computer) to display or draw a specified *character, the style and size of which is determined by the device's internal circuitry. This drastically reduces the complexity of the information transmitted. Instead of having to describe each character in terms of a number of dots or strokes, a single code of typically 7 or 8 bits represents each character. By means of special control codes, the size, slant, brightness, etc., of the hardware characters may often be altered.

hardwired logic Logic circuitry that forms all or part of an *integrated circuit and is thus permanently interconnected. Its function cannot therefore be changed.

hashing A technique used for organizing *tables or *files of information to permit rapid *searching or *table look-up. It is particularly useful for random-access *files and for tables to which items are added in an unpredictable manner, such as the *symbol table of a compiler. Each item of information to be placed in the table or file has a unique *key*. A special *hashing algorithm* uses the key to allocate a position to each item, the collection of items being distributed fairly evenly over the table or file. The same algorithm is used to yield the starting point for a search for the key.

hash total *See* control total.

HDX *Short for* half-duplex.

head The part of a peripheral device that is in contact with the data medium, or very close to it, and that is responsible for writing data on the medium or for reading or erasing data. For example, *disk drives and *tape units have *magnetic heads*; a magnetic head may be a *read head*, a *write head*, an *erase head*, or a *read/write head*, depending on its function.

head crash (disk crash) The accidental and disastrous contact of a read/write head with the surface of a hard disk as it rotates in a *disk drive. (Normally the head flies just above the surface.) A crash is often caused by the head passing over a particle of dust on the surface. The contact destroys the track so affected – and the data stored in that track. Particles of surface material produced by the contact rapidly spread around and cause other tracks to be destroyed. The damaged disk has to be thrown away. The possibility of a head crash is reduced by using the disk in dust-free or filtered air kept at a controlled temperature and humidity. Disks should be *backed up at regular intervals so that in the event of a crash a duplicate is available.

header label (header) *See* tape label.

heuristic Employing a 'self-learning' approach to the solution of a problem. A heuristic system is constructed so that it can acquire the knowledge needed to produce the required solution. This approach is adopted, for instance, when there is no good *algorithm to yield the solution. It may involve the knowledge, gained through experience, of when best to use a particular strategy. Heuristic methods have been employed, for example, to control the routing of data through computer *networks: the actual performance of a network is used to influence subsequent decisions on routing. Heuristic techniques have also been applied to problems in *artificial intelligence.

hex *Short for* hexadecimal notation or hexadecimal.

hexadecimal notation (hex) A number system that uses 16 digits and thus has *base 16. The 16 digits are represented by

0, 1, 2, ... 9, A, B, C, D, E, F

It is a positional notation (*see* number system), positional values increasing from right to left by powers of 16. Hex is a convenient shorthand by which people (rather than computers) can handle binary numbers. Each hex digit corresponds to a group of 4 binary digits, or bits, as shown in the table. Conversion of

binary	hex	binary	hex
0000	0	1000	8
0001	1	1001	9
0010	2	1010	A
0011	3	1011	B
0100	4	1100	C
0101	5	1101	D
0110	6	1110	E
0111	7	1111	F

Hexadecimal and binary equivalents

binary to hex is done by marking off groups of 4 bits in the binary number (starting from the right) and replacing each group by its hex equivalent. Conversion of hex to binary is done by replacing each hex digit by its equivalent binary group. *See also* binary notation.

hierarchy of operators The *order of precedence of *operators in a particular programming language.

high-level language A kind of *programming language whose features reflect the requirements of the programmer. It achieves this by being designed for the solution of problems in one or more areas of application. High-level languages are thus described as *applications-orientated* (or *problem-orientated*). They are easier for the programmer to use than *low-level languages, being closer to natural language and to the language of mathematics.

The programmer needs little knowledge of the computer on which the program is to run: unlike a low-level language a high-level language does not reflect the facilities provided by computer hardware. Before being run on a particular computer, however, programs written in a high-level language must be translated into a form that can be accepted by that computer, i.e. they must be converted into *machine code. This is achieved by means of a special program – either a *compiler or an *interpreter. Each statement in the original program – called the *source program* – is translated into many machine instructions. A source program can be translated into different machine codes using different compilers or interpreters. As a result, programs written in high-level languages can be moved from, say, one microcomputer to another.

The first high-level languages were released in the late 1950s. The number and variety now available is large and still growing. Examples include *Basic, *Cobol, *Fortran, *Algol, *Pascal, *Ada, and *Prolog. Some high-level languages are aimed at specific areas of application. Cobol, for instance, was developed for commercial data processing while Fortran is widely used for scientific computation. Other languages, such as Basic, Pascal, and Ada, are designed to be of more general use.

Hollerith code A code whereby the 26 letters of the alphabet and the digits 0–9 are represented as patterns of holes punched in cards. Each character is encoded by a hole (for the digits) or by two holes (for the letters) punched in a particular row or combination of rows within a column; each column has 12 rows. The code was devised by Herman Hollerith in the 1880s and used originally to speed up the process of recording and analysing the results of the 1890 US census. It is still used on 80-column *punched cards.

host computer (host) A computer that is attached to a *network and whose main function is to provide services to the network users rather than being involved in the operation of the network (*compare* node). Hosts can range from small microcomputers to mainframes. The latter may provide powerful computation facilities, a large *filestore, special programs or programming languages, and access to one or more *databases.

housekeeping Actions performed within a program or within a computer system in order to maintain internal orderliness. In the case of a program it may, for example, involve the management of storage space by freeing areas no longer required (*see* garbage). In the context of an entire computer system, housekeeping involves *backing up the *filestore, deleting files that are no longer required or whose expiry dates have passed, copying disks to reduce *fragmentation, and many other mundane but essential tasks.

human-computer interface (HCI) *Another name for* man-machine interface.

human-system interface (HSI) *Another name for* man-machine interface.

hybrid computer *See* analog computer.

I

IAR *Abbrev. for* instruction address register.

IAS *Abbrev. for* immediate access store.

IBG *Abbrev. for* interblock gap. *See* block.

IC *Abbrev. for* integrated circuit.

icon or **ikon** A pictorial symbol used in a *menu to avoid dependence on natural language.

identifier A *string of one or more letters, digits, or other characters selected by a programmer to identify some element in a program. An identifier can be a *name or a *label. The kind of element that can be identified depends on the programming language. It could, for example, be a *variable, an *array, a *procedure, or a *statement. When the program is compiled or assembled, prior to execution, identifiers are converted to machine addresses using a *symbol table. *See also* literal; reserved word.

idle time Time during which the central processor of a computer system is performing no useful function. It usually occurs when the workload on the system is insufficient to keep the processor fully occupied, or when the demands on the input/output components of the system are such that the processor runs out of work before outstanding input/output is completed.

IF, IF THEN *See* Basic.

if then else statement A simple conditional *control structure that appears in most programming languages and allows selection between two alternatives; the choice is dependent on whether a given condition is true or not. An example is

if it rains this afternoon
then we go to the cinema
else we go for a walk

Most languages also provide an *if then* structure to allow conditional execution of a single statement or group of statements, for example

if you have a dog with you
then put it on a lead

Primitive languages, like earlier versions of Fortran or Basic, restrict this facility to a conditional transfer of control, for example

110 IF A = 0 THEN 20

See also case statement.

if then statement *See* if then else statement.

ikon *See* icon.

illegal character A character, possibly in a binary representation, that is not in the *character set of a particular computer or of a particular programming language.

illegal instruction A *machine instruction whose *operation code cannot be recognized by a particular computer with the result that the instruction cannot be executed by the computer. Since neither a *compiler nor an *assembler ought to be able to generate an illegal instruction, a message from the *operating system claiming that one has been encountered is usually caused by accidentally using part of the main store containing instructions to store data, and subsequently trying to execute the data.

image processing (picture processing) The analysis and manipulation of information contained in images. The original subject can be an actual object or scene, a photograph, drawing, etc. A numerical version of this subject is obtained electronically: the original is effectively divided into a large number of tiny individual portions, and a set of numbers is produced, corresponding to the measured brightness and colour of these portions. The original is thus converted into a two-dimensional *array of data. The individual portions are known as *pixels*; the greater the number of pixels per image, the greater the detail available. The original is said to have been *digitized.*

This numerical version of the original is usually stored in a computer and can be manipulated in various ways to highlight different aspects of the original. For example, a specified range of brightness can be increased, or two slightly different images can be compared or superimposed. The final form of the image can be produced on a screen, photographic film, or plotter, and information derived from the image can appear in graphs or tables and can be further analysed.

immediate access store (IAS) *Another name for* main store, indicating the very great speed with which data can be retrieved from main store.

immediate addressing The process by which the data needed as the *operand for an operation is actually held in the associated *machine instruction. Although the data contained there is usually restricted in size, immediate addressing provides a convenient and quick way of loading small numbers into a *register or *accumulator. *See also* addressing mode.

impact printer *See* printer.

implementation 1. The working version of a given design of a system.

2. The processes involved in developing a working version of a system from a given design.

3. The way in which some part of a system is made to fulfil its function.

index 1. A set of *pointers that can be used to locate records in an *indexed file or an *indexed sequential file.

2. The value held in an *index register.

3. **(subscript)** A value, usually an integer or integer expression, that is used in selecting a particular element in an *array.

indexed addressing (indexing) An *addressing mode in which the address given in a *machine instruction is modified by the contents of one or more *index registers; the contents of the index register(s) are usually added to the address. The result identifies a storage location. The address specified in the machine instruction is called an *indexed address*. It may be an actual address or an address of an address (*see* direct addressing; indirect addressing).

indexed file A *data file in which records can be

accessed by means of an *index. This is a separate portion of the file in which the locations of the records are stored. In the simplest form of an indexed file, an entry in the index points directly to the position of an individual record or of a group of records. This can give rise to a long search time in a large file, and a more complex (multilevel) index is then usually used. An indexed file has characteristics of a random-access file. *See also* file; indexed sequential file.

indexed sequential file A *file whose records are organized in such a way that they are written sequentially and can be read sequentially or by means of an index (*see* file, indexed file). The index can be used to read data randomly or to skip over unwanted records in a sequential read. The records are accessed by means of an *indexed sequential access method (ISAM)*. An indexed sequential file is similar to a textbook – which can be read in chunks or straight through, or specific information can be found using an alphabetical index.

indexing 1. *Another name for* indexed addressing.
2. Selecting an element from an *array by means of its *index.

index register A *register that can be specified by machine instructions using *indexed addressing. Data can be loaded into the index register by a variety of methods, depending on the type of computer; it may for example be loaded from the *accumulator.

indirect addressing An *addressing mode in which the address specified in a *machine instruction identifies a storage location that itself holds an address. The address part of the instruction is thus an address of an address. It is called an *indirect address*. The second location identified generally holds the required item of data, but may however hold a further address.

infinite loop A *loop in a program from which, under certain circumstances, there is no exit except by terminating the program. This can be done accidentally, perhaps by a while loop whose condition can never be untrue, or deliberately when a program is to repeat a sequence of actions until stopped by some external event such as an interrupt or the switching off of the computer.

infix notation A form of notation in which an *operator is placed between its *operands, as in the arithmetic expression

$$a + b * c$$

If no brackets are used the expression is evaluated in a computer according to the *order of precedence of the programming language. *See also* reverse Polish.

information Data that has been processed into a more useful or intelligible form, by a computer or by some other means, and so carries meaning. *See also* data.

information processing The organization and manipulation of pieces of information in order to derive additional information. Information processing is the principal means of increasing the amount and variety of information. The computer is an information-processing machine.

information retrieval The process of recovering information from a computer system. The aim is to access only the information required, and to do so in the minimum time with a minimum of simple instructions to the system. *See also* information storage.

information storage The recording of information, usually on magnetic tape or disk, so that it may be used at some later time. There are various methods of organizing and labelling the information so that it may be readily accessed. *See also* information retrieval.

information technology (IT) Any form of technology, i.e. any equipment or technique, used by people to handle information. Although the abacus and the printing press are examples of IT, the term usually refers to modern technology based on electronics. It thus incorporates both the technology of computing and of telephony, television, and other means of telecommunication. It has applications in industry, commerce, education, science, medicine, and in the home. The development of IT is recognized worldwide as being of major importance, especially since cost reductions have made large-scale IT systems economically possible.

initialize To set *counters, contents of storage *locations, *variables, etc., to zero or to some other specific value before the start of some operation, usually at the beginning of a program or program unit. The value set is known as the *initial value*. Many programming languages provide a facility for specifying initial values of variables when the variable is first declared.

ink-jet printer A type of *printer in which fine drops of quick-drying ink are projected on to the paper to form the characters. It is thus a nonimpact matrix printer (*see* printer) and is much quieter in operation than an impact printer. In one design the print head contains a column of nozzles, each capable of ejecting a single drop of ink at a time. As the head moves along the line to be printed, the appropriate characters are built up. In another design the head has only a single nozzle that emits a jet of ink. The jet is made to break up into droplets, and each droplet is electrically charged; this charge enables a droplet to be deflected vertically as it flies towards the paper. As the head moves along the line to be printed, the appropriate characters are built up. This latter design is slower than the design with the column of nozzles, which can print up to 400 characters per second. Colour ink-jets can produce a large number of colours by mixing the inks as they print.

input 1. The data or programs entered into a computer system by means of an *input device.

2. The signal – voltage, current, or power – fed into an electric circuit.

3. To enter data, programs, or signals into a system.

INPUT *See* Basic.

input device Any device that transfers data, programs, or signals into a computer system. Examples include *keyboards, graphical devices such as a *mouse or *digitizing pad, *voice input devices, and *document readers. An input device need not be operated by a person – it could for example be a temperature sensor. The data, programs, or signals are fed into the input device in a suitable form, and are then converted by the device into electrical signals that are transmitted to the *central processor of the computer. There may be many input devices in a computer system, each device providing some means of communication with the computer; input devices used by people are said to provide a *man-machine interface. *Compare* output device.

input medium *See* media.

input/output (I/O) Components or processes in a computer system that are concerned with the passing of information into and out of the system, and thus link the system with the outside world.

input/output bus (I/O bus) *See* bus.

input/output device (I/O device) Any device in a computer system that can function both as an *input device and an *output device, and can thus be used both as an entry point and as an exit point for information. *Terminals are I/O devices.

input/output file (I/O file) A *file used to hold information immediately after input from or immediately before output to an *input/output device.

input/output processor (I/O processor) *See* direct memory access.

instruction *See* machine instruction.

instruction address register (IAR) A *register, i.e. a temporary location, in the *control unit from whose contents the *address of the next machine instruction is derived. It thus stores in turn the addresses of the instructions that the computer has to carry out. Each time the control unit fetches an instruction, it automatically increases the contents of the IAR by one. If the sequence of the instructions is altered by an unconditional *jump instruction, the contents of the IAR are subsequently changed to the address indicated by the jump instruction; in the case of a *conditional jump instruction, the contents of the IAR are changed only if the condition is met.

Since the contents of the IAR are incremented so as to point to the start of the next instruction, the IAR is a *counter and hence is also called an *instruction counter* or a *program counter*.

instruction counter *Another name for* instruction address register.

instruction cycle *Another name for* fetch-execute cycle.

instruction format The layout of a *machine instruction, showing its constituent parts.

instruction overlap *See* control unit.

instruction pre-fetch *See* control unit.

instruction register (IR) A *register (i.e. a temporary location) usually in the *control unit, used for holding the *machine instruction that is currently being performed or is about to be performed. Once the control unit has finished execution of one instruction, it obtains the address of the next instruction from the *instruction address register, fetches this instruction from main store (via the *memory data register), and places it in the instruction register. The control unit can then interpret the instruction in the instruction register and cause the instruction to be executed. *See also* microprogram.

instruction set All the instructions that are available in a particular *machine code or *assembly language, i.e. all the instructions that a particular computer is capable of performing. *See* machine instruction.

INT *See* Basic.

integer Any positive or negative whole number, or zero. Integers belong to the set

. . . −4, −3, −2, −1, 0, +1, +2, +3, +4, . . .
Negative integers carry a minus sign to distinguish them from positive integers. Positive integers do not necessarily carry a plus sign. Any integer without a sign is said to be *unsigned.*

Unsigned integers are stored in a computer in *binary notation, i.e. as a sequence of bits making up a *word; the sequence is the binary equivalent of the integer. In a machine with an 8-bit word, 2^8 (i.e. 256) possible values can be stored, ranging from 00000000 to 11111111. These represent the integers from 0 to $2^8 - 1$, i.e. from 0 to 255. Signed integers are usually stored in two's complement (*see* complement), and an 8-bit word then stores values from -2^7 to $+(2^7 - 1)$, i.e. from −128 to +127. *See also* integer arithmetic; real number.

operation	integer result	remainder	normal result
9 ÷ 4	2	1	2.250
47 ÷ 3	15	2	15.666
98 ÷ 5	19	3	19.60
1 ÷ 2	0	1	0.50

Integer division

integer arithmetic Arithmetic involving only *integers. The addition, subtraction, and multiplication of integers always produces an integer as a result. In integer arithmetic, *integer division* also always produces an integer result, unlike normal arithmetic. This is achieved by ignoring the *remainder*. Hence in integer division 7 divided by 2 equals 3 (rather than 3.5). Other examples are shown in the table.

In a *modulo* operation the result is the *remainder* after

one integer is divided by another. This is usually written i modulo j for the division of integer i by integer j. Hence 47 modulo 3 is equal to 2.

Many programming languages have special operators and functions to perform integer arithmetic. Pascal has div and mod operators for integer division and remaindering (i div j and i mod j where i and j are integers); Fortran assumes integer division if both operands are integers (I/J gives an integer result if I and J are integers), but has a special function for the remainder (MOD(I,J)). The original Basic had no concept of integers as such, but most modern dialects remedy this in one way or another.

integer division *See* integer arithmetic.

integrated circuit (IC) A complete electronic circuit that is manufactured as a single package: all the individual devices required to realize the function of the circuit are fabricated on a single *chip of semiconductor, usually silicon. Components (mainly transistors and diodes) can be combined to make a wide variety of circuits, including *logic circuits and *semiconductor memory.

Integrated circuits can be fabricated using either *MOS technology* or *bipolar technology*. MOS devices in general use less power and are more densely packed with components than bipolar devices, but cannot operate as quickly as bipolar devices. Bipolar technology is used to produce the components of central processors in large computers. As these two fabrication technologies have advanced, ICs have become cheaper, with improved performance and reliability. In addition, the number of components that can be fabricated on a single chip is continuously and rapidly increasing; the greatest density is now over one million per chip.

IC technology can be classified as *VLSI (very large scale integration)*, producing the largest numbers of components per chip, and *LSI (large scale integration)*, producing somewhat lower numbers. *MSI (medium scale integration)* and *SSI (small scale integration)* are used for smaller densities.

integrated office system A program that performs several functions concerned with office tasks. It combines some of the functions previously performed by single-purpose programs, such as *word processors, *spreadsheets, *database management systems, or programs to create graphs and charts. The results of the various sections can usually be merged to form a final document containing textual, pictorial, and tabular material.

integrity of data. A measure of the correctness of data following processing. For data to have integrity, it should not have been accidentally altered or destroyed during processing by errors arising in the hardware or software of the system. (Neither should it have been deliberately altered or destroyed by an unauthorized person.) System errors do occur from time to time. Normally, therefore, protective *dumps are organized on a regular basis. This ensures the existence of a valid copy of a recent version of every file stored in the system. *See also* security; privacy.

intelligent terminal *See* terminal.

interactive Denoting a device, system, application, etc., in which there is a response by the computer to instructions as they are input by the user. The instructions can be presented by means of, say, a keyboard, a light pen, or a digitizing pad. The response usually occurs sufficiently rapidly that the user can work almost continuously; this mode of operation, involving apparently continuous communication between user and computer, is thus often called *conversational mode*. *See also* multiaccess system.

interblock gap (IBG) *See* block.

interface In general, a common boundary between two devices, two systems, or two constituent parts of a large program. The word is usually used to describe the electronic circuitry plus associated software that is required to connect two computer systems or two components of a computer system such as a peripheral device and the central processor. The interface compensates for differences in the speed of working of the interconnected units and, if different *character encodings are used in the two units, will translate from one encoding to the other.

Several interfaces are classified as *standard interfaces*; these may be developed by, say, a national electronics association or an international body, or they may be industry standards. All the characteristics of a standard interface are in accordance with a set of predetermined values. Use of a standard interface allows computer systems and components from different manufacturers to be interconnected.

An example of a standard interface is the *RS232C interface*, which was developed by the Electronic Industries Association (EIA) in the USA. This can be used for making the connection between two computers, between a computer and a *modem, or between a computer and a printer or some other peripheral device.

interface card (interface board) *See* expansion card.

interpreter A means of converting a program written in a *high-level language into a form that can be accepted and executed by a computer. An interpreter is a program that analyses each line of code in the high-level language program – the *source program* – and then carries out the specified actions. In contrast to a *compiler, an interpreter does not translate the whole program prior to execution. Program run times are much slower than when a compiler is used. An interpreter does, however, simplify the process of loading and running source programs and changing source programs. A high-level language may be translated by an interpreter on some computers or by a compiler on others. *Basic, for example, is usually translated by an interpreter. More sophisticated languages tend to be compiled.

interrupt A signal that is sent to a processor, making it suspend its current task and start another. The main features of interrupts are that (a) they include information as to what caused the interrupt, (b) there are different procedures – *interrupt service routines* – to be executed for each kind of interrupt, and (c) when the correct action has been taken, control is returned to the task that was being processed when the interrupt occurred.

Interrupts can be caused by an external event, such as a key being depressed on a keyboard. They can also be caused by internal conditions in the processor, such as the detection of an attempt to divide by zero. Each interrupt has a priority: higher-priority interrupts may interrupt the servicing of lower-priority interrupts but not the other way round.

inverse video *Another name for* reverse video.

inverter *Another name for* NOT gate.

I/O *Abbrev. for* input/output.

IR *Abbrev. for* instruction register.

ISAM *Abbrev. for* indexed sequential access method. *See* indexed sequential file.

ISO The International Organization for Standardization, the body that establishes international standards in industry, etc., including those required to allow data to be transmitted from one country to another and to be transmitted between equipment made by different manufacturers.

ISO-7 A *character encoding scheme developed by *ISO and hence internationally agreed. ISO-7 uses 7 bits for each character, and hence provides 2^7, i.e. 128, different bit patterns. Certain bit patterns are reserved for national use, allowing countries to include the symbols used for their currency, the accents used above and below letters, etc. The US version is *ASCII, which is the code widely used in computing.

IT *Abbrev. for* information technology.

iteration (iterative process) Any process in which a sequence of operations is performed either a predetermined number of times or until some condition is satisfied. The repetition of the sequence can be executed by means of a *loop in a program. Iteration is used, for example, to obtain a numerical result: as the sequence of operations is repeated, the result of each cycle comes closer and closer to the desired value.

An iteration (in Basic) for calculating the sum of the squares of numbers from 1 to 100 is as follows:

```
100    FOR I = 1 to 100
110    S = S + X(I) ↑ 2
120    NEXT I
```

iterative Involving repetition. *See* iteration; control structure; loop.

J

JCL *Abbrev. for* job control language.

job A set of programs and the data to be manipulated by these programs, regarded by a computer system as a unit of work. The complete description of a job, required for its execution, is written in a *job control language.

job control language (JCL) A special kind of programming language by means of which a user can communicate with the *operating system of a computer. It is employed more often in connection with *batch processing than *interactive computing.

JCL is used to write the sequence of commands that will control the running of a *job on a particular computer: an initial command identifies the job while subsequent commands are each an instruction for the operating system to take some action on behalf of the user.

For example, there are usually commands to run a specified program (such as a *compiler or an *object program), find input data at a specified source, output results at some specified destination. The objects manipulated in JCL are thus not *variables as in a normal programming language but can, for example, be complete programs or the input or output streams for these programs. A JCL command can be obeyed as soon as it is keyed. Alternatively a complete set of JCL commands can be stored and executed later. *See also* command language.

joystick A device for generating signals that can cause the *cursor or some other symbol to be moved about rapidly on a display. It is a shaft a few inches in height that is mounted in an upright position in a base and can be pushed or pulled by the operator's fingers in any direction. Normally the joystick is actually tilted to produce the corresponding direction of motion of the cursor.

jump (branch) A departure from the normal sequential execution of program instructions. It is used when writing a program in *assembly language or *machine code. Instead of performing instruction 1, then instructions 2, 3, 4, and so on, there could be a jump from, say, instruction 3 to instruction 19. This departure from normal program flow is specified by using a special instruction in a program, known as a *jump instruction* (or *branch instruction*).

A jump can be either *unconditional* or *conditional*. An unconditional jump takes place whenever the instruction specifying it is executed (*see* instruction address register). A conditional jump takes place only if specified conditions are met, for example if the contents of the accumulator equal zero or if the value of some variable exceeds a stated number.

Jump instructions offer the only way of controlling the flow of events when using assembly language or machine code. This can lead to programming errors.

Most high-level languages offer improved facilities in the form of a variety of *control structures. *See also* GOTO statement.

jump instruction (branch instruction) *See* jump.

justify 1. To control the positions of printed or typed characters so that regular vertical margins to a page or column of text are obtained; the lines are then said to be *justified.* In some cases only one margin is aligned; the lines are then said to be left-justified when the left-hand margin is regular or *right-justified* when the right-hand margin is regular. When both margins are to be aligned, the spaces between words (and sometimes between letters) is adjusted until each line fills the distance between the two specified margins. Hyphenation of a word can be used if the space in a line is too great. Many *word processing systems allow the user to specify both the right and the left margin, between which text is automatically justified as it is typed in; hyphenation is often offered as an option.

2. To shift the contents of a *register, if necessary, so that the bit at a specified end (right-hand or left-hand) of the data entered in the register is at a specified position (usually the right- or left-hand end) of the register. The contents are then said to be *right-justified* or *left-justified,* as the case may be.

K

K (or k) A symbol used in computing for *kilo-, or sometimes for kilobyte or kilobit.

key 1. A labelled button or marked area on a *keyboard.

2. A value held in one of the fields of a *record and used to identify that record in a collection of records (usually a *file or *table). *See also* searching; sorting.

keyboard A manually operated input device for converting letters, digits, and other characters into coded

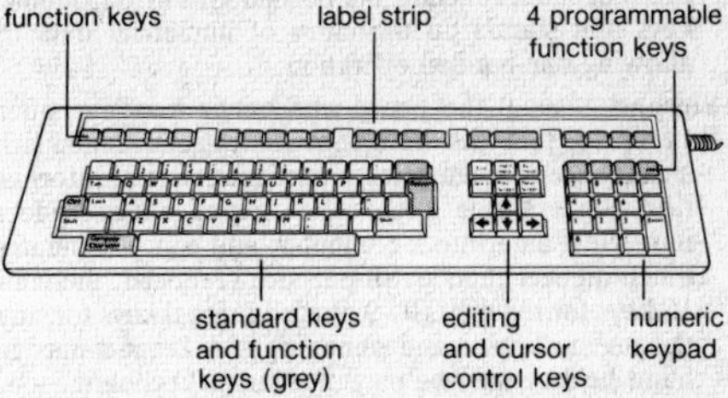

A typical keyboard

form. It is the most commonly used means by which people can communicate with a computer. It consists of an array of labelled *keys* that are operated by pressure applied by the fingers, as in a typewriter. In current devices the operation of a particular key generates a coded electrical signal that can be fed directly into a computer. The characters that have been keyed may be displayed on a *VDU screen. In earlier devices depression of a key led to the code being produced by, for example, the punching of holes in a punched card.

A computer keyboard consists of the standard typewriter layout – the QWERTY keyboard – plus some additional keys (see diagram). These can include a *control key, function keys, cursor keys,* and a *numerical keypad.* The control key operates in the same way as a shift key but allows non-character information to be sent to the computer, such as 'carriage return' or 'clear screen'; the function keys send not one but a whole sequence of characters to the computer at a time, and can often be programmed by the user to send commonly used sequences; the cursor keys are used to move the screen *cursor to a new position; the numerical *keypad duplicates the normal typewriter number keys and speeds up the entry of numerical data by allowing one-handed operation.

keypad A small *keyboard with only a few keys, often 12 or 16, that can be operated with one hand. It is usually used for encoding a particular sort of information. For example, a *numerical keypad* is used to feed numerical data into a computer, and can be operated much quicker than an all-purpose keyboard; there are 10 keys for the digits 0–9 plus additional keys for, say, the decimal point and minus sign. A keypad may be hand-held or may be part of a larger keyboard.

keypunch *See* card punch.

key to disk A system of data entry in which the data entered by a number of keyboard operators is recorded on a magnetic disk under the control of a small computer. The data from each keyboard is routed by the computer to the appropriate file on the disk. The data encoded on the disk is verified, often by comparing it with data entered by a second operator working from the same source. The disk can then be transferred to the computer on which the data is to be processed. Alternatively the data can be transferred to a magnetic tape.

key to tape A system of data entry in which the data entered by a keyboard operator is recorded on a magnetic tape. The data encoded on the tape is then verified, often by comparing it with data entered by a second operator working from the same document. The tape can then be transferred to a computer so that the data can be processed. When there are a number of keyboards available, associated data on individual tapes can be merged on to one tape before input to the computer.

kilo- A prefix indicating a multiple of 1000 (i.e. 10^3) or, loosely, a multiple of 2^{10} (i.e. 1024). In science and technology decimal notation is usually used and powers of 10 are thus encountered – 10^3, 10^6, etc. The symbol k is used for kilo-, as in kV for kilovolt. In communications, kilo- (as in kilobaud) means 1000. Binary notation is generally used in computing and so the power of 2 nearest to 10^3 has assumed the meaning of kilo-.

The prefix is most frequently encountered in computing in the context of storage *capacity. With magnetic disks, magnetic tape, and main store, the capacity is normally reckoned in terms of the number of *bytes that can be stored, and the word *kilobyte* is used to mean 2^{10} bytes; kilobyte is usually abbreviated to K byte or just to K, thus a 256 K byte main store can hold 262 144 bytes. *Semiconductor memory – RAM or ROM – is sometimes considered in terms of the number of bits that can be stored in the device, and the word *kilobit* is used to mean 2^{10} bits. A 64 K RAM chip thus can store 65 536 bits.

Kilo- is part of a sequence

kilo-, mega-, giga-, tera-, . . .

of increasing powers of 10^3 (or of 2^{10}).

Kimball tag A type of *punched tag used in shops.

L

label 1. An *identifier associated with a *statement in a program and used in other parts of the program to refer to that statement.

2. *See* tape label.

LAN *Abbrev. for* local area network.

language *See* programming language.

laser printer A type of *printer in which a page-sized image is produced in the form of a pattern of very fine dots by the action of a laser beam. The principle is similar to that used in many office copiers. The laser beam writes the image on the surface of a drum or band in the form of a pattern of electric charge. This charge pattern is transferred to paper and a permanent visible image is produced. Laser printers work quietly and at high speed, generating up to 150 pages per minute of high-quality print. They readily produce graphs and diagrams and a wide variety of typestyles.

latency *See* access time.

LCD *Abbrev. for* liquid crystal display. A device used in many digital watches, calculators, small computers, etc., to display numbers, letters, and sometimes other characters. The characters are formed from groups of segments or dots. The segments or dots contain a liquid that is usually transparent. Individual segments or dots can be darkened however (by applying an electric field) to form the shape of a particular character. Note that LCDs do not emit light, and can only be seen because light reflected from behind the display makes the dark characters stand out. LCD screens can now display all the characters available on VDUs. A simple *seven-segment display can produce the numbers 0–9 and some letters. LCDs require less electrical power than *LED displays.

least significant digit (lsd) The digit in the least significant, i.e. rightmost, position in the representation of a number, and thus making the smallest contribution to the value of the number. With a binary number, this digit is referred to as the *least significant bit (lsb).*

LED display A device used in some calculators, digital clocks, etc., to display numbers and letters. The characters are formed from groups of segments. The segments are small electronic components called LEDs, i.e. *light-emitting diodes.* Individual LEDs can be made to emit light (usually red) so as to form the shape of a particular character. A simple *seven-segment display can display the numbers 0–9 and some letters. LED displays require more electrical power than *LCDs.

left-justified *See* justify.

LEO *Abbrev. for* Lyons Electronic Office. *See* first generation computers.

LET *See* Basic.

lexical analysis The initial phase in the *compilation of a program during which the program is split up into meaningful units. These units could, for example, be *names, *constants, *reserved words, or *operators. The part of the compiler program that does this analysis is called a *lexical analyser*. The units recognized by the analyser are known as *tokens*. They are output in some conveniently coded form for further processing by the compiler. *See also* syntax analysis.

library *See* program library; subroutine library.

library program *See* program library.

LIFO *Abbrev. for* last in first out. *See* stack.

light-emitting diode *See* LED display.

light pen A hand-held penlike instrument used together with a *display device for the input of data to a computer graphics system. (The display has to be a *refreshed cathode-ray tube.) The main function of the light pen is to point to small areas of the screen, such as a single character or a small graphical object, and can for example indicate a selection from a displayed list (a *menu). It can also be used to draw shapes on the screen.

The light pen is connected by cable to the computer, and has a switch by which it is activated by the operator. The pen is held perpendicular and close to the screen. Having been positioned and activated, the computer can rapidly identify the position of the pen: light from the selected area of screen enters the pen, is sensed by an electronic light detector, and an electrical signal is sent to the computer. The pen position is passed to the graphics program and action is taken based on commands previously entered by the operator.

line editor *See* text editor.

line feed **1.** A control mechanism on a *printer, or a programmed instruction, that causes the paper to move up a specified distance (i.e. a specified number of lines on the paper) until the printing mechanism is opposite the next line to be printed. *See also* paper throw.

2. A means by which the *cursor on a screen is moved down one line. If that would result in the cursor dropping off the bottom, the whole display moves up one line and the cursor is placed on a new blank bottom line.

line printer A *printer that produces a complete line of characters at a time, or more precisely produces a complete line during one cycle of its operation. Printing rates range from 150 to 3000 lines per minute (lpm). There are normally between 80 and 160 character positions on a line. Each line is first assembled in the printer's memory and then printed. Once the line has been printed the paper is moved so that the next line is opposite the printing mechanism.

Line printers may be impact or nonimpact printers (*see* printer). There are two main types of impact line printers, both producing solid characters. These are *barrel printers* (also known as *drum printers*) and *band printers*. Simplified versions of the printing mechanisms are shown in the diagram.

A barrel printer involves a horizontal cylinder with rows of characters embossed along its length. The cylinder rotates continuously at high speed, and one line is printed during each rotation. The paper is positioned between the cylinder and a set of print hammers; there is one hammer for each printing position along a line, i.e. for every character in a row on the cylinder. The complete character set that can be printed is provided at each printing position. During one rotation of the cylinder all the characters of one sort are printed at the same time; for example, all the As in a line are printed, then all the Bs, then all the Cs, and so on.

A band printer involves a steel band with characters embossed along its length. The band forms a loop and is rotated continuously at high speed. The band moves

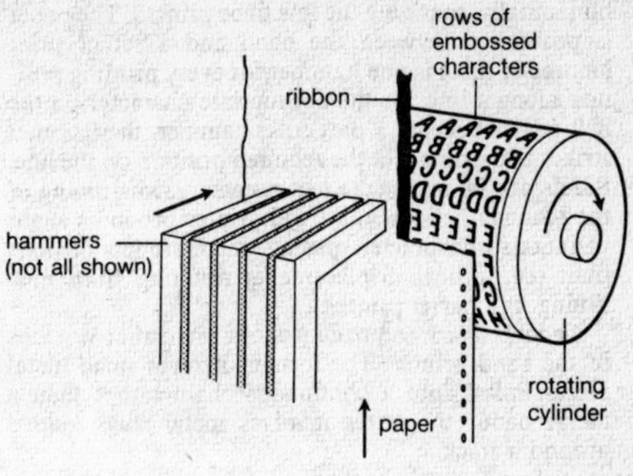

Barrel printer

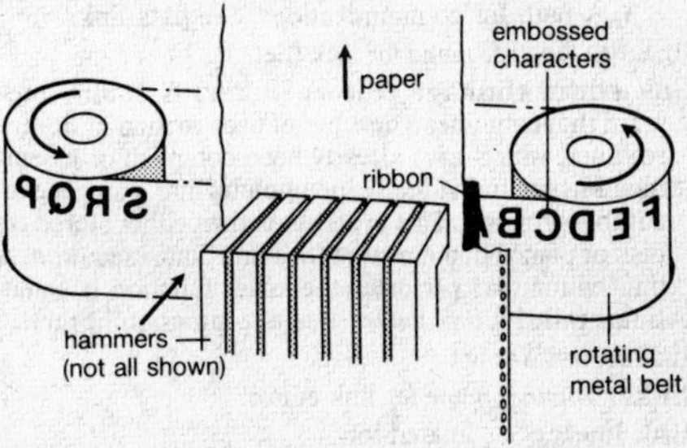

Band printer

horizontally, spanning the line to be printed. The paper is positioned between the band and a set of print hammers; there is one hammer for every printing position along a line. As the appropriate character on the belt passes beneath a particular hammer, the hammer strikes and prints it in the required position on the line. Bands can be replaced when necessary. Mis-timing of the hammer actions in a band printer produces slight variations in character spacing; these are less obvious than the vertical displacements resulting from mistiming in a barrel printer.

Chain printers and *train printers* are earlier versions of the band printer. The former involves small metal plates linked into a continuous chain rather than a metal band; the latter involves metal slugs guided around a track.

link 1. (linkage) The part of a computer program, possibly a single instruction or address, that passes control and *parameters between separate portions of the program.

2. (pointer) A character or group of characters that indicates the *location of an item of data in memory.

3. A path for communications. *See* data link.

linkage *Another name for* link (def. 1).

link editor (linkage editor; linker) A *utility program that combines a number of user-written or library routines, which have already been compiled or assembled but are individually incomplete, into a single executable program. This program is then either stored on disk or placed in main store for immediate execution. A link editor that performs the latter function is sometimes called a *link loader*. *See also* program library.

linked list *See* list.

linker *Another name for* link editor.

link loader *See* link editor.

liquid crystal display *See* LCD.

Lisp A high-level programming language whose name is

derived from **list** **pro**cessing. It was developed in the early 1960s. Lisp was designed specifically for the manipulation of *list and *tree structures of various kinds and has an unusual *syntax. It was later taken up by those working in the emergent field of *artificial intelligence. There are now a number of dialects of Lisp, extended in various directions and available on microcomputers as well as larger machines. Lisp programs are generally translated by an *interpreter.

list One form in which a collection of data items can be held in computer memory. The items themselves are in a particular order. The items could all be integers, for example, or real numbers, or letters, or they could be a mixture of, say, integers and real numbers. If all the items are of the same type then the list is a one-dimensional *array.

There are two commonly used forms in which this collection of data items is held in memory. In a *sequentially allocated list* the items are stored in their correct order in adjacent *locations. In a *linked list* each location contains a data item and a *link containing the address of the next item in the list; the last item has a special link indicating that there are no more items in the list. Various operations can be performed on the list components without moving the data items; only the links are modified. For example, a new item can be inserted in its correct place by having the preceding item link to the new item and the new item link to the succeeding item.

listing An output from a printer of a computer system. The word is usually qualified in some way to give a more precise idea of the contents, as in *program listing* or *error listing*.

literal A character or group of characters that stands for itself, i.e. is to be taken literally, rather than being a *name for something else. Numbers are always taken as literals. When letters are used as literals they must be placed within some form of quotation marks to distinguish them from letters used as names. For example, X may be the name given to a *variable in a program written in Basic.

```
100   PRINT X
```

would then mean print the value assigned to that variable.

```
100   PRINT "X"
```

would mean print the letter X.

load 1. To enter data into the appropriate *registers in a processor or into the appropriate storage *locations in main store.

2. To copy a program from backing store into main store so that it may be executed.

loader A *utility program that *loads a program into main store ready for execution. The program loaded is an *object program that is read from backing store and that has previously been combined with any required library programs by a *link editor. *See also* program library.

local area network (LAN) A relatively cheap and simple communication system linking a number of computers – usually microcomputers – within a defined and small locality. This locality may be, say, an office building, an industrial site, or a university. Linking the computers together allows single and/or expensive resources such as *hard disks, a *line printer, or an automatic telephone exchange, to be shared between them, allows *data files and *databases to be shared, and permits messages to be sent between the computers by *electronic mail.

The computers in the network are directly connected to the transmission medium by electrical *interfaces; normally the medium is in the form of electric cables or optical fibres. The computers may be organized as a ring network or as a bus network (*see* network). These two structures differ mainly in the way in which the computers are allowed to transmit information onto the network. The system may be controlled overall by a more powerful computer.

Local area networks generally provide high-speed data communications (up to a hundred million bits per second) and have very low *error rates. It is possible to interconnect two or more local networks, and to connect a local network to a longer-distance network, i.e. to a *wide-area network.

local variable *See* scope.

location (storage location) In general, any place in which information can be stored in a computer – in *main store or *backing store. A storage location is an area within a computer memory capable of storing a single unit of information in binary form. Each location can be identified by an *address, allowing an item of information to be stored there or retrieved from there. In most cases it is possible to change the stored value during execution of the program. The words location and address are often used as synonyms, as in ordinary speech.

Main store is divided into either *words or *bytes: in some computers each location holds a word; in other machines each location holds a byte. The memory is said to be *word-addressable* or *byte-addressable*. A word is now generally 32 or 16 bits and is usually large enough to contain a *machine instruction. A byte is almost always 8 bits and thus is the storage space required to hold a *character.

Locations on disk and tape tend to hold a number of bytes and are addressed by *track and *sector or by *block, respectively. Tapes are a *serial-access medium, however, and so it is a case of starting at the beginning and counting blocks until the desired one is reached.

logic *See* binary logic; digital logic.

logical error *See* error.

logical expression *Another name for* Boolean expression.

logical function *Another name for* Boolean function. *See* Boolean expression.

logical instruction *See* logic instruction.

logical operation *See* logic operation.

logical operator *See* logic operator.

logical record *See* record.

logical shift *See* shift.

logical value *See* truth value.

logic circuit (logic network) An electronic circuit consisting of interconnected *logic gates and possibly other components (such as *flip-flops). These elements are connected by paths that carry electrical signals from one to another. A circuit consisting only of logic gates is shown in the diagram, *logic symbols being used to represent the different gates. The inputs to one gate in a circuit are usually the outputs of other gates, or signals from, say, a peripheral device. The output of a gate can be fed to another gate or to some other unit in the computer system.

Logic circuits are found in all types of computer devices, including the *central processor where they perform various arithmetic, logic, and control operations, and in memory devices (such as *ROM and *RAM) and *counters.

A *truth table can be drawn up to determine the output of a *combinational logic circuit for all possible combinations of inputs (see diagram). It can also be used to obtain an expression of the logical function of the circuit. In the circuit and truth table shown, +, ., and ¯ are the OR, AND, and NOT *operators. The expression derived for the circuit output indicates that it is an *equivalence gate.

logic diagram A diagram in which *logic symbols are used to show how the inputs and outputs of components are connected together in a *logic circuit. It thus displays the design of the circuit but gives no indication of the electronics involved.

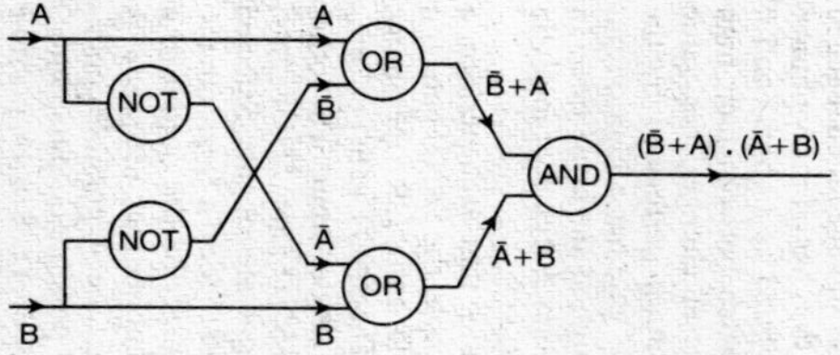

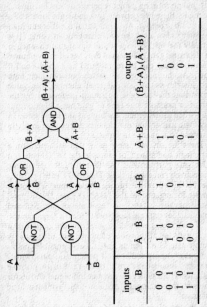

inputs A	B	Ā	B̄	$A+\bar{B}$	$\bar{A}+B$	output $(\bar{B}+A).(\bar{A}+B)$
0	0	1	1	1	1	1
0	1	1	0	0	1	0
1	0	0	1	1	0	0
1	1	0	0	1	1	1

Logic circuit and truth table of this circuit

logic element A *logic gate or combination of gates.

logic gate A device, almost always electronic, that is used to control the flow of signals in a computer. It does this by performing *logic operations on its inputs. Normally there are between two and eight inputs to a gate and one output. An input signal is either at a high level or at a low level, the level changing with time. (It is actually the voltage level of the signal that changes in an electronic gate.) The signal thus has a binary nature; the two values can be represented as 1 (high) and 0 (low). As the input signals switch between their high and low levels, the output level changes, the value depending on the logic operation performed by the gate. For example, one type of gate has a high output only when all its inputs are high at the same time. In any logic gate the output changes extremely rapidly in response to a change in input.

There are several simple gates that each perform a basic logic operation. For example, the *AND gate and *OR gate perform the *AND and *OR operations, respectively, on their inputs. The *NOT gate performs the *NOT operation on its single input. The other simple logic gates are the *NAND gate, *NOR gate, *nonequivalence gate, and *equivalence gate. Selected gates can be connected together to form a *logic circuit.

*Truth tables are used to describe the output of a logic gate for all possible combinations of inputs. A simple gate with 2 inputs has 2^2, i.e. 4, possible combinations of inputs and hence 4 possible outputs; with 3 or with 4 inputs there are 2^3 or 2^4, i.e. 8 or 16, possible outputs. Truth tables are given at individual entries for gates in the dictionary. *See also* logic symbols; logic diagram.

logic instruction A *machine instruction specifying a *logic operation and the *operand or operands on which the logic operation is to be performed. An example, expressed in *assembly language, might be

```
OR A,B
```

This is an instruction to perform the OR operation between the contents of registers A and B, placing the result in A. *See also* arithmetic instruction.

logic network *Another name for* logic circuit.

logic operation An operation performed on quantities (*operands) that can be assigned a truth value; this value is either *true* or *false*. The result of the operation is in accordance with the rules of *Boolean algebra, and again has a value *true* or *false*. The operands may be statements or formulae, such as

It is July
the wire is less than 10 cm long
x + 2 = 16

The operands of a logic operation can be represented by letters. For example, in

P AND Q, P OR Q, NOT (P OR Q)

P and Q are the operands and AND, OR, and NOT are *logic operators that represent three commonly used logic operations, namely the *AND, *OR, and *NOT operations. Logic operations can be described by means of *truth tables. *Logic gates are constructed so as to perform logic operations on their input signals.

logic operator A symbol representing a *logic operation such as the AND or OR operation. A logic operator has logical quantities as its *operands and delivers a logical result. For example, the expression

'I have no money' and 'it is Tuesday'

is true if both the operands are true, otherwise it is false. In programming languages logic operators are either spelt out in full (with dots at each end in Fortran) or various symbols are used; some of these are shown in the table overleaf.

An example of how logic operators are used, in Basic, is as follows:

```
10    IF (A=3) AND (X<10) THEN A=0
```

See also order of precedence.

logic seeking *See* character printer.

<table>
<tr><th>operation</th><th>operators</th></tr>
<tr><td>AND</td><td>AND .AND. & .</td></tr>
<tr><td>OR</td><td>OR .OR. ! | +</td></tr>
<tr><td>NOT</td><td>NOT .NOT. ¬ ! ¯ ′</td></tr>
</table>

Logic operators

logic symbols The symbols used in a *logic diagram to represent the various *logic gates and the other possible components in a *logic circuit. One set that is used to represent logic gates is shown in the diagram: the logic

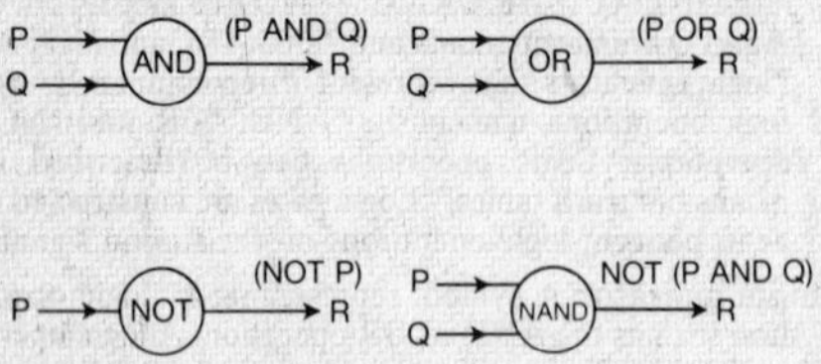

Logic symbols for gates

operation performed by the gate is printed inside a circle, and arrowed lines labelled by letters represent the inputs and output. In another set (widely used in technical literature) the shape of the symbol is used to indicate its function.

log in *See* log on.

Logo A *programming language developed in the 1960s by Seymour Papert for use in teaching young children. Logo is a simple but powerful language. It incorporates the concepts of *procedures and *lists, and helps children to think algorithmically. Logo includes *turtle graphics: the turtle is a simple pen-plotter that can be steered around a large piece of paper on the floor, under program control, allowing the children to create complex patterns. In some microcomputer implementations the turtle pictures may be drawn on the screen. This is cheaper but perhaps not so effective.

log off or **log out** To inform a computer system from a *terminal that one's work is finished for the moment. This *log off* or *log out* process is required in any *multiaccess system for security and accounting purposes. After a user has logged off, the computer system will not be available on that terminal until someone has *logged on there.

log on or **log in** To identify oneself to a computer system when wishing to enter the system from a computer *terminal. This *log on* or *log in* process is required in any *multiaccess system. The log on sequence involves first saying who one is by means of one's name or account number and then entering one's *password. In some cases where, say, security is very strict, there may be more to do. *See also* log off.

log out *See* log off.

look-up table A *table used in table look-up.

loop A statement or group of statements whose execution is repeated either a specified number of times or while or until some condition is met. Both types of loop are iterative *control structures, and appear in various forms in almost every programming language.

The *for loop* appears in several languages and permits a specified number of repetitions to occur. An example, in Pascal, is

for i := 1 **to** 10 **do** *statement*

This causes the *statement* to be executed 10 times. In Basic this would be written

```
10    FOR I = 1 TO 10
```

statement
50 NEXT I

The *do loop* is another form of the fixed-count loop and appears, for example, in Fortran.

There are two main forms of the second type of loop, i.e. the conditional-type loop. In one form the condition is given at the beginning of the loop and execution continues while this condition is satisfied. This is commonly referred to as a *while loop* or a *while do loop*. For example, Pascal has

while *condition* **do** *statement*

The statement or statements will not be executed at all if the condition does not hold the first time round. The other form is the *repeat until loop*, which is executed at least once since the condition is given at the end of the loop, causing it to terminate when necessary. For example, Pascal has

repeat *statement* **until** *condition*

It is possible for one or more loops to be included within a loop; the incorporated loop or loops are referred to as *nested loop(s)*. The nesting must be such that each inner loop is entirely contained within the outer loop or loops.

low-level language A kind of *programming language whose features directly reflect the facilities provided by a particular computer or class of computers. It is designed mainly around the set of instructions (i.e. the *instruction set) that a particular computer or computer class is able to perform: low-level languages are thus described as *machine-orientated* (or *computer-orientated*). Each instruction in a low-level language program corresponds to a *machine instruction. Low-level languages are generally *assembly languages. *See also* high-level language.

lpm *Abbrev. for* lines per minute, used in describing the rate of output of *line printers.

lsd, lsb *See* least significant digit.

LSI *Abbrev. for* large scale integration. *See* integrated circuit.

M

M The symbol used for *mega-, or sometimes for megabyte.

machine An actual computer, or sometimes a model of a computer used in theoretical studies.

machine address A unique number that specifies a unique storage *location (or in some computers a particular *register or *input/output device). A machine address contains a fixed number of bits, *n*, and hence can identify 2^n different locations. The number of distinct locations to which a machine address can refer is known as the *address space*. A machine address is determined by the computer hardware and when specified in a *machine instruction can be used directly by the hardware. A machine address is thus an *absolute address. *See also* address.

machine code The code used to represent the instructions in the *instruction set of a particular computer. It is therefore specific to a particular computer. It is the form in which programs must be recorded on, say, magnetic disk and entered into main storage, and is the form subsequently used for processing. Machine code consists of a sequence of *machine instructions. In order for the computer hardware to handle it, machine code is expressed in binary form: every operation, every address, every item of data consists of a particular sequence of bits.

It is very slow and tedious for a person to write a program in machine code, and very difficult to read and understand such a program. Instead a programmer normally uses a *high-level language (such as Basic or Pascal), which is translated into machine code by a program – either a *compiler or an *interpreter. A large number of machine code instructions are required for each high-level language statement. Another less easy alternative is for the programmer to use *assembly language, which gives a 'readable' and hence more convenient representation of machine code; a program written in assembly language is converted into machine code by a program known as an *assembler.

machine instruction (computer instruction) An instruction that can be recognized by the processing unit of a computer. It is written in the *machine code designed for that particular computer, and can be interpreted and executed directly by the *control unit and the *arithmetic and logic unit of that computer. A machine instruction consists of a statement of the *operation to be performed, and some method of specifying the object upon which the operation is to be performed (i.e. the *operand) together with an indication of where the result is to go. There may be more than one operand involved.

The portion of the machine instruction in which the operation is specified is known as the *operation part*. The operand or operands are generally specified in the instruction by stating their actual *address(es) in main store, or by some other scheme such as *indirect addressing, *indexed addressing, or *relative addressing; in *immediate addressing the operand itself is stated explicitly in the instruction. This information about the operand or operands is given in the *address part* or *parts* of the instruction.

In addition to the operation and address parts, special bit positions are required in the machine instruction to indicate whether a particular addressing mode is to be used. There are thus bit positions to specify indirect addressing, the use of index registers for indexed addressing, or the use of base registers in relative addressing. Additional bits may be used for other purposes.

The layout of a machine instruction, showing its constituent parts, is known as the *instruction format*. It is laid down by the computer manufacturer, and specifies the number of bits allocated to each part – operation part, address part or parts, etc. – and the relative positions of each of these parts.

machine-orientated language *See* low-level language.

machine word *See* word.

macro-instruction (macro) A named sequence of instructions in an assembly-language program that is inserted into the source code by the *assembler each time the *name is encountered. A macro is thus a convenient shorthand for the programmer.

magnetic disk A storage medium in the form of a flat circular plate that can be rotated by some means and that is covered on one or both sides with a magnetic film. Data is recorded in concentric tracks in the film (see below). Disks can be either rigid or flexible, leading to the two categories of *hard disk and *floppy disk. *Winchester disks are a type of hard disk. The storage *capacity depends on a number of factors including type and size of disk, the number of tracks per disk, and the recording density along the tracks.

A considerable advantage of magnetic disk over *magnetic tape is that there is *random access to disk: items of data can be located directly, independently, and within a very short period of time (the *access time) of some tens of milliseconds. It follows that *files of data can be stored on disk either in an ordered sequence or in a random manner. In addition, data within a file can be accessed either in sequential order or randomly.

The access time to disks is brief enough for *on-line processing, which is not the case for magnetic tape. Magnetic disks are in fact used as *backing store in the whole range of computers. Hard disks are employed in the larger computers while floppy disks or small Winchesters are used in smaller ones.

Data is recorded and retrieved when a disk is rotating rapidly in a peripheral device known as a *disk drive, and is achieved by means of read/write heads. When the head is to write data on the disk it receives a coded electrical signal. This signal causes magnetization of tiny regions in the magnetic film immediately below the head. The regions are magnetized in either of two directions; magnetization in one direction represents a binary 1 and in the other direction a binary 0. A letter, digit, or other character can therefore be encoded as a particular sequence of magnetized spots (*see* binary representation). This pattern of spots is produced along the concentric tracks.

The data is written on the disk in different *sectors of the tracks. The sectors may be in a continuous sequence or scattered in different tracks. When the head is to read data from a specified track and sector, it senses the magnetized patterns there and converts them into a corresponding electrical signal. This signal is then transmitted to another device. Items of data can be deleted from a disk and new data added – magnetic disk is a reusable resource.

See also disk pack; disk cartridge; multiplate disk.

magnetic drum A type of *backing store that has now been displaced by the *magnetic disk. It is a cylindrical storage device whose curved outer surface is coated with a magnetic material in which data can be recorded. The data is recorded in parallel tracks around the surface. The drum is permanently positioned in a peripheral device. When data is to be read or written, the drum is rotated at a high but constant speed past read/write heads. In the most recent devices the heads are fixed in position very close to the curved surface, with one head per track. The drum is typically half a metre in length and may have several hundred tracks. There is *random access to the data. Track selection is achieved very rapidly by electronic switching between the heads. Since the heads are not moved, drums have a much faster *access time than disks. Disks however have a higher storage *capacity.

magnetic ink character recognition *See* MICR.

magnetic media Material on which data can be recorded in the form of a magnetic pattern on the surface of a magnetizable film. The data is represented in binary form by the direction in which points on the surface are magnetized. Magnetic media form the recording basis of *magnetic disks, *magnetic tape, *magnetic stripes, and *bubble memory.

magnetic stripe (magnetic strip) A strip of magnetic film on a plastic card on which machine-readable data is encoded. The most common application of magnetic stripes is for identification and security purposes; they are found for example on credit cards.

magnetic tape A cheap robust storage medium consisting of a flexible plastic tape with a magnetic coating on one side. It is essentially the same as that found in domestic audio or video cassettes. The tape is held either on reels of between 300 and 2400 foot capacity, or in various designs of *tape cartridges or *cassettes. The information is stored in a series of parallel tracks that run along the length of the tape (see below). *Serial access must be used for storage and retrieval from tape. Domestic microcomputers may use ordinary audio cassettes to hold a few kilobytes of information. With a mainframe system 140 megabytes or more may be stored on a 2400 foot reel of ½ inch tape with 9 tracks.

When magnetic tape was first used in computer systems in the 1950s it was the only form of high-speed *backing store. It is still the cheapest way of storing very large amounts of information, especially when the information is accessed rarely, as in *file archives or *backup copies of information held on *magnetic disk. Recent advances in tape technology have been made largely in response to the need to take backup copies of new kinds of disks. Tapes are also used to transfer information from one computer system to another, although the advent of computer *networks is reducing this usage.

Items of data are recorded on and retrieved from magnetic tape by read and write heads operating in a device known as a *tape unit. The write head receives a coded electrical signal. This signal causes magnetization of tiny regions in the magnetic film immediately below the head. Each spot represents one *bit: a spot magnetized in one direction represents a binary 0 while a spot magnetized in the opposite direction represents a binary 1. A letter, digit, or other character is encoded as a row of magnetized spots across the tape (*see* binary representation). The same number of spots occurs in each row, thus making up the parallel tracks on the tape.

The data is written on the tape in *blocks; a sequence of blocks makes up a *file. When data is to be read from a block, the read head senses the magnetized patterns there and converts them into a corresponding electrical signal. Blocks of data can be erased from tape and new data added – magnetic tape is a reusable resource. The *formats, i.e. structures, in which data can be recorded on tape – as magnetic patterns – are strictly defined and are accepted internationally. This allows data to be interchanged between different computer systems.

magnetic tape unit (MTU) *See* tape unit.

mainframe Any large general-purpose computer system, as opposed to the smaller and less powerful *minicomputers and *microcomputers. Mainframes costing several million dollars are used by large commercial organizations such as banks and insurance companies, or by government tax, research, or defence establishments. Smaller mainframes, costing under $1m, cater for medium-sized businesses and universities with, say, 100 to 200 simultaneously active users.

main memory *Another name for* main store.

main store (main storage; main memory) The storage closely associated with the *processor (or processors) of a computer and from which program instructions and data can be retrieved extremely rapidly and copied directly into the processor registers, and in which the resulting data is stored prior to being transferred to *backing store or *output device. Main store thus stores instructions waiting to be obeyed or currently being obeyed, and data awaiting processing, being processed, or resulting from processing.

Programs can only be executed when they are in main store. Programs and associated data are not, however, retained permanently in main store. They are kept in backing store until required by the processor. The backing store in a particular computer (large or small) has a larger storage *capacity and is also less expensive (in terms of cost per bit stored) than the main store in that computer.

In computers manufactured now, main store consists of *semiconductor memory. (This replaced *core store.) There is *random access to data in main store, whether it is core store or semiconductor RAM or ROM. With semiconductor memory, however, the operating speeds are very much higher: the average *access time is less than a millionth of a second, a typical value being 0.5 microsecond. Semiconductor memory is also very reliable and is becoming highly miniaturized.

Main store can be divided into various portions that are used for different purposes, e.g. for the storage of data awaiting processing, awaiting output, or currently being processed. A single item of data is stored in a particular *location in main store. In most computers each location holds a fixed number of *bits; this number is the same for all locations in the main store of a particular computer, and is usually 8, 16, or 32 bits. Each location can be identified by its *address.

maintenance 1. Any activity, including tests, measurements, adjustments, replacements, and repairs, that aims to prevent the occurrence of faults in hardware or corrects an existing hardware fault. *See* preventative maintenance; corrective maintenance.

2. (program maintenance) *See* program.

malfunction The occurrence of a *fault, usually a hardware fault.

Manchester Mark I *See* first generation computers.

man-machine interface (MMI) The means of communication between a human user and a computer system, referring in particular to the use of input/output devices with supporting software.

mantissa *See* floating-point notation.

MAR *Abbrev. for* memory address register.

mark reading *Short for* optical mark reading. *See* OMR. *See also* document reader.

mark sensing A process of data entry to a computer in which a machine senses pencil marks made by a person in his or her choice of indicated positions on a document. The pencil marks are electrically conductive and can thus be sensed by electrical methods. Mark sensing has been displaced by optical mark reading, i.e. *OMR, which employs more reliable (photoelectric) sensing methods.

mask 1. A pattern of bits that is stored in a *register and is used to modify or identify part of a byte, word, etc., with the same number of bits. An operation, such as an *AND operation or an *OR operation, is performed on corresponding pairs of bits in the two patterns; this operation is called *masking*. For example, with an AND operation a 1 in the mask will retain the value of the corresponding bit in the byte, word, etc., for subsequent processing, while a 0 in the mask will set or keep the corresponding bit as a 0. Thus an AND on a byte containing a character with a mask of 01111111 will clear the *parity bit.

2. A chemical shield used to determine the pattern of interconnections in an *integrated circuit.

mass storage device Any backing storage device that contains one or more high-capacity disk drives used primarily as *filestore. *See also* capacity.

master file A *data file that is subject to frequent requests for data and frequent updating of the values stored. It can therefore be considered an authoritative source of information. A master file can be updated by being completely rewritten by the system. The version prior to a particular update is called the *father file*, while the one before that is the *grandfather file*. The father file, and often the grandfather file, are retained as *backup copies of the master file. *See also* file updating.

matrix A two-dimensional *array.

matrix printer *See* printer. *See also* dot matrix printer; ink-jet printer.

MBR *Abbrev. for* memory buffer register.

MDR *Abbrev. for* memory data register.

mean In general, a number representing the average or typical value of a group of numerical values, such as measurements of a quantity. If the values are represented by

$$x_1, x_2, x_3, \ldots x_n$$

so that there are n values in all, then their mean (symbol: $\bar{x}$) is given by the formula

$$\bar{x} = (x_1 + x_2 + x_3 + \ldots + x_n)/n$$

The mean of 8 numbers is thus the sum of those numbers divided by 8. For example, with the numbers

2, 5, 3, 7, 5, 1, 3, 2

the mean is 3.5

The amount of variation within the group is indicated by its *standard deviation.

media (singular: **medium**) Materials used in the entry or storage of data in a computer, or in the recording of results from a computer. The latter group are known as *output media*, the former as *input media* and *storage* *media*. Input and storage media include *magnetic media, *paper tape, and *punched cards. Data is represented in coded form on these media. Output media include the *continuous stationery used in *printers, the paper or transparent film used in *plotters, and the microfiche used in *COM.

mega- A prefix indicating a multiple of a million (i.e. 1 000 000 or 10^6) or, loosely, a multiple of 2^{20} (i.e. 1 048 576). In science and technology decimal notation is usually used and powers of 10 are thus encountered – 10^3, 10^6, etc. The symbol M is used for mega-, as in MV for megavolt. In communications mega- (as in megabaud) means a million. Binary notation is generally used in computing and so the power of 2 nearest to 10^6 has assumed the meaning of mega-.

The prefix is most frequently encountered in computing in the context of storage *capacity. With magnetic disks, magnetic tape, and main store, the capacity is normally reckoned in terms of the number of *bytes that can be stored, and the word *megabyte* is used to mean 2^{20} bytes; megabyte is usually abbreviated to M byte or just to M, thus a 16 M byte disk can hold 16 777 216 bytes.

Mega- is part of a sequence

kilo-, mega-, giga-, tera-, . . .

of increasing powers of 10^3 (or 2^{10}).

memory A device or medium in which data or program instructions can be held for subsequent use by a computer. The word is synonymous with *store* and *storage* but is most frequently used in the terms random-access memory (*RAM) and read-only memory (*ROM), i.e. semiconductor memory used for *main store. The word memory by itself is sometimes used to mean main store. *See also* storage device; media.

memory address register (MAR) A *register (i.e. a temporary location) in the central processor, used for holding the address of the next location in main store to be accessed. Whenever the main store is to be used, the required address must be sent to the MAR. The corresponding storage location can then be selected automatically, and data read from there or stored there. *See also* memory data register.

memory buffer register (MBR) *Another name for* memory data register.

memory card (memory board) *See* expansion card.

memory data register (MDR) A *register (i.e. a temporary location) used for holding all instructions and data items as they are transferred between main store and central processor. It thus acts as a *buffer, and is therefore also called *memory buffer register (MBR). See also* memory address register.

memory mapping 1. A technique allowing a processor to access more memory than it is ordinarily capable of addressing. Different banks of memory are electronically switched so that they appear to the processor to have the same address.

2. In microcomputers, a way of making input/output devices appear to be memory locations so that instructions that would normally store or retrieve information from main store perform output or input to an external device.

menu A list of options, usually displayed on a screen, from which a choice can be made by the user. The list may be displayed with a different letter or number opposite each option, and the selection made by typing in the appropriate letter or number using a keyboard. The selection can also be made by positioning the *cursor on the selected option using, for instance, cursor keys on a *keyboard, a *joystick, or a *mouse, by positioning a *light pen over a suitable area of the screen, or by touching a selected area of a *touch-sensitive screen. The selected item will often be highlighted in some way; *reverse video or blinking are commonly used.

Any program that obtains input from a user by

means of a menu is said to be *menu-driven*.

message switching A process whereby information (in digital form) can be sent automatically from one computer on a *network to any other, the information being switched from one communication line to another until it reaches its specified destination. The information to be communicated is known as a *message*. A message may be of any length, and is transmitted as a whole rather than being split up. At each switching point along its route the message is checked for errors, stored temporarily, and forwarded to the next point when the necessary resources become available. *Compare* packet switching.

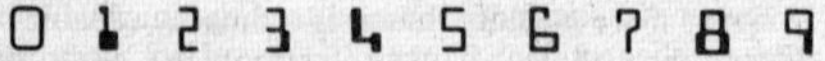

Digits that can be used in MICR

MICR *Abbrev. for* magnetic ink character recognition. A process in which a machine recognizes characters printed on a document in *magnetic ink* and converts them into a code that can be fed straight into a computer. The machine is called a *magnetic ink character reader*. The characters can be read not only by the machine but also by people: they may be digits, letters, or other symbols. The ink contains a magnetic substance. When the document is fed into the machine the ink is magnetized, enabling each character to be sensed by magnetic read heads. For the machine to recognize and encode the characters, they must be of an appropriate shape and size and have a high print quality; one standardized and widely used set of type is rectangular in appearance with thickened vertical sections (see diagram). The most common application of MICR is in the handling of cheques by banks; cheque number, branch number, and account number are printed in magnetic ink characters along the bottom of the cheque, the amount of the cheque being added later by the bank. *See also* OCR; OMR.

micro *Short for* microcomputer.

micro- 1. A prefix to a unit, indicating a submultiple of one millionth (i.e. 10^{-6}) of that unit, as in *micrometre*, *microsecond*, or *microvolt*. The Greek letter μ (mu) is used as the symbol for micro-; micrometre, microsecond, and microvolt are thus often written μm, μs, μV. Micro- is part of a sequence

milli-, micro-, nano-, pico-, . . .

of decreasing powers of 1000.

2. A prefix indicating smallness or comparative smallness, or something concerned with small objects, quantities, etc.

microcode 1. The code in which microinstructions of a *microprogram are written. It is used to create the microprogram, which defines exactly what each *machine instruction does.

2. A sequence of microinstructions.

microcomputer (micro) A computer system that uses a *microprocessor as its processing unit. The central control and arithmetic element is thus fabricated on (usually) one tiny *chip of semiconductor material. In addition a microcomputer contains storage and input/output facilities for data and programs, possibly all on the same chip as the microprocessor.

Microcomputers were originally rather limited in what they could do. With the emergence of more sophisticated systems they are now regarded as serious problem-solving tools in many fields, including business, science, and engineering. The capability of the system depends not only on the characteristics of the microprocessor employed but also on the amount of storage provided, the types of peripheral devices that can be used, the possibility of expanding the system with add-on peripherals and additional storage, and other possible options.

The storage capacity of *main store in a microcomputer is many tens or hundreds of times lower than that of larger *minicomputers and *mainframes (although it has a similar *access time). *Backing store consists typically of cheap but low-capacity *floppy disks, although *Winchester disks may be used in more expensive machines. Data and programs are entered on a *keyboard or read from floppy disk; data can also be fed in using a *computer graphics device. Information is displayed on a *VDU, which is an integral part of the microcomputer (rather than remote from it as in larger computer systems). A *printer can usually be connected for a more permanent form of output. It is also possible for data to be transferred between microcomputers, or between a micro and a larger more powerful computer.

microfiche, microfilm *See* COM.

microfloppy *See* floppy disk.

microinstruction *See* microprogram.

microprocessor The physical realization of the *central processor of a computer on a single chip of semiconductor, or on a small number of chips. It forms the basis of the *microcomputer. The *integrated circuit manufactured on the chip or chips implements – at the very least – the functions of an *arithmetic and logic unit and a *control unit. Normally there are other sections such as semiconductor memory in the form of *RAM (random-access memory) for data and *ROM (read-only memory) for programs, plus special *registers and input/output circuits.

Microprocessors are characterized by a combination of their speed (i.e. *cycle time), their *word length, their *instruction set, and their *architecture (i.e. storage organization and addressing methods, I/O operation, etc.). They are used not just in microcomputers but are embedded in a wide variety of devices.

The first microprocessor – the Intel 4004, produced

by the US company Intel – appeared in 1971. It had a 4-bit word length, 4.5 kilobytes of memory, and 45 instructions. Its 8-bit counterpart, the Intel 8008, was introduced in 1974 and its improved derivative, the Zilog Z80, in 1976. By this time there were over 50 microprocessors on the market. The number of microprocessors, and their sophistication, has increased rapidly – alongside developments in the fabrication technology of integrated circuits. Many of those now commercially available use a 16-bit word length and some have a 32-bit word length.

microprogram A sequence of fundamental instructions, known as *microinstructions*, that describe all the steps involved in a particular computer operation. It is the means by which an operation is accomplished. A microprogram is set into action once a *machine instruction is loaded into the *instruction register of a computer. One part of the instruction – the operation part – specifies the operation to be performed, and the microprogram for that operation can then be executed. Almost all processors in both large and small computers are now *microprogrammed*, i.e. controlled by microprograms. (It is often thought, mistakenly, that only *micro*computers use *micro*programs.)

The memory in which microprograms are stored forms part of the *control unit or *arithmetic and logic unit of the computer. It is sometimes referred to as *control store*. It must be very fast (i.e. have a very short *storage cycle) and not prone to errors. Semiconductor *ROM (read-only memory) is almost always used. The contents are therefore fixed, and the circuitry itself is usually permanently connected. In larger computers semiconductor *RAM (random-access memory) can be used to store microprograms, either instead of or in addition to ROM. Use of RAM allows modifications to be made and specialized microinstructions to be introduced.

milli- A prefix to a unit, indicating a submultiple of one thousandth (i.e. 10^{-3}) of that unit, as in *millimetre, millisecond*, or *millivolt*. The symbol m is used for milli-; millimetre, millisecond, and millivolt are thus often written mm, ms, mV. Milli- is part of a sequence

milli-, micro-, nano-, pico-, . . .

of decreasing powers of 1000.

mini *Short for* minicomputer.

minicomputer (mini) Loosely, a medium-size computer, i.e. one that is usually considered to be smaller and less capable in terms of performance than a contemporary *mainframe computer, and hence cheaper. A modern minicomputer might well operate faster than many of the mainframes used in the 1970s. Again, it might be out-performed by a sophisticated *microcomputer. Minicomputers came on the scene before microcomputers and the boundary between the two is no longer clear.

Minicomputers are often to be found in laboratories built into complex experiments, or controlling industrial processes. They are also used for small multiuser systems where *personal computers would be inappropriate because of the need to share data or programs. Mainframe computers often have a number of minicomputers to perform such tasks as input/output or communications, thus freeing the power of the mainframe CPU for more demanding tasks.

minifloppy *See* floppy disk.

mod *Short for* modulo. *See* integer arithmetic.

modem *Short for* modulator/demodulator. A device that converts a *digital signal into an *analog signal suitable for transmission over an analog communication channel, and that converts an incoming analog signal back into a digital signal. It does this by *modulation of the digital signal and demodulation of the incoming analog signal. A pair of modems can thus be used to connect two units – two computers, say, or a computer and a terminal – across a telephone line; the streams of bits from each unit are digital signals that are converted by the modems into continuously varying signals suitable for transmission. (Telephones cannot at present accept digital signals.)

modular programming A style of programming in which the complete program is broken down into a set of components, called *modules*. Each module is of manageable size, has a well-defined purpose, and has a well-defined boundary. Almost all programs are modular in structure. The basis on which a program is broken down could be that, for example, each module involves one specific task to be performed by the computer. Alternatively each module could involve a single design decision. It should be possible for the modules to be developed, tested, and *debugged independently. Modules can then be brought together and tested to see if they operate together correctly. Finally the whole program can be tested to ensure that it is performing in the desired way. A modular program is easy to amend or update, in many cases the modifications being necessary in just one module.

modulation The process of altering one *signal (called the *carrier*) according to a pattern provided by another signal. The device used to achieve this is known as a *modulator*. The carrier is usually a continuously and regularly varying *analog signal. The other signal may for instance be a *digital signal, e.g. a stream of bits. The pattern conveyed by this signal is superimposed on the carrier by varying one of the properties of the carrier, e.g. its frequency, amplitude, or phase. This modified analog signal – the *modulated* signal – can then be transmitted.

Demodulation is the reverse process to modulation: a signal is obtained from a modulated signal (by means of a *demodulator*) and has the same shape as the original modulating signal.

See also modem.

modulator *See* modulation.

module 1. A largely self-contained component of a program. *See* modular programming.

2. A unit of hardware that has a specific function or carries out a specific task and is designed for use with other modules.

modulo *See* integer arithmetic.

modulo-*n* check (checksum; remainder check) A type of *check, i.e. an error-detecting process performed on an item of information. In the simplest case the individual bits making up the item are added together and divided by a number *n* to generate a remainder. For example, in a modulo-5 check the number *n* is 5 and the remainder will be 0, 1, 2, 3, or 4. This remainder is added as an additional digit – the *check digit* – to the item of information. The check digit can be recomputed after the item has been transferred or otherwise manipulated. The new value is compared with the received value, and most simple bit errors (certainly all single bit errors) will be detected.

If the number *n* is made equal to 2, then the process is known as a *parity check and the check digit is the parity bit.

monadic operator (unary operator) *See* operator.

monitor 1. (TV monitor) A simple TV that can be used as one of the components of a microcomputer system. Monitors can be either *monochrome*, with white, green, or amber characters, or *colour*. Monochrome monitors are driven by *composite video signals*, colour monitors by *RGB (red-green-blue) signals*. The computer and monitor must use the same kind of signals. A domestic TV is fed UHF (ultra high frequency) signals and is not therefore a monitor. Again, a monitor is not designed to accept broadcast (UHF) signals.

2. *Another name for* operating system, or for the portion of an operating system that resides permanently in main store, i.e. the supervisor.

monochrome Using or involving only one colour. For

example, a *monochrome screen* uses white, green, or possibly amber characters and may have a facility allowing *monochrome graphics* in the same colour.

MOS *Abbrev. for* metal oxide semiconductor. *See* integrated circuit.

most significant digit (msd) The digit in the most significant, i.e. leftmost, position in the representation of a number, and thus making the largest contribution to the value of the number. With a binary number this digit is referred to as the *most significant bit (msb).*

mother board A *printed circuit board into which other boards can be plugged. In some microcomputer systems, the mother board carries all the major functional elements, e.g. the processor and some of the memory; additional boards plugged into the mother board perform specific tasks such as memory extension or disk control.

mouse A pointing device that is moved by hand around a flat surface: the movements on the surface are communicated to a computer and cause corresponding movements of the *cursor on the display. The mouse has one or more buttons to indicate to the computer that the cursor has reached a desired position. It is normally connected by cable to the computer; a 'tail-less' mouse communicates by means of infrared rather than electrical signals (as occurs in a TV remote control system).

MP/M *See* CP/M.

msd, msb *See* most significant digit.

MS-DOS *Trademark* An *operating system produced by Microsoft Corp. It is intended for use on microcomputers that are based on the Intel 8086 family of microprocessors and support a single user at any one time.

MTBF *Abbrev. for* mean time between failures. *See* failure.

MTU *Abbrev. for* magnetic tape unit. *See* tape unit.

multiaccess system (multiuser system) A system

allowing several people to make apparently simultaneous use of one computer. The system is based on the technique of *time sharing and is used mainly for *interactive working. Each user has a *terminal, usually a VDU plus keyboard. The terminals are connected to a *multiplexer or to a *front-end processor, both of which transmit the data, etc., from the various terminals to the computer in a controlled way. The *operating system of the computer is responsible for sharing main store, processor, and other resources among the terminals in use.

An operating system providing multiaccess is fairly complex in comparison with, say, one handling *batch processing or a single-user interactive system. As the number of users increases at any one time, the *response time of the computer gets longer. A multiaccess system is an example of a *multiprogramming system.

multifunction card (multifunction board) *See* expansion card.

multiplate disk A disk storage medium in which there is more than one plate on which data can be stored. A *disk pack is an example. Again, a fixed *disk drive may use a multiplate disk.

multiplexer (MUX) A device that merges information from several input channels so that it can be transmitted on a single output channel. One transmission channel can thus be shared among multiple sources of information or multiple users. This can be achieved by allocating to each source or user a specific time slot in which to use the transmission channel; this is known as *time division multiplexing (TDM)*. Alternatively the transmission channel can be divided into channels of smaller bandwidth – frequency range – and each source or user is given exclusive use of one of these channels; this is known as *frequency division multiplexing (FDM)*. Multiplexers are often used in pairs, connected by a single transmission channel and allowing contact to be made between any of a large choice of points at each end.

multiprocessing system A computer system in which two or more *processors may be active at any particular time. Two or more programs can therefore be executed at the same time – a multiprocessing system is thus also a *multiprogramming system. The processors share some or all of main store. They must also share other resources such as input/output devices and parts of the system software. The allocation and release of resources is under the control of the *operating system.

multiprogramming system A computer system in which several individual programs may be executed at the same time. A *multiprocessing system, containing several processors, is a multiprogramming system. It is also feasible for a multiprogramming system to be operated with only one processor. On any processor only one processing task can take place at a particular time. In a multiprogramming system there is rapid switching between the tasks to be performed for each of the programs running. For example, while one program is waiting for an input or output operation to be completed, another program can be allocated use of the processor. This switching procedure is under the control of the *operating system, which also controls the allocation and release of other resources in the system.

Multiprogramming enables optimum use to be made of the computer resources as a whole: a processor operates very much faster than its peripheral devices, and valuable processor time is wasted if the processor remains idle while a program uses a peripheral.

multiuser system A computer system that is apparently serving more than one user simultaneously, i.e. a *multiprogramming or a *multiprocessing system.

MUX *Short for* multiplexer.

N

name A means of referring to or identifying some element in a computer program, in a computer *network, or in some other system. For example, *variables, *arrays, and *procedures in a program would be named, as would be the *nodes in a network. In many programming languages a name must be a simple *identifier consisting of a string of one or more characters. In most of these languages names can be chosen quite freely by the programmer. The names used in a program are stated in a series of *declarations. When the program is compiled or assembled, prior to execution, names are converted to *machine addresses by means of a *symbol table. *Compare* literal.

A	B	output
0	0	1
0	1	1
1	0	1
1	1	0

Truth table for NAND gate

NAND gate A *logic gate whose output is low only when all (two or more) inputs are high, otherwise the output is high. It can thus be regarded as an *AND gate followed by a *NOT gate: it effectively first performs the AND operation on its inputs then negates the output, i.e. performs the NOT operation on it. The *truth table for a NAND gate with two inputs (A, B) is shown, where 0 represents a low signal level and 1 a high level. The *logic operation implemented by the gate is known as the *NAND operation* and can be written as A NAND B for inputs A and B.

The NAND gate is important because any logic gate can in theory be constructed from a suitable combination of NAND gates. For example, a two-input NAND gate with one input kept permanently high acts as a NOT gate. An AND gate is produced by feeding the output of a NAND gate through such a NOT gate, i.e.

NOT (A NAND B) = A AND B

This can be checked by means of the NAND and AND truth tables. Again, an *OR gate is produced if each of the two inputs to a NAND gate is first fed through a NOT gate, i.e.

(NOT A) NAND (NOT B) = A OR B

See also NOR gate.

NAND operation *See* NAND gate.

nano- A prefix to a unit, indicating a submultiple of one thousand millionth (i.e. 10^{-9}) of that unit, as in *nanometre* or *nanosecond*. The symbol n is used for nano-; nanometre and nanosecond are thus often written nm and ns. Nano- is part of a sequence

milli-, micro-, nano-, pico-, . . .

of decreasing powers of 1000.

negation 1. In computing, a *NOT operation, the performance of a NOT operation, or the result of a NOT operation. The NOT operation can be performed, for example, on a binary digit or number or a logic statement. The outcome is the *complement of that entity. (It should be noted that if a number is stored in two's complement, then to negate it is to take two's complement.)

2. The changing of the sign of a nonzero number or quantity. The negation of +42 is −42; the negation of −42 is +42; the negation of 0 is 0.

negative acknowledgment *See* acknowledgment.

NEQ gate *Short for* nonequivalence gate.

nested structure A programming structure that is incorporated into another structure of the same kind.

More than one structure, of the same kind, can be incorporated. For instance, one or more *loops can be nested in another loop and one or more *subroutines can be nested in another subroutine.

network Loosely, a group of computer systems that are situated at different places, and are interconnected in such a way that they can exchange information by following agreed procedures (*see* protocol). The computer systems must be capable of transmitting information onto and receiving information from the connected system. The information is sent as an encoded signal, and is transmitted along communication lines such as telephone lines, satellite channels, electric cables, and optical fibres.

It is not sensible (in terms of cost and efficiency) for each computer to be directly connected to every other computer on the network: communication lines are expensive to provide and maintain and would be unused for much of the time. Direct connections are made only at certain points in the network, called *nodes. (Strictly, a network is a set of interconnected nodes.) Computing facilities are attached to some or all of the nodes. Nodes may be at a junction of two or more communication lines or may be at an endpoint of a line. A particular piece of information has to be routed along a set of lines to reach its specified destination, being *switched* at the nodes from one line to another, often by a computer. A particular destination is specified by its *address, which is indicated by the sender and forms part of the transmitted signal.

The computers on a network may be organized in several ways (see diagram). In a *star* structure all communication lines connect directly to a single central or controlling node. The endpoints on each line cannot therefore communicate directly. In a *ring* structure there is a single loop of communication lines (usually electric cables) between the various nodes on the network. Each node is thus connected to two adjacent

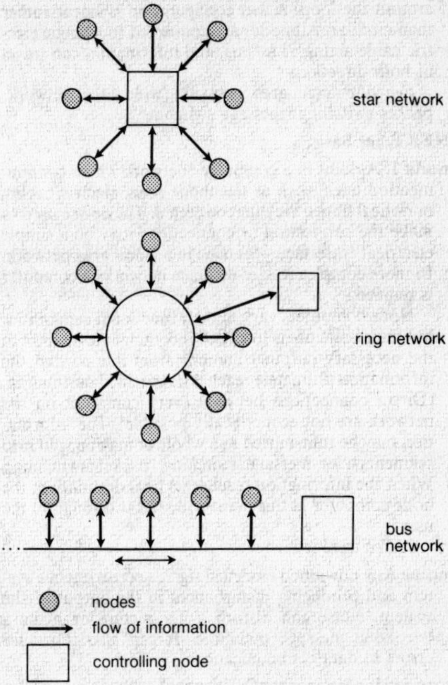

Types of network configuration

ones. Information can pass in only one direction around the loop. A *bus* configuration is linear rather than circular. All nodes are connected to a single electric cable acting as a *bus, and information can travel in both directions.

See also local area network; wide area network; packet switching; message switching.

NEXT *See* Basic.

node 1. A point in a computer *network where communication lines, such as telephone lines, electric cables, or optical fibres, are interconnected. The device used to make the connection or connections may be a simple electrical *interface – as used in a *local area network. In more complex longer-distance networks a computer is required.

Node computers vary in their functional capabilities but their basic use is to switch incoming information to the necessary output communication line so that the information ultimately reaches its specified destination. (Direct connections between every computer on the network are not economically possible). The information may be transmitted as a whole or may be split into segments (*see* message switching, packet switching). When the information reaches its final destination, the node computer at this point will send it through to the user.

2. *See* tree.

noise Any unwanted electrical signals occurring in a system and producing disturbances in the output of the system. Noise can disturb a TV picture or make a telephone message inaudible. It can also introduce errors in data communications.

nonequivalence gate (NEQ gate) A *logic gate whose output is high only when one of its (two or more) inputs is high and the rest are low; otherwise the output is low. It effectively performs the operation of *equivalence on its inputs and then negates the output, i.e. performs the

A	B	output
0	0	0
0	1	1
1	0	1
1	1	0

Truth table for NEQ gate

*NOT operation on it. The *truth table for a gate with two inputs (A, B) is shown, where 0 represents a low signal level and 1 a high level.

The NEQ gate is also called the *exclusive-OR* (or *XOR*) *gate*: it excludes the possibility (allowed in the *OR gate) that the output is high when more than one input is high. *See also* equivalence gate.

nonimpact printer *See* printer. *See also* ink-jet printer; thermal printer; laser printer.

nonlocal variable *See* scope.

nonvolatile memory A type of memory whose contents are not lost when the power supply to the memory is switched off. *ROM is nonvolatile memory. *Compare* volatile memory.

no-op instruction (do-nothing operation) An instruction whose execution causes no action to take place in a computer. The computer just proceeds to the next instruction to be executed.

NOR gate A *logic gate whose output is high only when all (two or more) inputs are low, otherwise the output is low. It can thus be regarded as an *OR gate followed by a *NOT gate: it effectively first performs the OR operation on its inputs then negates the output, i.e. performs the NOT operation on it. The *truth table for a NOR gate with two inputs (A, B) is shown, where 0 repre-

A	B	output
0	0	1
0	1	0
1	0	0
1	1	0

Truth table for NOR gate

sents a low signal level and 1 a high level. The *logic operation implemented by the gate is known as the *NOR operation* and can be written as A NOR B for inputs A and B.

The NOR gate is important because any logic gate can in theory be constructed from a suitable combination of NOR gates. For example, a two-input NOR gate with one input kept permanently low (i.e. earthed) acts as a NOT gate. An OR gate is produced by feeding the output of a NOR gate through such a NOT gate, i.e.

NOT (A NOR B) = A OR B

This can be checked by means of the NOR and OR truth tables. Again, an *AND gate is produced if each of the two inputs to a NOR gate is first fed through a NOT gate, i.e.

(NOT A) NOR (NOT B) = A AND B

See also NAND gate.

NOR operation *See* NOR gate.

NOT gate (inverter) The only *logic gate with a single input. When the input is high then the output is low; when the input is low the output is high. The NOT gate thus performs the *NOT operation on its input and has the same *truth table. The truth table is shown in the diagram, where 0 represents a low signal level and 1 a high level.

A	output/outcome
0	1
1	0

Truth table for NOT gate and NOT operation

NOT operation A *logic operation with only one *operand. When applied to an operand A (a statement or formula, for instance), the outcome is false if A is true and is true if A is false. It thus negates the truth value of A. The *truth table is shown in the diagram, where the two truth values are represented as 0 (false) and 1 (true). The operation can be written in several ways, including

NOT A $\neg A$ $\bar{A}$ $\sim A$ A′

The symbol next to the operand A (i.e. NOT, $\neg$, etc.) is a *logic operator for the NOT operation.

In a computer the NOT operation is used in *high-level languages to negate a logical expression. It is used in *low-level languages on a *byte or *word, producing a result by performing the NOT operation on each bit in turn. If 8-bit words are used, then for example with the operand

01010001

the outcome of the NOT operation is

10101110

See also NOT gate.

null string *Another name for* empty string.

number cruncher *Informal* Any powerful computer designed or used mainly for numerical and mathematical work, usually of a scientific or technical nature. *See also* supercomputer.

number system Any of various systems used to represent and manipulate numbers. A particular system is characterized by its *base, i.e. the number of digits (and possibly letters) used to represent the numbers. All present-day number systems are *positional notations*. In such a notation the value of a number is determined not only by the digits it contains but also by the position of the digits in the number. The positional value increases from right to left by powers of the base; in *binary notation, for example, the positional value increases by powers of 2. *See also* octal notation; hexadecimal notation; floating-point notation.

numerical control The control, by means of a computer, of a manufacturing process. It typically involves a machine tool used in metal-working, such as a milling machine, lathe, or welding machine. Numerical control systems range from very simple to quite complex. The principal variable that is controlled is the position of the machine tool during the manufacturing process. The desired positions are calculated and stored in numerical form on, for example, paper or plastic tape or a magnetic storage medium, together with other necessary information. When fed into the computer associated with the machine tool, this information is converted into signals that operate servomechanisms that in turn guide the tool through the desired sequence of positions.

numerical keypad *See* keypad.

O

object code *See* object program.

object program The program that is output by a *compiler or *assembler and is ready to be loaded into a computer for execution. The program is in the form of *object code*. It is the translation of a *source program.

OCR *Abbrev. for* optical character recognition. A process in which a machine scans a document and is able to convert the characters that it recognizes into a code that can be fed straight into a computer. The machine is called an *optical character reader*, also sometimes abbreviated to OCR. The characters can be read not only by the machine but also by a person: they can be letters, digits, punctuation, and other symbols.

Machine recognition involves special optical methods and requires characters to be of an appropriate shape, size, and print quality. Early optical character readers could only recognize a limited number of rather stylized characters. Current devices can now recognize characters produced by a variety of typewriters, printers, etc., and may even recognize handwritten characters. OCR is widely used in billing and banking, optical characters being used for example on gas and electricity bills. *See also* MICR; OMR.

binary	000	001	010	011	100	101	110	111
octal	0	1	2	3	4	5	6	7

Octal and binary equivalents

octal notation (octal) A number system that uses 8 digits, 0–7, and thus has *base 8. It is a positional notation (*see* number system), positional values increasing from right to left by powers of 8. Octal is a convenient shorthand by which people (rather than machines) can handle binary numbers. Each octal digit corresponds to a group of 3 binary digits, or bits, as shown in the table. Conversion of binary to octal is done by marking off groups of 3 bits in the binary number (starting from the right) and replacing each group by its octal equivalent. Conversion of octal to binary is done by replacing each octal digit by its equivalent binary group. *See also* binary notation.

odd parity *See* parity check.

OEM *Abbrev. for* original equipment manufacturer. Usually, an organization that purchases equipment, such as electronic circuitry, that is to be built into one of its products. In some cases the term is used to refer to the supplier of the equipment.

off-line 1. Of *peripheral devices or *files: not under the control of the processing unit of a computer, i.e. not connected to a computer system or not usable. A peripheral device may be connected to a computer but is off-line if the system has been instructed not to use it.

2. Involving peripheral devices or files that are off-line (as in *off-line processing* or *off-line storage*).

Compare on-line.

OMR *Abbrev. for* optical mark reading (or recognition). A process of data entry to a computer in which a machine detects marks made by a person in his or her choice of indicated positions on a document. The marks could be put for example in one or more chosen columns of a table or in selected areas of a multiple-choice answer sheet. OMR displaced the less reliable but similar process of *mark sensing. In OMR each mark is detected photoelectrically, usually by the reduction in intensity of a narrow light beam after reflection by the mark rather than the less absorbent paper or card. The positions of a mark on a document indicate the input data. Once a mark has been detected, the relevant data is converted into a code that can be fed straight into the computer. *See also* OCR; MICR.

one's complement *See* complement.

on-line 1. Of *peripheral devices or *files: under the control of the processing unit of a computer, i.e. connected to the computer and usable.

2. Involving peripheral devices or files that are on-line (as in *on-line processing* or *on-line storage*).

Compare off-line.

op code *Short for* operation code.

operand 1. In general, a quantity or function upon which an arithmetic or *logic operation is performed. For example, in

$$(3 + 5)/2$$

3, 5, and 2 are the operands. The symbols + and / are called *operators.

2. The parts of a *machine instruction that specify the objects upon which the operation is to be performed. For instance, in the instruction

ADD A,B

A and B are the operands and could be *registers in the central processor, or actual values, or *addresses of values, or even addresses of addresses of values. *See also* addressing mode.

operating system A program or collection of programs used for managing the hardware and software resources of a computer system on behalf of the user. Every general-purpose computer has an operating system. In all but the smallest microcomputers a portion of the operating system is resident in *main store; the rest is kept on *backing store and is read into main store when required.

The operating system provides the *user interface that interprets commands typed on the user's *keyboard and provides information about the current state of the system on the *VDU. It also manages queues for slower devices such as *printers and *plotters, keeps track of where *files are stored, what they are named, and who they belong to, and transfers files between disks or between disks and main store when instructed. In *multiprogramming systems the operating system is responsible for deciding in what order and for how long each processing task it to have the central processor, and what sections of memory they are to use. All communications are managed by the operating system – not only links between the *terminals and the computer but also links to other computers.

operation code (op code) The code that can be placed in the operation part of a *machine instruction and that specifies the operation to be performed.

operation part (function part; operator part) The part of a *machine instruction in which the operation to be performed is specified.

operator 1. A symbol representing the operation that is to be performed on one or more *operands so as to yield a result. An operator taking one operand is called a *monadic operator* or *unary operator*. A monadic operator usually precedes the operand, as in – 1, NOT P. An operator taking two operands is called a *dyadic operator* or *binary operator*. A dyadic operator usually appears between the operands, as in 1 + 1, 3/X; in certain notations, however, it appears before or after the operands. *See* reverse Polish. *See also* arithmetic operator; logic operator; relational operator; order of precedence.

2. A person responsible for the supervision of the hardware of a computer system.

operator part *Another name for* operation part. *See* machine instruction.

optical character recognition *See* OCR.

optical disk A recently developed storage device in the form of a disk covered (usually on one surface only at present) with a special layer on which data or images can be stored and retrieved by optical means. It is similar to a video disk. A light beam from a (semiconductor) laser is focused as a tiny spot on the sensitive layer. When writing information, the laser has sufficient power to heat each tiny region on which it is focused and to change the optical properties so that binary information can be recorded. When reading, the power of the laser beam is lower so that it cannot affect the surface; the scanning beam is reflected from the surface (or in some cases transmitted), and the contents of each tiny storage location (binary 0 or binary 1) can be determined. The storage *capacity can be extremely high. The information is stored and retrieved by *random access.

There are three broad classes of optical disk: *read-only* disks, to which information is added at the time of manufacture and cannot subsequently be changed; *write-once* disks, where information is added by the customer but once written cannot be erased; *erasable* disks, where recorded data or images can be erased and rewritten. The high capacity of the optical disk means that it can provide low-cost storage. It is also a robust medium: the sensitive recording layer is covered by a clear protective layer; the laser is out of focus on this outer layer so that it is reasonably insensitive to scratches or dust that occur there. The presence of flaws in the recording layer do however require elaborate error correcting techniques.

The information is retrieved from optical disk (and in some cases written to it) by *optical disk drives*. The disk is rotated in the disk drive and the laser beam is moved radially for reading/writing purposes. (It is thus similar in operation to a magnetic *disk drive.) Optical disk drives became commercially available in the mid-1980s. In nearly all cases the disks are exchangeable rather than fixed permanently within the disk drive.

optical fibre *See* fibre optics transmission.

optical mark reading *See* OMR.

Oracle *Trademark* Independent Television's *teletext service in the UK.

order of precedence The order in which *arithmetic or *logic operations are performed in an expression. Programs treat expressions in parentheses as a unit to be calculated. In a set of nested parentheses, the innermost ones are handled first. For instance, in evaluating the expression

$$((3*(6+(4-2)))/5)+7$$

the program first subtracts 2 from 4, then adds 6 to the

result, multiplies this value by 3, divides the result by 5, and finally adds 7. Sets of nested parentheses can always be used in programs to make the expression unambiguous.

operation
unary minus
exponentiation
multiplication division
addition subtraction
relationals
NOT
AND
OR

Typical order of precedence

When no parentheses are used, arithmetic and logic operations are performed in a particular order. This means that the *operators are applied in a particular order. This order of precedence is not the same for all programming languages. A typical order is shown in the table; the operator symbols are not included since they vary from one language to another.

There are always several levels of precedence, some operations/operators lying on the same level and thus having the same precedence. When an expression is to be evaluated, operations of the highest precedence are performed first, then the next highest, and so on. With the order shown, *unary minus would be done first, i.e. all negative numbers would be set as such before any *exponentiation, multiplication, division, etc., was performed. Operations on the same level are usually performed from left to right (for instance, all multiplications before any division) but in some languages the order is undefined. Again, in some languages the *relational operators, (less than, greater than, etc.) come after the logic operations (NOT, AND, OR, etc.); the relationals do not always have the same precedence.

OR gate A *logic gate whose output is low only when all (two or more) inputs are low, otherwise the output is high. It thus performs the *OR operation on its inputs and has the same *truth table. The truth table for a gate with two inputs (A, B) is shown, where 0 represents a low signal level and 1 a high level.

A	B	output/outcome
0	0	0
0	1	1
1	0	1
1	1	1

Truth table for OR gate and OR operation

OR operation A *logic operation combining two statements or formulae, A and B, in such a way that the outcome is false only when A and B are both false; otherwise the outcome is true. The *truth table is shown in the diagram, where the two truth values are represented by 0 (false) and 1 (true). The operation can be written in several ways, including

A OR B   A ! B   A | B   A + B

A and B are known as the *operands and the symbol between them (OR, !, |, +) is a *logic operator for the OR operation.

In a computer the OR operation is used in *high-level languages to combine two logical expressions according to the rules stated above. It is used in *low-level languages to combine two *bytes or *words, producing a result by performing the OR operation on each corresponding pair of bits in turn. If 8-bit words are used, then for example with operands

01010001
11110000

the outcome of the OR operation is

11110001

See also OR gate.

output 1. The results obtained from a computer system following some processing activity. Computer output may be in a form that people can understand and use, such as words or pictures that are displayed on a screen or printed or drawn on paper. Alternatively, it may be written on, say, a magnetic tape or disk so that it can be fed back into the computer system – or into another system. *See also* output device.

2. The signal – voltage, current, or power – obtained from an electric circuit.

3. To produce a signal or some other form of information.

output device Any device that converts the electrical signals representing information within a computer system into a form that can be understood and used by people. *Printers, *VDUs, and *plotters are the most common types of output device. Devices giving a spoken output are now available. An output device may also convert internal signals into a coded form on, say, magnetic disk that can be fed back into a computer system at a later date. *Compare* input device.

output medium *See* media.

overflow The condition arising when the result of an arithmetic operation in a computer exceeds the size of the location allocated to it. For example, a number represented by 9 bits would not fit in an 8-bit word. If there were no means to detect overflow, results would be unreliable and might be incorrect. Facilities are therefore provided to detect overflow: a particular bit, known as an *overflow flag* or *bit*, is set to 1 when overflow occurs. The overflow can then be corrected. *See also* underflow.

overlay 1. Part of a program, i.e. a section of code, that is loaded into *main store during the execution of that program, overwriting what was previously there. The section of code is thus not permanently resident in main store but is held in *backing store until required by the processor. The parts of the program to be used as overlays, and the other parts that these are allowed to overwrite, are determined by instructions to the *link editor at link time. This has to be done with care: if an overlay tries to use a procedure in a part of the code it has just overwritten, then the program will fail.

In general several overlays are loaded into the same area of main store at different stages of the program, each erasing the code already there but no longer needed. This process of repeatedly using the same area of store during program execution overcomes space limitations in main store. The technique, which is called *overlaying*, is used mainly in systems that do not have *virtual storage – microcomputers and some older mainframes.

2. A piece of card or plastic placed over or around a *keyboard to indicate what special functions have been assigned to particular keys.

overwrite 1. To destroy the contents of a storage location by writing a new item of data to that location.

2. To write a new version of a file on backing store on top of the existing version.

P

pack To store data in a compact form in order to reduce the amount of storage space required. The process of packing data is called *data compression*. There are several ways of packing data, making use of the characteristics of the storage medium or of the data itself. For example, several *bytes may be stored in one *word, or multiple occurrences of a character or word may be replaced by a single instance of the character or word and an indication of the number of times it occurs. The original data can be recovered from its packed form by *unpacking* it.

package *See* application package.

packet *See* packet switching.

packet assembler/disassembler (PAD) The device that builds packets of information in order to transmit them across a *packet-switching network, and breaks up incoming packets. A computer wishing to use a packet-switching network may either have an internal PAD, allowing it to be connected directly to the network, or it may communicate with a PAD belonging to the provider of the network.

packet switching A process whereby information (in digital form) can be sent automatically from one computer on a *network to any other, the information being switched from one communication line to another until it reaches its specified destination. The information is transmitted in units known as *packets*. A packet is a group of bits of fixed maximum length. If the information to be communicated exceeds the packet size it is split up into a number of packets. Each packet is switched as a composite whole from one communication line to another. At each switching point along its route the packet is checked for errors, stored temporarily, and forwarded to the next point when the necessary resources become available. The packets of a partitioned message, document, etc., are reassembled when they reach their final destination (*see* packet assembler/disassembler).

National and international packet switching services

have recently been set up, or are being set up, by many of the national governmental bodies that provide communication services. British Telecom's packet switching service is called *PSS* (packet switch stream) and has been available for public use since 1981. These services allow data to be transmitted at very high speeds (up to about two million bits per second).

Compare message switching.

packing density **1.** The number of components, or *logic gates, per unit area of an *integrated circuit.

2. The amount of information in a given dimension of a storage medium, for example the number of bits per inch of magnetic tape.

PAD *Abbrev. for* packet switching network.

page The unit of interchange between main store and a backing-store device used for *swapping. A page contains instructions or data, or both, and generally the number of words or bytes is fixed for a given computer system. *See also* virtual storage.

page printer A *printer that produces a complete page at a time, an example being the *laser printer.

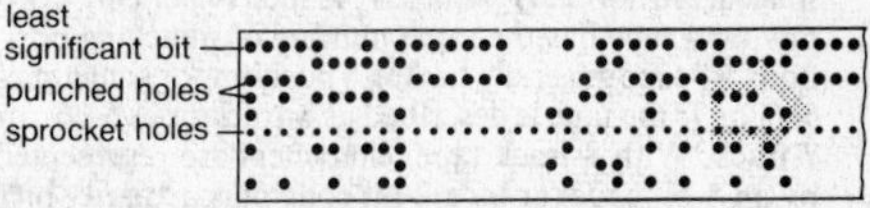

Section of paper tape

paper tape A continuous strip of paper of uniform width and thickness on which data can be encoded by punching patterns of holes (see diagram); materials of greater strength are also used such as laminates of paper and polyester. All these forms can be referred to as *punched tape*. Punched tape was once widely used for the input, output, and storage of data, especially in scientific and engineering applications, and in fact was used for data communications (telex) before its use in computing. Although still employed for example in the programmed control of some industrial processes and equipment, it has been largely superseded by more recent devices such as the magnetic disk.

The holes are punched in rows across the tape. Since a hole can either be present or absent, it can be used to represent a binary 1 or a binary 0. A row of holes and spaces on the tape can thus represent a particular sequence of 1s and 0s that identifies a letter, digit, or some other character (*see* binary representation). The holes are punched one row at a time by a device known as a *tape punch*. To input data to a computer the punched tape is first fed into a *tape reader*. This device senses the holes in each row (achieved by photoelectric methods in current devices) and converts the punched data into the corresponding binary code of 1s and 0s that can then be fed to the computer. Signals from a computer can be fed to a tape punch to produce computer output on punched tape.

The tape used in computing is usually 1 inch (2.5 cm) wide and comes wound on reels; 10 rows, equally spaced, are normally punched per inch (4 per cm). Each row on a tape has the same number of punching positions, 1″ tape generally having 8 positions or sometimes 5, 6, or 7; the tape is described as 8-track or as 5-, 6-, or 7-track. With 8-track tape, characters are represented by an 8-bit code (or by a 7-bit code plus a *parity bit). In addition to the data tracks there is also a line of smaller holes running down the middle (between the 3rd and 4th tracks in 8-track tape) and punched at the same time; these are called *sprocket holes* or *feed holes*. Originally used to advance the tape through the tape punch and tape reader, the sprocket holes are now used for timing purposes.

Punched tape is a robust medium and is good for data transfer. It does however have several disadvantages compared with more recent alternatives. It has a low storage *capacity; it has a long preparation time and very slow input speeds, rarely exceeding 1500 characters per second; it can only be used to store one lot of data; insertion and deletion of data usually requires a new tape to be punched.

paper throw A rapid and continuous movement of the paper in a *line printer through a distance of several lines without any printing. In high-performance printers the rate of movement may be almost two metres per second. A paper throw may be used, for example, to print the next line on a new page – described as *throwing a page.*

parallel processing Strictly, the execution of two or more *processes at the same time in a single computer system. This implies that two or more *processors are in operation at the same time. The term is often loosely applied to a situation in which a number of processes are potentially active, but only one is actually being run at any particular instant. *See also* multiprocessing system.

parallel transmission A method of sending data between devices, typically a computer and its peripherals, in which all the *bits associated with a unit of data (e.g. a character) are transmitted at the same time along different paths. For example, if two devices wish to communicate a 16-bit unit of data, the sending device would transmit all the 16 bits at the same time, one bit per wire. More than 16 wires are required, however, since control signals are sent simultaneously, again one bit per wire, indicating that data was available (*see* handshake). The receiving device would then signal that the data had been received. *See also* serial transmission.

parameter 1. A quantity whose value is selected according to the application or the circumstances.
2. Information passed to a *procedure, *subroutine,

or *function. Different parameters may be provided for each *call of the procedure, subroutine, or function. The *actual parameters* (or *arguments*) are those supplied at the time of a particular call. The mechanism by which the parameters are supplied is known as *parameter passing*. Normally this involves either passing the value of the actual parameter or passing the address of the location in which the actual parameter is stored.

parameter passing *See* parameter.

parity bit *See* parity check.

parity check A simple *check used to detect *errors in items of information in binary form. The item may represent a piece of data or part of a program, and may be a single *character, *byte, or *word. An extra *bit, called the *parity bit*, is added to the leftmost end of the item. There are two kinds of parity: *even parity* and *odd parity*. In the former, the parity bit is used to make the total number of 1s an even number; in the latter, the parity bit is used to make the total number of 1s an odd number. For example, the 7-bit *ASCII code for W is 1010111. The number of 1s is 5; the parity bit for even parity is thus a 1, making the number of 1s up to 6 (an even number) and the ASCII code 11010111.

The parity bit is recomputed after the augmented item – original item plus parity bit – has been transferred or otherwise manipulated. The new value is compared with the received value, and most simple bit errors (certainly all single bit errors) will be detected.

parsing, parser *See* syntax analysis.

Pascal A *programming language named after the French philosopher and mathematician Blaise Pascal and developed by Niklaus Wirth in the late 1960s. Pascal was intended to be used for teaching students the principles and practice of programming, and is a relatively small concise *high-level language with what were at the time a number of novel features. Pascal has certain drawbacks when it comes to large-scale programming but is nevertheless very popular and has been implemented on all sizes of computer. It now has an international standard.

password A means of verifying the identity of someone wishing to gain access to a computer system or to certain parts of a system. A password is a particular sequence of characters (letters, numbers, etc.) that is allocated to or chosen by an authorized user and is unique to that person. A potential user must feed his or her password into the computer to establish identity. The password entered is checked against the stored version of the password. Only if the two sequences agree will the person be granted access.

Passwords form part of the *log on sequence in most modern computer systems. They are used, for example, in systems that hold sensitive data (i.e. for security reasons) or when charges are made for use of system resources. Passwords can also be granted to programs in order to control access to data.

Methods commonly used to make a password system more effective are:
1. the passwords are stored on the computer in code so that unauthorized people looking at the password file cannot read the passwords;
2. the password does not appear on the screen when it is typed in, thus making it harder to discover users' passwords by watching them log on;
3. users are urged, and in some cases forced by the system, to change their passwords frequently.

patch A small section of code, often provided by a software supplier, that allows a user to correct or modify a program. It is used for purposes of convenience and speed of change. The patch may be written in *machine code and introduced into the compiled (or assembled) version of a program, i.e. the *object program.

pause instruction An instruction that specifies that the execution of a program is to be suspended. After a pause, a program may be continued from where it left off or abandoned. For example, a program might pause to allow the screen to be read, or so that the ribbon, paper, or print wheel may be changed on a printer.

PC *Abbrev. for* personal computer, printed circuit.

PCB or **pcb** *Abbrev. for* printed circuit board.

PC-DOS *Trademark* An *operating system produced by Microsoft Corp. for IBM and intended for use on the IBM Personal Computer. It is essentially the same as *MS-DOS, but makes assumptions about the underlying hardware that are only fully justified on IBM PCs.

peek To examine the contents of a storage *location in main store using a high-level language. This is usually achieved by means of a *function of this name whose *argument is the address in question. The process is used mainly in microcomputers. *See also* poke.

peripheral device (peripheral) Any device that can be connected to and controlled by a computer. It is external to the *central processor of the computer. Peripherals may be *input devices, *output devices, or *backing store.

personal computer (PC) A general-purpose computer designed for operation and use by one person at a time. Such a device became a reality when *microcomputers became available. All personal computers are microcomputers, but microcomputers are not necessarily personal computers. Personal computers range from cheap domestic machines of limited capability to expensive and highly sophisticated systems. The ratio of computing power to cost is sufficiently high, however, so that PCs do not have to be used continuously to be cost-effective – unlike larger minicomputers and mainframes.

personal identification device (PID) A device issued to an authorized user of a computer system and containing a machine-readable sequence of characters that identifies that person. It may be a card or badge. The PID must be inserted into a terminal of the computer system before access to the system is granted. In many cases a person must use a PID in conjunction with a PIN (*personal identification number) to gain access.

personal identification number (PIN) A number that is allocated to an authorized user of a computer system, that is unique to that person, and that he or she must feed into the computer system in order to establish identity. A PIN is a form of *password. It is often used in conjunction with a PID (*personal identification device). PINs and PIDs are used, for example, at cash dispensers in banks.

physical record *See* block; record.

pico- A prefix to a unit, indicating a submultiple of one million millionth (i.e. 10^{-12}) of that unit, as in *picosecond.* The symbol p is used for pico-; picosecond can thus be written ps. Pico- is part of a sequence

milli-, micro-, nano-, pico-, . . .

of decreasing powers of 1000.

picture processing *Another name for* image processing.

PID *Abbrev. for* personal identification device.

PIN *Abbrev. for* personal identification number.

pin header A device similar in form to a *DIP but containing no circuitry. Instead each leg is extended vertically through the package allowing pins to be connected together in any configuration by soldering small pieces of wire across the relevant pins. A pin header is more flexible but clumsier than a *DIL switch.

pipelining *See* control unit.

pixel *Short for* picture element. In computer graphics, the smallest element of a *VDU with graphics capability. In general it is an element in a large *array that is holding pictorial information. It contains data representing the brightness, the colour, or some other property of a small region of an image. The *resolution of a graphics display is measured in terms of how many pixels there are across and down the screen.

PL/I A high-level *programming language whose name

is derived from **P**rogramming **L**anguage **I** (one). It was developed by IBM in the late 1960s to combine what were considered the best features of *Fortran, *Algol-60, and *Cobol, and was intended to replace all three. PL/I is a very large comprehensive language, and although it is used fairly widely in IBM installations it was never taken up to any large extent by other manufacturers.

plasma display (plasma panel display) *See* display.

plotter An *output device that converts coded information from a computer into graphs or pictures drawn on paper or transparent film by means of one or more pens. There are many types of plotter, varying in the accuracy, quality, and speed of production of the graphs or pictures, the size produced, and the use (if any) of colour.

Two basic designs of plotter are the *flatbed plotter* and the *drum plotter*. Simplified versions are shown in the diagram. In both cases the pen is mounted on a bar that spans the width of the paper. The pen can be moved to precise positions along the bar. In the flatbed plotter the bar can be moved on tracks running up and down the length of the sheet of paper or film. The pen can therefore be moved to any specified point on the surface of the paper or film to make a mark. It can either touch the surface as it moves so that it makes a line, or it can be lifted off the surface as it moves.

In the drum plotter the bar is fixed in position and it is the paper that is moved. The bar is parallel to the axis of a drum. The paper is wrapped around part of the surface of the drum; the holes down each side of the paper engage with pegs on the drum. Rotating movements of the drum cause the paper to move, and different positions down the length of the paper can be brought precisely under the pen. As in the flatbed plotter the pen can be moved along the bar to the required position across the width of the paper, and it can be lifted off the surface of the paper if necessary.

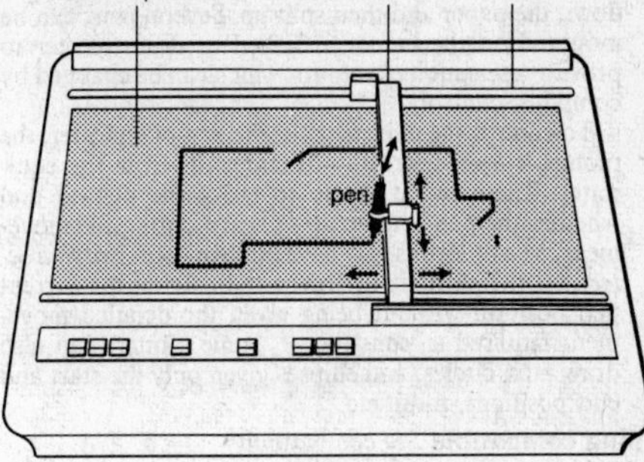

Flatbed plotter

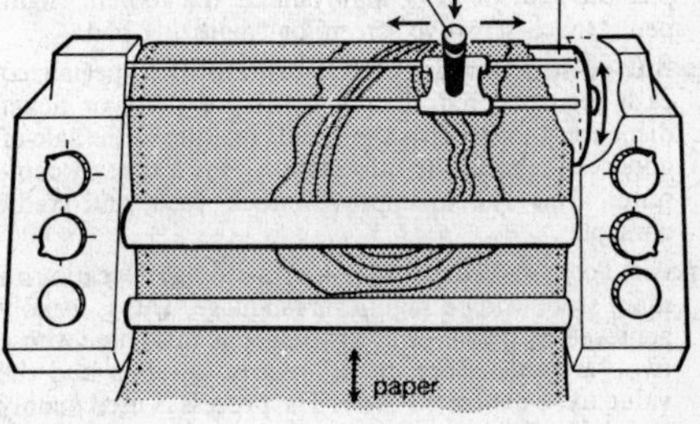

Drum plotter

The drum plotter is used when large numbers of drawings are required; these can be plotted in sequence down the paper and then split up. Several pens can be mounted on the bar of a flatbed or drum plotter to provide a selection of colours, which can be changed by computer control.

To control the movement of the pen of a plotter, the plotter is sent a stream of commands from the computer. These tell it where to move the pen to and whether the pen is to be up or down during the movement. Most plotters also have built-in *hardware characters*, i.e. the plotter will draw a character at the current pen position without being given the detailed movement required to construct it. Some plotters can also draw arcs, circles, and ellipses given only the start and end positions, radii, etc.

plug compatible *See* compatibility.

pointer (link) A character or group of characters that indicates the *location of an item of data in memory.

pointing device Any device that identifies a point on a *VDU and transmits its location to a computer. Examples are *cursor keys, a *joystick, *trackerball, *light pen, *touch-sensitive screen, or *digitizing pad.

point-of-sale terminal (POS terminal) A specialized cash register, credit-card recording system, or ticket dispenser that records the details relating to the sale of goods and feeds the information into a central computer. This system improves stock, cash, and credit control.

poke To modify the contents of a storage *location in main store using a high-level language. This is usually achieved by means of a *procedure of this name whose two *arguments are the address in question and the value to be deposited there. The process is used mainly in microcomputers. *See also* peek.

polling A technique whereby a computer checks each of a number of input devices in rotation to see if any data is waiting to be read. Polling depends for its success on each device being checked at least as frequently as the data is arriving; in addition the time spent processing any data that has arrived must not be too long so that data on other devices is missed. Polling can be contrasted with the use of *interrupts, where it is the devices that inform the processor when they have data available. In some systems an interrupt will alert the processor to the fact that one of a number of devices has data available, and the processor then polls the devices to find out which one it is.

pop *See* stack.

port 1. A point at which a connection can be made between an input/output device and the central processor of a computer system, allowing data to be passed.
2. A point through which data can enter or leave a computer *network. It forms part of a *node.
3. To move a program, usually written in a *portable form, to another computer system.

portable Denoting programs that can be readily transferred from one computer to other computers. For maximum portability a program should be written in a *high-level language possessing an internationally agreed standard, and any extensions or deviations permitted by a particular *compiler should be avoided. Where it is absolutely necessary to make some reference to particular hardware or to include system-dependent features, then these should be concentrated in a few well-documented routines and not scattered throughout the program. *See also* configure.

positional notation *See* number system.

positive acknowledgment *See* acknowledgment.

power-fail recovery *See* recovery.

power on To switch on a piece of computing equipment.

precedence *See* order of precedence.

precision The degree of exactness to which a numerical value is stated, usually based on the number of digits to which the number is represented. The value of some quantity given to 6 digits thus has 6-digit precision. For example, π to 6-digit precision and to 8-digit precision is respectively

3.141 59 and 3.141 5927

In a computer each item of information must fit into a *word, which contains a fixed number of bits. This sets a limit on the precision to which a number can be represented.

Many programming languages offer *extended precision* (for *floating-point numbers). More powerful computers will perform extended-precision floating-point arithmetic in hardware. In the simplest case two words can be operated as a single *double-length word*; this doubles the number of bits available to represent a number, and leads to what is known as *double precision*. (The use of only one word is then called *single precision*.) The increased number of bits is normally added to the mantissa section of the word, leaving the exponent section unchanged in length.

Prestel *Trademark* The public *videotex system run by British Telecom.

preventative maintenance *Maintenance that is performed on a regular basis and is intended to prevent failures or to detect failures that are just about to happen. For example, routine lubrication, cleaning, and replacement of air filters, fans, etc., can prevent failures in devices with moving magnetic media, i.e. disk drives and tape units. When the performance of, say, an electric circuit is suspect, the circuit can be checked by deliberately trying to induce a failure. *Compare* corrective maintenance.

primary store *Another name for* main store. Backing store is then often referred to as *secondary store*.

PRINT *See* Basic.

printed circuit board (PCB) A thin rigid board of insulating material, usually fibreglass, with electronic

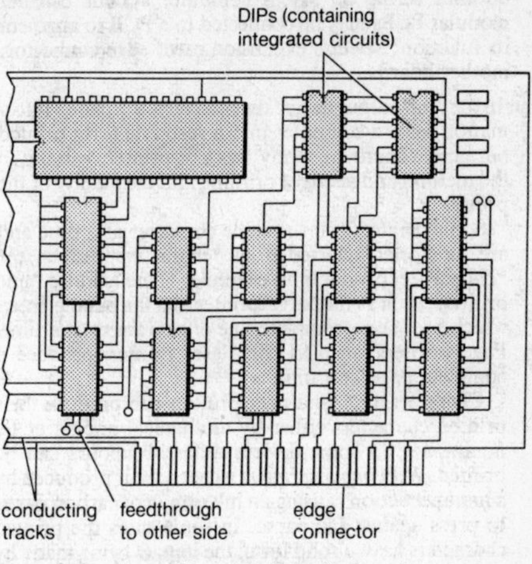

Part of a printed circuit board

components and interconnections on one or both sides (see diagram). A specific pattern of metal strips is chemically formed on the board in accordance with the circuit design; the metal strips are conducting tracks. The components, usually *integrated circuits, are then soldered into position between the appropriate conducting tracks to complete the circuit. Double-sided PCBs are commonly produced; these have components and some of the conducting tracks on one side of the board with additional tracks on the other, interconnections being made through the board.

A PCB connects via an appropriate socket to the

internal wiring of, say, a computer system. Smaller modular PCBs may be connected to a PCB to augment its function. *See also* expansion card; edge connector; mother board.

printer An *output device that converts the coded information from a computer into a readable form printed on paper. There are many types of printer, varying in the method and speed of printing and the quality of the print.

Some printers print a single character at a time and are thus often referred to as *character printers; the *daisywheel printer is an example. There are also *line printers, such as the barrel printer and the band printer, which produce a complete line of characters at a time. Page printers, such as the *laser printer, produce a complete page at a time.

Character, line, and page printers can produce their printed characters either by mechanical impact or by nonimpact; in some devices different colours can be printed. With *impact printers* a character is produced by a hammer action causing an ink ribbon or carbon paper to press against the paper. In some cases the printed characters have a solid form, the impact being made by a print hammer on which the type character is embossed; the daisywheel printer is an example of this type of impact printer. Alternatively, characters may be built up as a pattern of closely spaced (or possibly overlapping) dots, each dot produced by the impact of a thin rod. In *nonimpact printers* characters are produced without the use of mechanical impact; examples include *ink-jet, *thermal, and laser printers. The characters are usually composed of fine dots.

Printers – either impact or nonimpact – that produce characters as a pattern of dots are known as *matrix printers*. The *dot matrix printer is a widely used impact printer. Matrix printers can produce a large selection of shapes and styles of letters and digits, and may also print Arabic characters or the ideograms of oriental languages. In addition to characters it is possible to produce diagrams, graphs, etc.

printer format *See* format.

printout The output of a *printer, either the printed matter itself or the paper – usually a stack of *continuous stationery – on which the matter is printed.

print wheel *See* daisywheel printer.

privacy of data. The protection of stored data against unauthorized reading. When privacy is required for data stored in a computer it implies that the data is confidential and that access to it should be limited. The data may be 'owned' in some way by a particular person or organization, for example it may be data derived from commercial research and development. More usually it is data about a particular person or organization. Personal data is protected by legislation in many countries (*see* data protection).

If a system has poor *security then the privacy of data is at risk. If the *integrity of the data is to be maintained in some way by the system, then the privacy is reduced because of the number of copies of the information that safe operation of a computer system demands.

problem-orientated language *See* high-level language.

procedure A section of a program that carries out a well-defined operation on data. The word procedure is generally used in the context of *high-level languages; the same concept appears in *assembly language but is then normally called a *subroutine*. The same procedure (or subroutine) can be used at different places in a program. Rather than repeating the same set of instructions at each place, the procedure (or subroutine) appears only once and is obeyed 'out of line'.

It is brought into effect by a *call: control is transferred to the procedure (or subroutine) and on its completion control reverts to the main program. This process saves storage space when the program is running. The actual data values to be used in the operation (or their addresses in memory) are specified at the time of call; these values or addresses are known as *parameters. Different parameters can be provided for each call.

In a large computer system with many users, a collection of procedures and subroutines can be held on backing store and made available for general use. *See also* function; program library; subroutine library.

process 1. In general, to perform a sequence of operations on something in order to produce a particular result. In computing, the operations are arithmetic calculations and *logic operations that are performed on data in accordance with instructions in a computer *program. The data is stored within the computer and is processed by the *processor (or processors) in the computer.

2. A sequence of operations or events defined by the result it produces or by its purpose. It can be considered as a particular task to be achieved. In computing the word is applied particularly to the task currently being executed by the *processor or awaiting execution.

process control The computer-based monitoring and control of a manufacturing or industrial process. Sensing instruments measure one or more variables. The input from these instruments is compared with the optimum values, and control devices are adjusted to maintain the process in an efficient and safe state. Any serious problems will cause automatic safety features to operate and human supervisors will be notified.

In industries concerned with fluids and bulk solids, such as chemical manufacture, petroleum refining, and food processing, the variables to be controlled include temperature, pressure, density, consistency, and composition. If sheeted or webbed materials are involved, as in the paper, plastics, and textile industries, the major variables are temperature, thickness, width, length, and weight per area. When discrete items are handled or manufactured, as in the car and aircraft industries, then position, dimensions, and other properties are controlled.

processing The performance of *arithmetic and *logic operations by the *processor (or processors) in a computer on data stored within the system. The operations are performed in accordance with the instructions in a computer *program.

processing unit *See* processor.

processor A piece of *hardware, or a combination of hardware and *firmware, whose function is to interpret and execute instructions. It may be the principal operating part of a computer, in which case it is also known as the *central processor. In larger and/or more complex computers there may be several processors, acting independently, each one performing some of the processing tasks or possibly having a specialized function. A processor may form part of a unit, as with an intelligent *terminal. The processor or set of processors in a computer is often called the *processing unit*. The words processor and computer are often used as synonyms. *See also* front-end processor; microprocessor.

program 1. A set of *statements that can be submitted as a unit to a computer system, and used to direct the way in which that system behaves. Since the program will be followed slavishly by the computer system, it must indicate precisely what is to be done, and is thus expressed in a formal notation. The *programming languages used for this purpose can be picked from a selection of *high-level languages or *low-level languages (usually *assembly language). Before it can be executed by a computer, however, the program must be converted into the appropriate *machine code.

The major part of any program consists of one or more *algorithms, each setting out the steps by which some calculation or other task can be performed. With all but the simplest programs, there are various stages in producing a program and maintaining it in the desired form. The first stage is to understand exactly the whole task under consideration so that the *requirements* of the program can be clearly stated. During the process of *program design*, a description is produced of the program itself, the major components of the program, the way in which the components are interrelated, and the main algorithms employed by the components.

The design acts as the basis from which a working version of the program is created. This *implementation* stage involves writing the program in the chosen language as well as *testing and *debugging it. If at any stage the design proves to be inadequate or wrong, then a return to the previous stage is made. Once testing and debugging have been satisfactorily completed the program can be released for *operational usage*, together with *documentation. During its working lifetime it may have to be modified or upgraded, and its documentation suitably amended. This forms part of *program maintenance*.

2. To design, write, test, and debug programs.

program counter *Another name for* instruction address register.

program design *See* program.

program file A *file containing one or more programs or program fragments, which may be written in *source code or *object code. *Compare* data file.

program flowchart *See* flowchart.

program library An organized collection of computer programs held on *backing store. It may be available for general use by all users of a particular computer system, in which case it is called the *system library*. The individual programs are known as *library programs*. A typical library might contain *compilers, *utility programs, *application packages, and *procedures or *subroutines. Usually it is only necessary to make a reference to a particular library program, i.e. indicate its *name, to cause it to be automatically incorporated in a user's program by the *link editor.

programmable ROM *See* PROM.

program maintenance *See* program.

programming The activities involved in producing a computer program. In the broadest sense of the word, this includes producing an accurate description of the requirements that some envisaged program is expected to meet, and all stages of program design and implementation (*see* program). In a much narrower sense, the activities involve simply the writing and testing of a program from some given design. This narrower usage is most common in commercial programming, where a distinction is often drawn between systems analysts and programmers. *See* systems analysis.

programming error *See* error.

programming language Any of a wide variety of notations designed for the precise description of computer *programs. With any programming language, the notation consists of a set of letters, digits, punctuation marks, and other *characters that can be assembled into various combinations, together with a strictly defined set of rules describing exactly which combinations are permitted. This set of rules is the *syntax of the language. The meaning of text constructed according to the syntax is also strictly defined – by the *semantics of the language. Programming languages are thus artificial languages in that there is no freedom of expression characteristic of a natural language like English. *See also* high-level language; low-level language.

program module *See* modular programming.

program unit (subprogram) A part of a program that performs a specific task and so in some sense is self-contained. A *procedure, *function, *subroutine, and program *module are examples of program units.

Prolog A *programming language whose name is derived from **pro**gramming in **log**ic. It was developed in Europe in about 1970 and is based on symbolic logic. It is widely used in the field of *artificial intelligence. Its structure is not at all like that of more conventional languages such as Pascal or Basic. It consists mainly of statements about relationships between objects, or implications derived from the statements, rather than instructions about how the objects are to be manipulated.

PROM *Abbrev. for* programmable read-only memory, i.e. programmable ROM. A type of *semiconductor memory that is fabricated in a similar way to *ROM. The contents required, however, are added after rather than during manufacture and cannot be altered from that time. These contents are fixed electronically by a device known as a *PROM programmer.* It is only outside a computer that a PROM can be programmed. Within a computer the contents cannot be changed; they can only be read. *See also* EPROM.

PROM programmer *See* PROM; EPROM.

prompt A short message displayed on a VDU and sent to the terminal user to indicate that additional data is required from the user to allow processing to continue. The prompt frequently has some mnemonic content to describe the type of data expected. Ideally a prompt should be explicit and informative for those unused to the system, but capable of being shortened to increase the speed of use for an experienced user. For example, a novice prompt may take the form

Enter the name of a file,
1 to 8 characters starting
with a letter:

The equivalent expert prompt could then be

Filename:

This state of affairs is seldom realized, and many operating systems in particular prompt with a single character such as > or $.

protection *See* data protection; file protection; storage protection.

protocol An agreement that governs the procedures used to exchange information between entities in a computer *network. In general, a protocol will govern the way in which information is encoded (*see* code), the generation of checking information (*see* check), and the *flow control of information, as well as actions to be taken in the event of *errors.

The agreement operates between entities that are physically remote and have no direct means of exchanging information. The information is passed across a series of *interfaces to so-called *lower-level* protocols until the *lowest, physical, level* is reached. The information is transferred to the remote location using the lowest-level protocol and then passes upwards, via the interfaces, until it reaches the corresponding level at the destination.

pseudoassembly language A programming language that is similar to *assembly language but has features that are machine-independent. These languages are used only for educational purposes. They may be regarded as assembly language for a hypothetical computer.

pseudocode A program-like but informal notation consisting of text in natural language (e.g. English) and used to describe the functioning of a procedure or a program. The flow of control is usually expressed in programming terms, e.g.

```
if ... then ... else ...
repeat ... until ...
```

while the actions are elaborated in prose. Pseudocode is used mainly as a design aid and is an alternative to *flowcharts.

pseudorandom numbers *See* random numbers.

PSS *Abbrev. for* packet switch stream. British Telecom's public *packet switching service.

punched card A rectangular paper card on which data can be encoded in the form of holes punched in columns. Since a hole can either be present or absent, it can be used to represent a binary 1 or a binary 0. A pattern of holes and spaces can therefore represent a sequence of 1s and 0s that in turn represents a character (*see* binary representation). Punched cards are little used in present-day computing but were employed extensively for the input, output, and storage of data in early computers. They were in fact used for data processing before computers were available.

Each letter, number, or other character is represented on a card by holes produced mechanically – by a *card punch* – in one or more rows within a column. When used for the input of data, the card punch is operated by means of a keyboard; it is then known as a *keypunch*. The presence of holes in a column, and their positions, is sensed (photoelectrically) by another machine – a *card reader*. The reader converts the punched data into a binary coding of 1s and 0s that can be fed into a computer. Binary data from a computer can be punched on to cards – again by a card punch – as output.

The 80-column card, 7.375 inches by 3.25 inches in size, has been the most commonly used punched card. Each of the 80 columns has 12 possible punching positions, i.e. 12 rows, the holes being rectangular in shape (see diagram). The ten digits 0–9 are represented by one hole punched in one of ten rows while the 26 letters of the alphabet require two holes – one punched in a digit row, the other in one of the two remaining rows; other characters require one, two, or sometimes three holes to be punched. The characters are printed across the top of the card so that the encoded data can be read by people as well as machine. Another punched card is

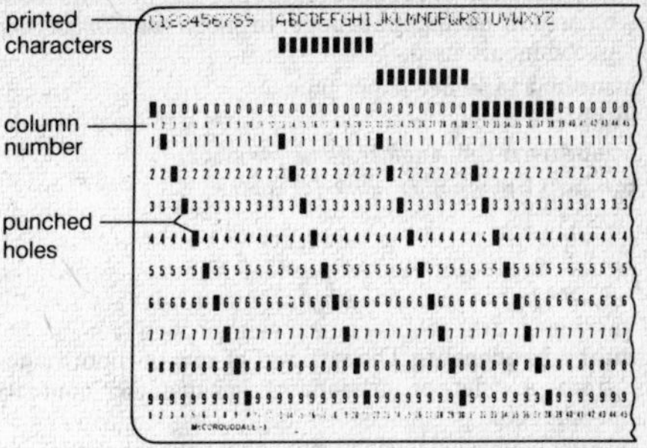

80-column punched card (complete card not shown)

the 96-column IBM card; this is smaller than the 80-column card and holds more data, encoded as combinations of round holes.

Punched cards have several disadvantages compared with more recent devices such as the magnetic disk. Cards are bulky, with only a small proportion of space being used for punched data; they have slow input speeds, rarely exceeding 2000 cards per minute (i.e. 3000 characters per second); they take some time to prepare for data input; although a stack of cards can be read repeatedly, and individual cards can be easily removed and possibly replaced by new cards, discarded cards cannot be reused.

punched tag A small cardboard tag that is attached to a product in a shop or possibly a factory and carries data on that product, encoded as a pattern of holes. When the product is sold or moved to a different location the tag, or part of it, is removed and subsequently fed into a machine that senses the holes. The data thus collected helps in stock or production control and provides sales records in retail applications. In shops the *Kimball tag* is commonly used.

punched tape *See* paper tape.

push *See* stack.

pushdown list *Another name for* stack.

pushup list *Another name for* queue.

Q

query processing The retrieval of one or more values from a *file or *database, leaving the contents unchanged.

queue (pushup list) A *list that is constructed and maintained in computer memory so that all insertions are made at one end of the list and all removals are made at the other end. The next item to be removed is thus the earliest to have been inserted, i.e. the queue works on a first in first out (FIFO) basis. In contrast, a *stack works on a last in first out (LIFO) basis. Queues may be used to store requests for access to peripherals such as disks or printers.

R

radix *Another name for* base.

radix point A symbol, usually a full stop, used to separate the integral part of a number from the fractional part. The radix point in decimal notation is called the *decimal point*.

RAM *Abbrev. for* random-access memory. A type of *semiconductor memory that can be read from and written to by the user, i.e. it is *read/write memory. The basic storage elements are microscopic electronic devices fabricated as an *integrated circuit. These elements, often referred to as *cells*, are arranged in a two-dimensional array, i.e. in rows and columns. A single cell can store one bit of information – either a binary 1 or a binary 0. Each cell can be identified uniquely by its row and column. It can therefore be accessed directly (and extremely rapidly), i.e. there is *random access to any cell. Since it is read/write memory, data can be both read from and written to the cells in the array. To preserve the contents, however, RAM requires its power supply to be maintained; it is thus *volatile memory.

RAM can be fabricated with thousands of cells on one small semiconductor chip. For example, a 64 K RAM chip stores a total of 64 kilobits (i.e. 65 536 bits) of information in its cells.

It should be noted that all kinds of semiconductor memory provide random access, including *ROM (read-only memory).

random access A method of retrieval or storage of data that does not require any other stored data to be read first. The storage locations can be accessed (read or written to) in any order. There is random access with *magnetic disk storage. There is also random access with *main storage, i.e. with *RAM and *ROM, but with a much shorter *access time than with disk storage. *See also* file. *Compare* serial access.

random-access file *See* file.

random-access memory *See* random access; RAM; ROM.

random numbers Numbers that are drawn from a set of permissible numbers and that have no detectable pattern or bias. Any number in the set should therefore have an equal probability of being selected. Random numbers are required, for example, when selecting the winners of the Premium Bond scheme. In a computer true random numbers are difficult to obtain. Instead programs are designed to generate what are known as *pseudorandom numbers*. In principle the numbers produced depend on their predecessors and so are not truly random; in practice the pseudorandom numbers generated by a particular program are sufficiently random for the purpose intended.

raster graphics A method of producing pictorial images in which the desired shape is built up line by line. Each line is composed of closely spaced elements that can be any one of a number of colours or shades. This is the technique used in most VDUs, in TV monitors, and also in some plotters. *Compare* vector graphics.

raw data Data in the form in which it reaches a computer system from the outside world. It is data that has not been vetted for correctness, nor sorted into any particular order, nor processed in any other way. *See also* data cleaning.

read 1. To sense and retrieve data from a storage medium such as *magnetic disk, *magnetic tape, or *semiconductor memory. This data can then be transferred to another storage medium or to an output medium. *See also* readout.

2. To sense and interpret data on an input medium such as *paper tape or a document, and to convert the data into an electrical signal that can be fed into a computer.

READ *See* Basic.

reader An *input device, such as a *document reader or *card reader, that is able to *read data, i.e. sense and interpret data, on an input medium.

read head *See* tape unit.

read instruction A *machine instruction that causes an item of data to be *read from a specified location in a memory device and copied into a *buffer store or into a *register.

read-only memory *See* ROM.

readout 1. Information retrieved from *main store after processing and displayed on a screen or copied into backing store.

2. The process of *reading data from a memory device. In most types of memory this does not alter the actual representation of the data; the readout is then described as *nondestructive.*

read/write head *See* head. *See also* disk drive; magnetic drum.

read/write memory A type of memory that in normal operation allows the user to read from or write to individual storage locations within the memory, i.e. to retrieve and store information. It may involve *serial access or *random access. *RAM is read/write memory.

real number (real) In computing, any number with a fractional part, such as 0.75, 57.3654, or 3.141 59... (i.e. π). As with *integers, reals can be unsigned or can carry a plus or minus sign. Real numbers are represented in a computer in *floating-point notation or sometimes in *fixed-point notation; they are thus represented and manipulated differently from integers. Only a subset of the real numbers can be represented in a computer. If n bits are reserved to store each real number then only 2^n different real numbers can be represented. (In practice the number will be smaller than this since not all combinations are valid floating-point numbers.)

real-time processing A method of using a computer where the rate of working of the computer is fast enough to keep up with the input data. For instance, a computer that could display musical notes on its screen as fast as someone played them on a keyboard would be performing real-time processing; one that displayed the notes only after the person had finished playing would not. Real-time processing is used when the time at which the computer produces its results is crucial.

Computers controlling industrial processes or telephone exchanges would both have to use this technique.

real-time system Any computer-based system, such as air-traffic control, *process control, or defence systems, in which the time at which the output is produced is of importance. The system must be able to respond to some external event (for example, some movement in the physical world) and be able to perform calculations and control functions within a specified and usually very brief time limit. This response time, i.e. the lag between input and output time, must be sufficiently small for the effective operation of the system, and can range from a few seconds to less than a microsecond.

reboot To reuse a *bootstrap program in a computer. An instruction to reboot the system can be given to the system when, say, the *operating system is not running properly or has been corrupted in some way. Rebooting loads a new copy of the operating system from backing store and allows the system a fresh start.

reconfiguration A change or redefinition of the configuration of a computer system, i.e. of the pieces of hardware making up the system and in some cases of the way in which they are interconnected. A reconfiguration may be necessary, for example, to bypass a defective unit or to provide a different overall function. The software may need to be reconfigured to reflect a change in the hardware (*see* configure).

record A collection of related items of data, treated as a unit. It consists of a number of parts, called *fields*, each field holding a particular category of data. In a person's hospital record, for example, there could be a field for the person's name, another for date of birth, and another for, say, the clinic attended; the *key field* holds a number allocated to the patient for ease of identification, and is used to find the record in a group of hospital records or to *sort the group into patient order. Normally one particular field in a record is used as the key field. It is also possible for there to be several key fields in a record.

A field may contain either a fixed or a variable number of *characters, and hence be of a fixed or variable length. A record may thus be of fixed length (with fixed-length or variable-length fields) or of variable length. Fixed-length records may lead to a wastage of storage space if used for data items of variable length, such as names. In a variable-length record the position of the beginning and end of each field has to be indicated in some way, with a comma, say; the beginning and end of the record have also to be indicated. The symbols used for this are called *delimiters* or *terminators.*

This collection of related data items is considered in terms of its contents or function rather than on how it is stored and moved in a computer. It is often referred to as a *logical record.* In contrast, a *physical record* is the unit in which data is transferred to and from peripheral devices; it is also called a *block. One logical record may be split up and held in different physical records. Several logical records or parts of logical records may be located in one physical record.

The record is one of the fundamental ways of collecting and organizing data. *Data files held in backing store are usually treated as sequences of records. Many programming languages permit operations on an entire record as well as on its individual components.

recovery The procedure whereby normal operation is restored after the occurrence of a *fault. *Power-fail recovery*, for example, deals with a loss of the incoming power supply to a computer system. The system is equipped to detect any long-term deviation of the power-supply voltage from acceptable limits. When such a deviation is detected, and before it can cause any problems, a signal (*interrupt) is sent to the processor and the sequence of instructions being carried out is suspended, relevant information is *dumped in *non-volatile memory, and processor activity is halted. When the voltage is restored the program or programs that had been running can be *restarted.

recursive routine A *procedure or *subroutine that *calls itself, resulting in a continued repetition of the operation that the procedure or subroutine is designed to perform. The call must occur as one possibility of a conditional *jump, otherwise there would be an endless series of calls. Recursion is not allowed in every programming language. Improper use can cause problems during program execution, being difficult to detect during compilation.

redundancy The provision of additional components in a system, over and above the minimum set of components required to perform the function of the system. This is done to increase the reliability of the system and, in the event of errors occurring, to increase its ability to recover from such situations. For example, two or three identical pieces of hardware may be used in a computer so that if a fault occurs in one piece that item can be replaced. Again, additional bits are attached to data when it is transferred from one location to another, enabling a *check to be performed – a *redundancy check* – and any errors occurring in the data during transfer to be detected.

reference file A *file that contains reference material and thus changes infrequently.

refreshed display A display in which the image lasts only a very short time and therefore has to be repeatedly redrawn electronically (every $^1/_{50}$ of a second in the UK). An ordinary TV screen is a refreshed display. If the same image is redrawn on a refreshed display then the display appears continuous, without flickering. Alternatively different information can be fed to the screen to give the appearance of motion in the image. A refreshed display can be used for instance to produce an animated cartoon.

register A storage device in the processing unit of a computer in which data has to be placed before it can be operated upon by instructions. It is therefore a temporary location, and has a *capacity of only a *word, a *byte, or a *bit. The registers within a processing unit are quite separate from the storage *locations in main store and backing store. Registers are either general-purpose devices or are intended for a special purpose. Special-purpose registers include the *instruction address register and *instruction register in the *control unit. In larger computer systems there may be several hundred registers.

Information must be stored in and retrieved from registers extremely rapidly. They are therefore high-speed semiconductor devices (usually a group of *flip-flops, each flip-flop storing one bit). In a personal computer the *access time for a register is typically 5 nanoseconds i.e. 5 billionths of a second; in a minicomputer or mainframe system the access time is even shorter – typically 2 nanoseconds and 0.2 nanoseconds respectively.

register transfer An operation whereby information is transferred between two particular *registers or between a specified storage *location in main store and a particular register. For example, the register needed to load the contents of address 10 in main store into the *accumulator would involve

(1) loading address 10 into the *memory address register,

(2) copying contents at address 10 to accumulator.

This can be written in symbolic form:

(1) 10 ⇒ MAR

(2) MEM ⇒ ACC

where the arrow symbol means 'is transferred to'.

relational operator (relational) A symbol representing a comparison operation. These operations take two *operands and provide a logical value *true* or *false* as

comparison	operator
less than	<
less than or equal to	<=
equal to	=
greater than or equal to	>=
greater than	>
not equal to	<>, #, !=, ¬=

Relational operators

their result. The operands may be of any type so long as like is compared with like. The common comparison operations are shown in the table, together with the relational operators normally used in computing; 'not equal' has many denotations. An example of how relationals are used, in Basic, is as follows:

```
100    IF (B↑2 < 4*A*C) THEN 2010
110    IF (A = 0) THEN 1000
```

See also order of precedence.

relative address An *address expressed as a difference with respect to some numerical value used as a reference. This reference is known as a *base address*. Addition of a base address to a relative address gives an *absolute address. The base address may, for example, be the address specified in the instruction currently in the *instruction address register, or it may be stored in a special-purpose register, the *base address register*. *See also* relative addressing.

relative addressing An *addressing mode in which a *relative address is used in a *machine instruction in order to identify the storage location to be accessed. An instruction to skip the next instruction would then merely cause an extra 1 to be added to the *instruction address register (IAR) rather than replacing its contents with an entirely new address. A backward jump could be made in a similar way, by subtracting the relevant amount from the IAR.

reliability A measure of the ability of a system – hardware or software – to provide its specified services for a given period or when demanded.

relocatable code The code making up a program or part of a program that can be loaded anywhere in main store. No *absolute addresses are used, except perhaps those of known operating system or I/O functions. All *jumps are made relative to the current instruction, the start of the code, or the contents of a *register, examples being

jump to the next instruction but one,
jump to the second instruction of the program,
call the procedure whose address is in register 5.

REM *See* Basic.

remainder check *Another name for* modulo-*n* check.

repeat until loop *See* loop.

report generator *See* generator.

requirements description *See* program.

rerun 1. To *run a program again from the start, usually as a result of a malfunction of the computer. *See also* restart.

2. A repeat run.

reserved word A word that has a specific role in a programming language and cannot therefore be used as an *identifier. For example, in many languages the words *if*, *then*, and *else* are used to separate the different parts of conditional statements. These are thus reserved words.

reset (restore) 1. To cause a device to take up an earlier value. For example, when a program is about to be *restarted on a processor, the contents of the working registers of the processor must be reset to the values they last held when the program was previously running.

2. To set the whole computer back to its initial condition when it was switched on. This process is used in smaller computers to clear faults that have corrupted the *operating system and made further processing impossible.

resolution In general, the amount of information or detail that can be produced by a device such as a VDU or plotter or can be revealed in an image. The device or image can be described qualitatively as having a *high resolution (hi res)* or a *low resolution*, etc. The resolution can also be given in numerical terms. The resolution of a display screen, for example, can be expressed as the number of lines (e.g. of text) that can be displayed. With a graphics display the resolution can be quoted as the number of *pixels (picture elements) that are available in the horizontal and vertical directions of the screen, e.g. 1024 by 768 pixels. The resolution of a plotter can be given as the smallest possible pen movement. The resolution of a character can be expressed as the number of dots or pixels available to define it, e.g. 7 by 5 or 9 by 7.

resource Any of the facilities that are available in a computer system and that are required by a processing activity. The resources in any computer system include the following devices: one or more *processors, some form of memory – *main store and *backing store – in which to store the instructions for the processor(s) and the data awaiting manipulation, and *input/output devices through which instructions and data are fed to the computer and information is fed back to the outside world. Program instructions and data are held on backing store as *files. Files are also resources.

Any facility required from the *operating system of a computer is regarded as a resource. These include programs for scheduling and supervising the running of users' programs on the computer.

resource allocation 1. The sharing of the *resources of

a computer system between various processing tasks. A resource, such as the processor, that can only be used by one task at a time, is shared by allowing each task in turn a set time period. In the case of storage devices, several tasks can use the resource at once since portions of storage can be allocated. A magnetic disk, for example, is shared by allocating to each task a suitable number of tracks. Resource allocation is under the control of the *operating system of the computer. With some operating systems the allocation can be changed while the system is running.

2. The sharing of *resources among the users of a computer system to prevent or reduce the unfair use of the system by some users at the expense of others. It can be done, for example, by allocating units of processor time to each user, depending on their status, work, etc., and by demanding more units at peak time rather than, say, at night.

response time Usually, the time that elapses from some action by a computer user to the receipt of some response or feedback from the computer. With a personal computer the response time depends entirely on the size of the task to be performed; there is a fast response for simple tasks like displaying the contents of a file on the screen and a slow response for, say, compiling a large program. When there are a large number of terminals linked to a computer the response time increases as the number of users increases; a lightly loaded mainframe responds extremely rapidly. *See also* interactive.

restart The resumption of the execution of a program after a temporary halt, using data *dumped at a particular point in the program. The program is said to be *restarted*. Much of the data from the previous *run is therefore preserved, and a restart is often described as a *warm start*. In contrast, there is a *cold start* when a program has to be rerun from the start. Some programming languages allow the programmer to specify the points at which a program can be restarted.

restore *See* reset.

RETURN *See* Basic.

return instruction *See* exit.

return key (enter key) A key on a *keyboard that sends a carriage return character to the computer. It is often used to signal that the current line of typing is complete and may be processed.

reverse Polish (RP) A notation used in a computer to evaluate arithmetic expressions. In RP the *arithmetic operator (e.g. +, −, ∗, /) is placed after its operands rather than between them as in conventional notation. The addition of two numbers, *a* and *b*, would thus be expressed as $ab+$.

Expressions in RP are scanned from left to right and the values of the operands stored until an operator is encountered. The operator is then applied to the last two values and replaces them by a single result, which may be used as a value for the next operator, and so on. Hence

$$ab-cd+*$$

would be evaluated as

$$(a-b)*(c+d)$$

i.e. *b* would first be subtracted from *a*; *c* and *d* would then be added together and the sum would finally be multiplied by $(a-b)$.

The translation of conventional notation to RP is achieved by an algorithm. A programmer would not have to write expressions in RP but a *compiler producing machine code from a high-level language might well use RP for expression evaluation.

reverse video (inverse video) A display attribute of most *VDUs, used to draw attention to a character. The character is displayed on the screen in the opposite contrast to surrounding information. For instance, with a screen that normally has bright characters on a dark background, a character in reverse video will be a dark character within a bright character-sized rectangle.

ribbon cable An electric cable in which a number of similar wires lie side by side in a flat plastic strip and are electrically insulated from each other. A ribbon cable provides a continuous path along which electrical signals can be conveyed from one point in a system to another. It can be used for *parallel transmission of data.

right-justified *See* justify.

ring network *See* network.

robot A programmable device that has been engineered to perform many simple repetitive tasks formerly done by human labour. It consists of one or more articulated mechanical manipulators, typically an arm and hand, that are linked to a computer and have considerable freedom of movement. In more advanced types there is also some form of sensory mechanism, such as a TV camera acting as an artificial eye. Most robots in current industrial use follow a fixed sequence of instructions but can be reprogrammed to carry out another task. They have little if any sensory capability. They are designed to be flexible and transportable and can be used, for example, for loading and unloading machines, positioning and transferring parts, and welding pieces of metal or plastic.

robustness A measure of the ability of a system – hardware or software – to recover from conditions caused by *errors. The errors may be external to the system or may occur within the system itself. The system can be described as robust or possibly highly robust if it recovers and continues to operate despite numerous error conditions.

rogue value *Another name for* terminator (def. 2).

roll-out roll-in *Another name for* swapping.

ROM *Abbrev. for* read-only memory. A type of *semiconductor memory that is fabricated in a similar way to

*RAM but whose contents are fixed during manufacture and cannot therefore be modified. The contents can only be read. As with RAM, ROM is composed of an array of cells, each of which can be identified uniquely by its position in the array. There is thus direct and extremely rapid access to any cell in ROM, i.e. there is *random access to any of the storage locations. Since the contents cannot be altered, ROM is *nonvolatile memory. *See also* PROM; EPROM.

ROM cartridge (ROM pack) A module containing software that is permanently stored as *ROM. The module can easily be plugged into and later removed from a microcomputer without the integrated circuitry being handled.

rotate *Another name for* circular shift. *See* shift.

rounding The process applied to a number whereby its length is reduced to a specified number of significant digits, the nearest approximation to its true value being taken. For example, rounding the number 3.257 69 to 5, to 4, and to 3 digits yields 3.2577, 3.258, and 3.26. The *registers in a computer can hold only a fixed number of binary digits (bits). When the result of an arithmetic operation requires more than this fixed number of bits, either rounding or *truncation will take place. Since the rounded value is an approximation to the true value of the number, a *rounding error* is introduced; this is less than the truncation error. Repeated rounding can cause a build-up of such errors and the programmer should try to minimize this problem.

routine *Another name for* subroutine (in assembly language) or procedure (in high-level language), used normally in combinations, as in *input routine*, *recursive routine*, *diagnostic routine*.

RP *Abbrev. for* reverse Polish.

RS232C interface *See* interface.

run 1. To execute a program, i.e. to carry out the program instructions. A program or part of a program that is currently being executed by the processor (or processors) is said to be *running* or *active*. Only one program or program section can be running at any one instant on a processor.

2. The act of executing a program, a set of programs, or some part of a program.

run time The period of time during which a program is actually being executed, or the time taken for execution. It does not include the time during which the program is loaded, or is compiled or assembled.

run-time error (execution error) An *error detected at *run time. The error may be *fatal*, in which case execution is terminated; a fatal error would result, for instance, from an attempt to divide by zero or read past the end of a file. Alternatively the error may be *nonfatal*, in which case a warning is generated and execution continues; a nonfatal error would result, say, from an attempt to calculate a real number too small to be stored – it would be replaced by zero.

run-time system A collection of *procedures that support programs derived from a high-level language at *run-time, providing services such as *storage allocation, *input/output, *debugging, etc., but are not actually a part of the program code as stored on disk. This avoids storing large numbers of copies of commonly used procedures, and allows new versions of them to be installed without the need to recompile all the programs that might use them. In computer systems where a number of high-level languages are supplied by a common manufacturer, it is often possible for a single run-time system to service programs written in any of these languages.

S

sampling 1. A process by which the value of an analog (i.e. continuous) signal is 'examined' at distinct intervals of time. The sampled value can, for example, be converted into a digital form using an *A/D converter for subsequent processing by a computer.

2. A process by which a group of people or items are selected for a particular study. Measurements made on the people or items in the sample will provide information on similar people or items not in the sample.

scheduling The method by which the use of a *processor is controlled, i.e. by which time on the processor is allocated. Scheduling is necessary in a system where the processor has to be shared between a number of programs; this occurs for example in a *multiaccess system. The choice of which processing activity should be granted access to the processor, and can safely be granted access, is determined by the *scheduling algorithm*. This is designed to ensure that the computer is used as efficiently as possible.

Schottky TTL *See* TTL.

scope The range of program code over which a *variable or some other element of a program is defined. The element can be described as *local*, *nonlocal*, or *global*. A local element is accessible only in a restricted part of the program, typically in a *procedure or *function. By contrast, nonlocal elements are accessible in a wider scope and global elements are accessible from all parts of the program. The scope of a variable or other element is normally indicated by the positioning of its *declaration.

scratchpad *Another name for* working space (in main store).

screen The front surface of a VDU or monitor on which computer text or graphics can be displayed. *See* display.

screen dump A way of transferring the entire graphical or textual contents of a VDU screen to a printer. Each row of *pixels in the screen memory is converted to a row of dots on the printer, and the entire contents of the screen appears on the printer a row at a time. *Dot matrix or *ink-jet printers are often used for this purpose, and colour screen dumps are possible if a colour printer is used. *See also* dump.

screen editor *See* text editor.

screen turtle *See* turtle graphics.

scroll To move the information displayed on a screen in a vertical direction, usually towards the top of the screen; it is sometimes also possible to move it in a horizontal direction, as when a *spreadsheet table is being examined. As information disappears at one edge of the screen, new information can become visible at the other edge or alternatively space is provided for the entry of new data.

searching The process of locating information held in a *file or *table by reference to a special field of each *record in the file or table. This field holds a *key* by which the record can be identified. The goal of the search is to discover a record (if any) with a given key value. Many different *algorithms can be used for searching.

The most simple search is a *sequential search*, in which the keys in the file or table are searched sequentially from the beginning until a match is found with the desired key. In a *binary search* the records in the file or table must be arranged with their keys in ascending order. The middle key is examined and, depending on whether this is less than or greater than the sought-for key, the top or bottom part of the file or table is examined. Again the middle key is checked against the desired key, and a smaller section – top or bottom – is indicated and re-examined. The process continues until the desired record is found or its absence discovered.

When a record is to be inserted in a table or file, with its own unique key, then a search must first be made to ensure that no existing record has the new key.

secondary store *Another name for* backing store. Main store is then often referred to as *primary store*.

second generation computers Computers designed in the mid and late 1950s and early 1960s, i.e. after the *first generation, and characterized in particular by the increasing use of discrete *transistors in addition to valves in their electronic circuitry. A wider range of *input/output equipment became available in the period, together with higher performance *magnetic tape and the first forms of on-line storage – *magnetic drums and early *magnetic disks. Magnetic *core store was introduced for main store. Initial efforts were made at *high-level programming languages, the earliest versions of *Fortran, for example, being issued in 1956 and 1958.

During the 1950s several companies, including IBM, had become active in developing computer systems and peripherals. In the late 1950s IBM designed and built a monster computer, called *Stretch*, which had very advanced hardware. It became available commercially in 1961 as the IBM 7030. The IBM 1401 (1959) and 1410 (1960) included early on-line disk storage.

Another important machine designed in this period was *Atlas*, which incorporated many features now considered standard. Its design was begun in 1956 by T. Kilburn at the University of Manchester and it became commercially available, from Ferranti Ltd., in 1963.

See also third, fourth, fifth generation computers.

sector A subdivision of a track on a *magnetic disk (or drum). The computer records data on a disk one sector at a time. The sector is thus the smallest addressable portion of the track: each sector has a unique *address that contains the track location and sector number. The disk is divided into sectors prior to any recording of data; the disk may be *hard-sectored*, in which case the sector positions are set at the time of manufacture, or *soft-sectored*, when sector lengths and positions are set by control information written on the disk by computer program. Once divided into sectors, the address plus other control information can be added to each one. This initial preparation of a disk is known as *formatting*.

security Prevention of or protection against (a) access to information by unauthorized recipients or (b) intentional but unauthorized alteration or destruction of that information. The measures taken to provide security in a computer system include the use of *passwords when logging on and the classifying of information in order to restrict the users who can access it. The security provided may guard against accidental access to sensitive information as well as deliberate access attempts. *See also* integrity; privacy.

seek time *See* access time.

semantics Part of the description of a *programming language, concerned with specifying the meaning of various constructs – *statements, *control structures, etc. These constructs must conform to the *syntax, or grammar, of the language; if they do not then they are meaningless. Most programming languages have their semantics defined by descriptions in English or some other natural language. Because natural language is imprecise and hence ambiguous, different interpretations of the semantics are possible in the early stages of development of a language.

semiconductor memory (solid-state memory) Any of various types of cheap compact memory composed of one or more *integrated circuits fabricated in semiconductor material, usually silicon. The integrated circuit is composed of an array of microscopic electronic devices, each of which can store one bit of data – either a binary 1 or a binary 0. There may be thousands of these storage locations within a single integrated circuit measuring only a few square millimetres in area. Data can be accessed extremely rapidly from these locations.

The categories of semiconductor memory include *RAM (which is read/write memory), *ROM (read-only memory), *PROM (programmable ROM), and *EPROM (erasable PROM). There is *random access to all these types of semiconductor memory. Semiconductor RAM has been used to build the *main store in computers since the early 1970s.

sentinel *See* flag.

separator A symbol that separates *statements in a program. The symbol used depends on the programming language. A semicolon is the separator in several languages, including Pascal:

begin read (x); y := x*x; write (x,y) **end**

Note that the final statement needs no semicolon. *Compare* terminator.

sequence control register (SCR) *Another name for* instruction address register, but whose use is diminishing.

sequential access *Another name for* serial access. *See also* file.

sequential file *See* file.

sequential flow *See* control structure.

serial access (sequential access) A method of retrieval or storage of data that must be used for example with magnetic tape. Blocks of data are read from the storage medium in the actual order in which they occur until the required item or storage location is found. The *access time thus depends on the location of the item. *Compare* random access.

serial transmission A method of sending data between devices, typically a computer and its peripherals, in which the individual *bits making up a unit of data (e.g. a character) are transmitted one after another along the same path. For example, if two devices wish to communicate an 8-bit unit of data, the sending device would transmit the 8 bits in sequence (perhaps with a *start bit* preceding them and a *stop bit* following to aid synchronization). The receiving device can then reassemble the stream of bits into the original 8-bit unit. *See also* parallel transmission; handshake.

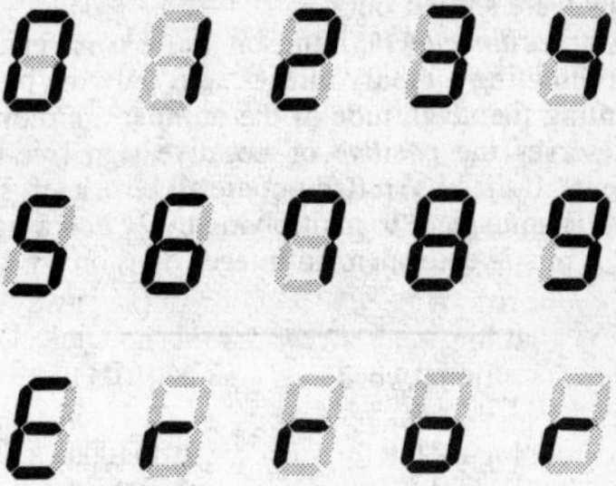

Characters in a seven-segment display

seven-segment display A simple display in which the numbers 0–9 and some letters can be formed from a group of seven segments (see diagram). The segments can be individually darkened or illuminated to form the different characters. The figure eight for instance uses all seven segments; the figure one uses only two segments. *See also* LCD; LED display.

SGN *See* Basic.

shift 1. A concerted movement of some or all of the bits held in a storage location in a specified direction, i.e. to the left or to the right. Shifts are performed in *shift registers. A left (or right) shift of, say, 3 bits means that 3 bits are removed from the left (or right) end of the register. The bits are said to be *shifted* left, right, out, etc.

There are three kinds of shift.

In a *logical shift* the bits shifted from the end of the register are lost, and 0s are shifted in at the opposite end.

In a *circular shift* the bits shifted from the end are reinserted at the opposite end, in the order in which they were shifted out.

In an *arithmetic shift* the bit pattern is regarded as representing a binary integer, and only the bits representing the magnitude of the number are moved; this preserves the positive or negative sign (*see* complement). If the bits shifted out are all zero, a left shift of n bits is equivalent to multiplying by 2^n and a right shift of n bits is equivalent to integer division by 2^n.

original word	00010111
logical left	10111000
logical right	00000010
circular left	10111000
circular right	11100010
arithmetic left	10111000
arithmetic right	00000010

Effects of different 3-bit shifts on an 8-bit word

The effects of different kinds of 3-bit shift on the same 8-bit word are shown in the table; the left arithmetic shift is equivalent to multiplication by 2^3 (i.e. 8), the right arithmetic shift to division by 2^3.

2. On a keyboard, a movement with a *shift key* enabling an alternate character or group of characters to be used. For example, it allows the capital rather than the lower case form of a letter to be typed.

shift instruction A *machine instruction specifying that the contents of a *shift register are to be shifted either to the left or to the right by a specified number of positions. The bits that are introduced as replacements at the opposite end of the register depend on the kind of *shift. In the case of a circular shift, the bits shifted off one end of the register are reintroduced at the other end. With a logical shift and an arithmetic shift, zeros are introduced and the bits shifted out are often discarded.

shift register A *register in which *shifts are performed.

signal A means of conveying data through, say, an electric circuit, a computer, or a communications system. A signal is usually a sequence of values of an electric voltage recorded against time. The value – the *amplitude* – varies either continuously or discretely (i.e. in steps). It is the amplitude that represents the data: the data can therefore be represented in discrete form (e.g. as integers) or in continuous form (as 'real' numbers). The amplitude can be recorded or displayed over a continuous period of time or it can be examined at discrete intervals. Discrete representations of both amplitude (i.e. data) and time are required by *digital computers. *Analog computers employ continuous representations. *See also* digital signal; digitized signal; analog signal.

sign bit A single bit used to represent the sign of a number; normally 0 represents + (plus) and 1 represents – (minus). *See* complement; sign-magnitude notation.

significant digits (significant figures) The digits in a number that make a contribution to the value of that number. The number 0.1234 has four significant digits: the zero does not contribute to its value. The number of significant digits can be reduced by *truncation or *rounding.

sign-magnitude notation A notation that can be used to represent positive and negative integers in a computer. Normally the leftmost bit in a *word is used to denote the sign (0 for +, 1 for −) and the remaining bits are used to represent the magnitude of the integer; the leftmost bit is called the *sign bit*. It is more usual, however, for a computer to use two's complement notation to represent signed integers. *See* complement.

sign off (or **sign on**) *Another term for* log off or log on.

simplex transmission One-way transmission of data between two endpoints. There is no possibility of data travelling in the opposite direction. Simplex transmission could be used to drive an output device such as a printer when it is known that the output device is faster than the transmission line and can therefore always keep up. *Compare* half-duplex transmission; duplex transmission.

simulation The imitation of the behaviour of a system, or of some aspect of that behaviour, by another system. The imitation may be in the form of a model, possibly quite abstract, that can be manipulated by a computer. Again, the imitation may be achieved by a device under the control of a computer and often employing components from the system being simulated – such as the controls in the flight deck of an aircraft. Any computer device or program that performs a simulation is called a *simulator*.

Simulation is widely used as a design aid for both large and small computer systems and for computer networks. It can also be used for more specific purposes, for example in weather forecasting to predict likely developments in the weather pattern. Simulators are extensively used in the training of airline pilots, military commanders, etc. Simulation is an important application of digital computers and is the major application of *analog computers. *Compare* emulation.

single precision *See* precision.

smart terminal *Another name for* intelligent terminal. *See* terminal.

soft keyboard A *keyboard in which the meaning of each key, i.e. the code to be generated by each key, can be allocated and possibly changed by program control. In many cases not all the keys are 'soft'; some are permanently wired so that they have a fixed meaning.

soft-sectored disk *See* sector.

software The programs that can be run on a computer system, as distinct from the physical components – the *hardware – of that computer system. There are two basic forms: *systems software and *applications programs. Systems software, which includes the *operating system, is an essential accompaniment to the hardware in providing an effective overall computer system; it is thus normally supplied by the computer manufacturer. The applications programs relate to the role that the computer system plays within a given organization. The *documentation associated with all these programs is also considered part of the software.

software engineering The entire range of activities involved in the design and development of software. The aim is to produce programs that are reliable and efficient by following standards of quality and adhering to specifications, as is done in other engineering disciplines.

software house A commercial organization whose main business is to produce software or assist in the production of software. Software houses may offer a range of services, including consultancy, the hiring out of suitably qualified personnel to work within a client's team, and a complete system design and development service.

software package *Another name for* application package.

software tool One of a set of programs that are used in the development, repair, or enhancement of other programs. All the programs in the tool set have a common mode of use and employ files and other facilities in a well-defined standard way. Originally, software tools were employed only in the actual production of programs. A typical set of tools might consist of a *text editor, *compiler, *link loader, and some form of *debug tool. It is now recognized that software tools can assist in the activities at all stages in the lifetime of programs. *See* program.

solid-state memory *See* semiconductor memory.

sorting The process of rearranging information into a desired order. This is achieved by means of *sort keys* that are associated with each *record of information. Sorting is achieved by comparing sort keys and rearranging the records accordingly. The sort keys are derived from the values stored in the fields of the records in such a way that by ordering the sort keys in ascending or descending sequence, the associated records will be placed in the desired order. For instance, if the sort key were to be derived from date of birth and surname, then the result of a sort would be to place the records in order of age, with those born on the same day in alphabetical order.

There are many methods of sorting. For example, in the *straight insertion sort* each sort key in a collection of records is checked in turn, and the record associated with the key is repositioned (if necessary) with respect to all previous sort keys. In a *bubble sort* a pair of records is interchanged if their sort keys are not in the correct order, different pairs being checked on different passes through the collection of records. This continues until no further interchanges are necessary.

sort key *See* sorting.

source code *See* source language.

source language The programming language in which

a *source program is written. The program is in the form of *source code*.

source program A program that is written by a programmer in a *programming language, but cannot be executed directly by a computer. It must first be converted into a suitable form by a specialized program. This program may be a *compiler, *interpreter, or *assembler. *See also* object program; high-level language.

space character A member of a *character set that is usually represented by a blank site on a screen, printout, etc. It causes the print or display position to move forward by one position without producing any mark. Within the computer a space is treated in exactly the same way as any other character.

special character A symbol in a *character set that is a *graphic character but is not a letter, nor a digit, nor (usually) a *space character. Punctuation marks, brackets, and arithmetic symbols are special characters. The special characters often vary from one country to another, and would include, for instance, the national currency symbol. *Compare* alphanumeric character; control character.

specification *See* system specification.

speech generation device A means of producing spoken messages in response to signals from a data processing or control system. The selection of messages are produced by assembling speech sounds from a set of fundamental sounds that may be artificial in origin or may have been extracted by processing human speech.

speech recognition The process whereby a computer interprets spoken words in order to determine their data content. *See also* voice input devices.

speech understanding The process of using *speech recognition in order to perform some task making use of speech, such as *voice input.

spool 1. The reel on which magnetic tape, paper tape, or printer ribbon is wound.

2. To transfer information intended for a slow peripheral device into an intermediate store on magnetic disk or tape. This process of *spooling* allows information to be sent to the peripheral (such as a printer) at a more convenient time: programs that produce printed output can then run even when the printer is busy or unavailable. Without spooling, the program would have to slow down so that its speed matched that of the slow peripheral, thus wasting valuable processor time.

spreadsheet (spreadsheet program) A program that manipulates tables consisting of rows and columns of *cells*, and displays them on a screen. The cells contain numerical information and formulae, or text. Each cell has a unique row and column identifier; different spreadsheets use different conventions so the top left-hand cell may be A1, 1A, or 1,1. The value in a numerical cell is either typed in or is calculated from a formula in the cell; this formula can involve other cells. Each time the value of a cell is changed by typing in a new value from the keyboard, the value of all other cells whose values depend on this one are recalculated. The ability of the cells to store text is used to annotate the table with column headings, titles, etc.

The spreadsheet is particularly suited to the microcomputer since it requires the fast and flexible display handling that is a feature of microcomputer systems. The common characteristic of all spreadsheets is the way in which the display screen of the computer acts as a *window on to the array of cells; if there are more rows and columns than will fit on the screen, then the spreadsheet can be scrolled horizontally or vertically to bring into view previously hidden rows or columns. To change a value it is only necessary to move the *cursor into the required cell displayed on the screen and type in the new value.

Spreadsheets can be used for storing and amending

accounts, 'what if?' financial projections, and many other applications involving tables of numbers with interdependent rows and columns. A spreadsheet is often a component of an *integrated office system.

SQR *See* Basic.

stack (pushdown list) A *list that is constructed and maintained in computer memory so that data items can only be inserted at or removed from one end of the list (called the *top*). The most recently inserted item is thus the first to be removed, i.e. the stack works on a last in first out (LIFO) basis. The operations *push* and *pop* refer respectively to the insertion and removal of items at the top of a stack. Stacks are frequently used in computing, especially in connection with subroutine *calls and *interrupt handling. *See also* queue.

stand-alone system A computer or a computer program whose operation is independent of any other device or program. A stand-alone microcomputer, for example, is capable of operation without being connected to any other piece of equipment. A diagnostic program that runs alone in a large computer system without even the operating system is also termed stand-alone.

standard deviation A measure of the amount of variation within a group of numerical values, such as measurements of a quantity. If the values are represented by

$$x_1, x_2, x_3, \ldots, x_n$$

so that there are n values in all,
their standard deviation is given by the formula

$$\sqrt{[1/n\,((x_1 - \bar{x})^2 + (x_2 - \bar{x})^2 + \ldots (x_n - \bar{x})^2)]}$$

where $\bar{x}$ is the *mean of the group. This formula is usually given in the form

$$\sqrt{[1/n\,\Sigma\,(x_i - \bar{x})^2]}$$

where i ranges from 1 to n and Σ is read as 'the sum of'. The square of the standard deviation (i.e. the above formulae without the square root) is called the *variance*.

standard interface *See* interface.

star network *See* network.

statement The basic building block of a programming language, *high-level or *low-level, and used in a *program for a particular purpose or function. It may be an *executable statement* and thus specify some operation to be performed by a computer. Alternatively it may, for example, be an input/output statement, describing the operations concerned with input and output, or it could be a *declaration, in which the names and types of variables are defined.

A program consists of a sequence of statements. It is translated into a sequence of *machine instructions by a *compiler, *assembler, or *interpreter. In the case of a high-level language, one statement is translated into many machine instructions, sometimes hundreds. A statement in an *assembly language is usually translated into one machine instruction.

static 1. Not changing or incapable of being changed over a period of time, usually while a system or device is in operation or a program is running. For example, a *static allocation* of a resource cannot be changed while processing is taking place, and *static RAM* is a type of semiconductor memory that retains its contents until written to.

2. Unable to take place during the execution of a program. For example, a *static dump* is usually taken at the end of a program run.

Compare dynamic.

STOP *See* Basic.

storage 1. (store; memory) A device or medium in which data or program instructions can be held for subsequent use by a computer. The two basic types of storage in a computer are *main store (or main storage) and *backing store (or backing storage). *See also* storage device; media.

2. The retention of data or program instructions in a *storage device or storage *medium.

3. The act of entering data in a *storage device or storage *medium.

storage allocation The allocation of specified areas of storage to the various processing tasks that are active in a computer. This controlled use of storage is necessary in a computer system in which several individual programs may be running. Each processing task is allocated sufficient *working space so that it does not interfere with another task's allocated working space. The allocation, and the amount of storage allocated, is controlled by the *operating system of the computer; with some operating systems the amount can be changed while a program is running. Storage allocation is one form of *resource allocation.

storage capacity *See* capacity.

storage cycle **1.** The sequence of events occurring when a unit of a storage device goes from one inactive state through a read and/or write phase, and back to an inactive state.

2. The minimum period of time required between successive accesses (read or write) to a storage device.

storage device A device that can receive data and retain it for subsequent use. Such devices cover a wide range of storage *capacities and speeds of *access. The semiconductor devices used as *main store have very fast speeds of access but the cost of storing each bit is high. In comparison the devices – *magnetic disks and *magnetic tapes – used as *backing store have a lower cost per bit and a greater storage capacity, but it takes somewhat longer to retrieve data.

storage location *See* location.

storage medium *See* media.

storage protection Any of many facilities that limit and hence control access to a storage device or to one or more storage locations. The intention is to prevent inadvertent interference by users and/or to provide system *security. It is achieved by prohibiting unauthorized reading or writing of data, or both. In storage devices that operate at high speed, protection is implemented by hardware (to maintain speed). For slower devices it may be done entirely by software.

store 1. (storage; memory) A device or medium in which data and program instructions can be placed and held for subsequent use by a computer. The two basic types of store in a computer are *main store and *backing store. *See also* storage device; media.

2. To enter or retain data or instructions for subsequent use by a computer.

stored program A set of instructions that can be submitted as a unit to some computer system and stored in its memory, in advance of being processed. It is then possible for instructions to be extracted automatically from memory at the appropriate time. This is done, without human intervention, by the *control unit of the computer.

The data to be manipulated by the computer, in accordance with the program instructions, is also stored in the computer memory. Instructions and data are both represented in binary form within the computer – i.e. as sequences of the binary digits 0 and 1 – and cannot be distinguished (*see* binary representation). As a result a program and the data handled by that program can be stored together, sharing the same storage space.

The idea of program and data sharing the same memory is fundamental to the great majority of modern digital computers. The concept of the stored program was documented in 1946 by John von Neumann, forming the basis of his design of EDVAC (*see* first generation computers). The concept was also considered by John W. Mauchley and J. Presper Eckert at about the same time. The first operational stored-program computers were the Manchester Mark I and

EDSAC.

The storage of programs and data in *read/write memory allows the stored data to be modified by the operations performed on it, and if necessary the program itself to be modified by the program instructions. Modifying a running program is normally avoided since it is a major source of error. The opportunities for program modification in present-day computers are reduced by dividing the program into two parts: one part must not be modified, and is therefore stored either in a software-protected area of memory or is permanently resident in read-only memory (*ROM, *PROM, or *EPROM); the other part may be modified, and is stored in an area of read/write memory.

straight insertion sort *See* sorting.

streamer *Short for* tape streamer.

Stretch *See* second generation computers.

string One form in which a collection of data items can be held in computer memory. A string is a list of letters, digits, or other *characters, examples being

cat
735
Sue Jones
COMP

It is therefore an item of textual data. Strings are in fact used mainly for handling text. The *length* of a string, i.e. the number of characters in it, is not fixed. There may be only one character. An *empty string is also a possibility. Any sequence of characters within a string is called a *substring*; *bc* and *abc* are possible substrings of *abcde*.

A string is represented in memory as a line of adjacent *locations; either the first location holds a number that gives the string length and the remaining locations hold the characters in correct order, or the string is terminated by a location containing a special noncharacter code. A string is denoted in a program by various means, depending on the programming language. In Basic, for example, a dollar sign ($) as the final character of a *variable name declares it to be a string. In many languages the characters making up a string are placed in quotation marks. An example in Basic would be

```
110    PET$ = "HORSE"
```

Various operations can be performed on strings in addition to input/output and storage. They can be joined together (*see* concatenation); they can be compared to find out if they differ; they can be searched to see if they contain a given sequence of characters; a given substring can be extracted and replaced by another sequence of characters. The operations that can be performed are known collectively as *string manipulation*, the choice of operations depending on the programming language.

string manipulation *See* string.

structured programming An approach to producing an actual program in a high-level language in which only three structures need be used to govern the flow of control in the program. These three structures – *control structures – allow for sequential, conditional, and iterative flow of control. Arbitrary transfer of control – in the form of the *GOTO statement – is expressly forbidden. As a result, for each statement or group of statements in a structured program there is precisely one entry point and one exit point. The program is thus (in theory) easy to follow, to debug, and to modify.

subprogram *Another name for* program unit.

subroutine A section of code in *assembly language (and in *Fortran) that corresponds in use and function to the *procedure, which is used in most high-level languages.

subroutine library A collection of *subroutines kept in the form of *object code in a single file on *backing store. A subroutine library will often consist entirely of routines connected with a common subject area such as graphics or numerical analysis. When a user program requiring library routines is combined with the library file by the *link editor, the library is *searched for the required routines, and only they are extracted. If searching is not used, all the library routines would be combined with the user program whether they were required or not. *See also* program library.

subscript (index) A value, usually an integer or integer expression, that is used in selecting a particular element in an *array. In computing, subscripts cannot be put in a subscript position (e.g. x_i), as the name suggests, and some other notation must be used. This usually involves brackets, as in x(i) or x[i].

substring *See* string.

suite A set of *programs or program *modules that is designed so as to meet some overall requirement, each program or module meeting some part of that requirement. For example, an accounting suite might consist of separate programs for stock control, inventory, payroll, etc.

supercomputer A computer that is capable of working at very great speed, and can thus process a very large amount of data within an acceptable time. Supercomputers are in fact now purpose-built to manipulate numbers, and are the most powerful form of *number cruncher. Present-day supercomputers can handle tens or hundreds of millions of floating-point operations per second. Even greater speeds will be possible with machines now under development. These machines are used, for example, in meteorology, engineering, nuclear physics, and astronomy. In mid-1985 there were less than 150 supercomputers in the world. Most of these were manufactured by two American companies, Cray Research and Control Data.

supervisor (executive) The part of a large *operating system that resides permanently in main store, as opposed to other sections of the operating system that are brought into main store when required. The supervisor is responsible for the supervision during some time period of many unconnected processing tasks running on the computer. It is directly concerned with controlling the use by these processing tasks of the physical components of the computer system. Different portions of the supervisor handle different components, such as storage devices or input/output devices.

swapping (roll-out roll-in) A method of handling *main store in which the contents of an area of main store are interchanged with the contents of an area of *backing store. The contents are written to backing store during periods when they are not required by the processor, and are read back into main store when needed. Swapping is controlled automatically by the *operating system of the computer and is used in systems where *virtual storage is available.

switching speed A measure of the rate at which an electronic *logic gate or *logic circuit can change the state of its output from high to low or vice versa in response to changes at its inputs. It is extremely fast but does depend on the fabrication technology; *TTL and *ECL devices have much higher speeds than *CMOS devices.

switch statement A conditional *control structure in certain programming languages (e.g. Algol-60, C) that allows a selection to be made between three or more choices. It is equivalent to the *case statement that appears, for example, in Pascal and the computed *GOTO in Fortran.

symbolic addressing A method of addressing in which reference to an *address is made in an instruction by means of some convenient symbol chosen by the programmer. The symbol may be one or more letters or other characters (appropriate to the programming language), generally bearing some relationship to the meaning of the data expected to be located at that address. This *symbolic address* is replaced by some form of computed or computable address (such as the *machine address) during the operation of an *assembler or *compiler. *See also* addressing mode.

symbol table A list kept by a *compiler or an *assembler of the *identifiers that have been used in a program. An identifier consists of a string of characters chosen by the programmer to identify a *variable, an *array, a *function, a *procedure, or some other element in the program. The properties of these identifiers, such as their address, value, or size, form part of the table.

As the translation of the source program proceeds, the compiler or assembler recognizes occurrences of identifiers – or symbols – in the text and looks them up in the table. If a symbol is already in the table, then the associated value is used by the compiler or assembler instead of the symbol. If the symbol is not in the table, then it is entered and eventually, when a definition of the symbol is found, the correct information is also entered. The compilation or assembly will terminate with errors unless all symbols are defined.

synchronous Involving or requiring a form of timing control in which sequential events or operations take place at fixed and predictable times, usually determined by an electronic signal generated by a *clock. This means that the length of time required by each set of events or operations must already be known.

Digital computers operate as synchronous machines: the start of every basic operation is under the control of the signal from an internal clock. The operations are therefore kept in synchrony – in step – with the clock signal (rather as the players in an orchestra are kept in time by the conductor's baton), and thus take place at regular and predictable times.

In *synchronous transmission* between two devices, the devices can operate continuously and each bit of data is transmitted at a fixed and predictable time. *Compare* asynchronous.

syntax Part of the description of a *programming language, akin to the grammar of English or some other natural language. The syntax of a language is the set of rules defining which combinations of letters, digits, and other characters are permitted in that language. The rules allow a valid sequence of characters to be distinguished from an invalid, i.e. a meaningless combination. They determine the form of the various constructs – *statements, *control structures, etc. – but say nothing about the meaning of the constructs. The syntax of a language can be expressed precisely and unambiguously, allowing *syntax errors to be detected. It is often expressed in a symbolic notation called *Backus-Naur form (BNF)* or some derivative of BNF. *See also* semantics.

syntax analysis (parsing) A phase in the *compilation of a program during which the program is checked for compliance with the *syntax of the programming language that has been used. If syntax errors are found then the compilation process is stopped and the errors can be corrected. Syntax analysis follows the process of *lexical analysis, and is achieved by means of a program known as a *syntax analyser* or *parser*. The input to the syntax analyser is a string of tokens from the lexical analyser.

syntax error A programming *error in which the grammatical rules of the programming language are broken, i.e. the program fails to obey the *syntax of the programming language. Syntax errors are generally detected during *compile time. The compiler would then normally produce information indicating both the location of the error(s) in the program and the kind of error involved – e.g. an unrecognized statement or an undeclared identifier.

system A set of related components that can be regarded as a collective entity. In computing the word is most widely used to mean a related set of hardware units, or programs, or both. For example, the hardware units may make up a working computer installation, or one under design, as in the terms *computer system*, *system design*; they may also be a range of computer equipment produced by a particular manufacturer, as with IBM's System/36. The programs making up a system may, for instance, be those jointly controlling the operation of a computer, i.e. the *operating system, or may be a group of programs used or required for a particular application. In the case of hardware units the word system may be broadened in meaning to include basic software, such as operating systems and compilers, associated with the hardware.

system crash *See* crash.

system design *See* systems analysis.

system flowchart (data flowchart) *See* flowchart.

system library *See* program library.

system life cycle The phases of development through which a computer system passes, usually a system providing information to its users rather than, for example, a control system. The phases have been defined in many different ways and in varying degrees of detail. Broadly speaking, they include initial conception of the system, definition of requirements, outline design, detailed design, programming, testing, implementation, maintenance, and modification.

systems analysis The analysis of the role of a computer system in, for example, fulfilling a particular job in a business, and the identification of a set of requirements that the system should meet. This can then be used as the starting point for an appropriate *system design*, from which a working version of the system is eventually produced.

In commercial programming, where the term systems analysis is most commonly used (with a variety of meanings), those involved in developing software can be described as either *systems analysts* or *programmers*. Systems analysts are responsible for identifying a set of requirements and for producing a design that meets those requirements. The design is concerned with the main components of the system and their roles and interrelationships, and sometimes with the internal structure and operation of individual components. The procedures detailed in the design by the analysts are then encoded by the programmers using a suitable programming language, usually *Cobol. The programmers are thus responsible for the production of the working version of a system, i.e. its implementation.

systems analyst *See* systems analysis.

system specification A precise and detailed statement of what a computer system – hardware or software – is to do, generally without any commitment as to how the system is to do it. A good system specification defines only the externally observable behaviour of the system, treating the system itself as a 'black box' whose internal makeup need not be considered. It is normally produced once the set of requirements to be met by the system has been identified. It is then used as a basis for the design of the system.

systems programmer, systems programming *See* systems software.

systems software The software required to produce a computer system acceptable to end-users, providing a good environment for writing, testing, running, and storing users' programs. It includes programs that are essential to the effective use of the system. *Operating systems, *compilers, *utility programs, *database management systems, and *communication systems are examples of systems software. Systems software is usually provided by the computer manufacturer and is bought together with the computer. It can also be produced or modified by competent users. The production, documentation, maintenance, and modification of systems software is known as *systems programming* and is performed by *systems programmers*. *Compare* applications program.

T

table A collection of data values, each one of which can be identified by some number. The values may be arranged in an *array and a particular item is then identified by one or more subscript values. Alternatively the data may be stored in the form of *records; one field in each record holds a *key, and the key is the means of identification.

Values can be extracted from tables using the method of *table look-up (TLU)*. The item number in the table is then the same as the value to be looked up. The table may, for example, be a list of square roots. The 4th entry in the table would then be the square root of 4, i.e. 2. Again, the table may consist of prices of numbered items on a menu. Entering the number of a particular dish gives its price; the table can thus be used to calculate the bill for a particular selection of dishes.

table look-up (TLU) *See* table.

tape *See* magnetic tape; paper tape.

tape cartridge Usually, a casing containing *magnetic tape and from which the tape is not normally removed. The casing therefore protects the tape. Some cartridges have no outer casing but have some other protective device, such as a collar. The cartridge can be loaded on a suitable *tape unit without the tape being handled. There are several types; some contain two reels while others have only one reel. Various widths of tape are used – ¼″, ½″, or wider; these widths come in various lengths. Cartridges are similar to *cassettes but are faster and have larger storage capacities.

tape cassette *See* cassette.

tape deck *Another name for* tape drive.

tape drive (tape transport; tape deck) A mechanism for moving *magnetic tape and controlling its movement. A tape drive together with magnetic read and write heads and associated electronics is known as a *tape unit. The term tape drive is often used however as another name for a tape unit.

tape format *See* format; magnetic tape.

tape label A section of coded information on *magnetic tape. A *volume label* is a *record at the very start of a magnetic tape. It holds the identity and other characteristic information about the tape itself, but not about the files stored on the tape. Volume labels are checked at run time by the *operating system to ensure that the specified tape is the one that has been mounted.

A *header label* occurs at the beginning of each file on a magnetic tape and contains information about the file as a whole, such as its name and length. A *trailer label* occurs at the end of a file and contains exactly the same information as the header label. This is a hangover from the time when some *tape units could read in either direction.

There are internationally recognized standards for the structure of tape labels.

tape punch *See* paper tape.

tape reader *See* paper tape.

tape streamer A type of *tape unit specifically designed for the rapid *backup of magnetic disks using *tape cartridges. The tape streamer is currently the only efficient way of backing up the fixed disk systems on microcomputers.

tape transport *Another name for* tape drive.

tape unit (magnetic tape unit, MTU) A peripheral device containing a mechanism for moving *magnetic tape and controlling its movement, together with recording and sensing *heads (and associated electronics) that cause data to be written to and read from the tape. Magnetic tape is held on reels or in *tape cartridges or *cassettes. The reel, cassette, or cartridge is mounted in the tape unit, and the tape is driven past the heads.

Data is recorded on the tape by the *write head*: the head receives an electrical signal coded with the data – from, say, a disk drive – and converts it into patterns of magnetization on the tape (*see* magnetic tape). Data on the tape can be sensed by the *read head*: the patterns of magnetization induce a coded electrical signal in the read head, and this signal can be fed, say, to a printer. Data is stored on and retrieved from magnetic tape by the method of *serial access, i.e. by first reading through all previous items of data on the tape until the required location is reached.

The writing of data takes place only when the tape is moving past the write head at the required speed; this speed is very high. Data is written in *blocks. After a block has been written, the tape is slowed down and stopped. It is accelerated to the right speed when the next block is to be written. The blocks are thus separated by a gap – the interblock gap – in which no data can be recorded. Writing can only occur when a device known as a *write-permit ring* is attached to the tape reel; this prevents data already on the tape being overwritten by mistake. Reading, like writing, takes place with the tape moving at constant high speed. Reading ceases when an interblock gap is sensed by the read head, and the tape is slowed down and stopped. It is subsequently accelerated for the next read.

teleconferencing A computer-based system enabling its users to participate in a conference or some other joint activity despite being at different places and/or communicating at different times. Users typically have access to computer *terminals interconnected by communication lines. A contribution made by any member of the conference will be brought to the attention of each of the other members when they next use their terminals. A record can be kept of the proceedings, to which participants can refer, and possibly votes can be taken and tabulated.

telesoftware Software transmitted by *teletext.

teletext A computer-based system for the one-way broadcasting of information using spare TV channel capacity and specially adapted domestic TV receivers. Information is provided on news, finance, sport, weather, travel, TV and radio programmes, etc. Both text and primitive graphics can be transmitted. A number of 'pages' of information are broadcast in a continuous cycle at the same time as the normal TV signal, leaving it unaffected when the receiver is used for normal viewing. Having chosen teletext mode on the control pad, a page number can then be selected. When the selected page next arrives in the transmission cycle, it is stored in local memory in the TV set and displayed on the screen. The teletext services available in the UK are *Ceefax* (BBC) and *Oracle* (ITV). *See also* videotex.

teletypewriter (typewriter terminal) A device that is similar to an electric typewriter but is used to communicate with a computer. The user can input instructions or queries to the computer by means of a keyboard, and receives output in the form of messages printed on paper by a *character printer. There may be a *paper tape punch and reader on the teletypewriter. Messages can then be transmitted directly to the computer or can be punched on paper tape for input at a later time; output can be printed or can be punched on paper tape for subsequent computer use.

Teletypewriters were once extensively used as computer *terminals, one of the most popular makes being the *Teletype*. They have been superseded by the *VDU plus keyboard.

television monitor *See* monitor.

terminal An input/output device that is used for communication with a computer from a remote site. (Some terminals are restricted to the output of data or to the input of data.) The terminal may be linked by cable to the computer, which may be in the next room or a nearby building, or the two may be connected over a telephone line. In larger computer systems there may be many terminals linked to one computer (*see* multiaccess system).

The most common type of terminal is the *VDU paired with a *keyboard: the user of the VDU types information to the computer and information from the computer is received on the VDU screen. Terminals can be designed for a particular application; examples include *point-of-sale terminals and cash dispensers at banks. If a terminal has a built-in capability to store and manipulate data – i.e. it contains a microcomputer – then it is classed as an *intelligent terminal*; without this capability it is described as *dumb*. The features of a VDU make it an intelligent terminal.

termination The end of execution of a program or some other processing task. A processing task that reaches a successful conclusion terminates by returning control to the *operating system; this is described as a *normal* termination. If the processing task reaches a point from which it cannot continue, it *aborts itself, or is aborted by the operating system; this is referred to as an *abnormal* termination.

terminator 1. A character or group of characters used to mark the end of a program *statement, *control structure, or some other item of data. For example, in Fortran every statement is terminated by an end of line while in the language C every statement must have a semicolon at the end. *Compare* separator.

2. (rogue value) A value that is added at the end of a list of data values and that is recognized by the computer as a signal to terminate some operation on the data. It must not be possible for the terminator to appear in the list of data values. If the data values consist of, say, numbers from 0 to 50, then 99 could be selected as the terminator.

test data *See* testing.

testing Any activity that checks whether a system – software or hardware – behaves in the desired manner. It is achieved by means of a *test run* in which the system is supplied with input data, and the system's responses are recorded for analysis. The input data is referred to as *test data*. Testing can be performed on individual components of the system in isolation; when the components are brought together, further testing can be performed to check that the components operate together correctly. Alternatively the behaviour of a system can be investigated without concern for individual components and their internal interfaces. Testing can never prove the correctness of a program. It can only show that the program works under certain circumstances. *See also* debugging.

test run *See* testing.

text editor A *utility program used specifically for input and modification of information in textual form. For example, a document in English can be keyed into a computer and a text editor used to create a *file. The same applies to a program in a high-level programming language. A text editor can also be used to inspect the contents of a file, and if necessary to modify them by inserting, deleting, or reordering data. Text editors are an essential means of communication between user and computer in an *interactive system. There is a considerable overlap between text editors and *word processing systems.

A *screen editor* is a text editor that enables a particular portion of a file to be displayed through a *window on a screen. The screen cursor can then be positioned at points where insertions, deletions, and other editing functions are to be performed. Since the window is movable, any portion of the file can be examined.

A *line editor* is used on terminals that do not have the ability to move the cursor around the screen, or on hardcopy terminals, or where delays inherent in long communication links (perhaps across computer *networks) make screen editing tedious.

text processing *Another name for* word processing.

thermal printer A type of nonimpact *printer – either a *line printer or a *character printer – in which the printing mechanism contains tiny heating elements. Localized heating of special heat-sensitive paper by the printing mechanism causes visible marks to appear on the paper in the shapes of the required characters. The *thermal transfer printer* is a later development in which localized heating causes special 'thermoplastic' ink to be transferred to the paper from a ribbon or film, producing an image that is more permanent and of better quality; this printer is either a character or a page printer. Thermal and thermal transfer printers are quiet in operation compared with impact printers.

third generation computers Computers designed in the 1960s or thereabouts. Since computer design is a continuous process by different groups in several countries, it is difficult to establish when a generation starts and finishes. One feature regarded as characterizing the third generation is the introduction of *integrated circuits, although discrete transistors were still used in most of this generation. Main store was almost exclusively magnetic *core store.

In general, *second generation computers were limited to what the engineers could put together and make work. Advances in electronic technology now made it possible to design a computer to suit the requirements of the tasks envisaged for the machine: the concept of computer *architecture thus became a reality with this generation. Most manufacturers introduced at least three members of a computer family, architecturally similar but differing in price and performance. The IBM 360 series, first introduced 1964, is an important example.

Comprehensive *operating systems became, more or less, part of third generation machines. *Multiprogramming was facilitated and much of the task of control of storage, input/output, and other resources became vested in the operating system or the machine itself. In addition new programming languages were introduced, such as *Cobol, and later versions of existing languages, such as *Fortran, came into use.

See also first, fourth, fifth generation computers.

throughput A measure of the overall performance of a computer system, i.e. of the amount of work performed in a given period. It can, for example, be measured in terms of *jobs per day.

time division multiplexing (TDM) *See* multiplexer.

timeout A condition that occurs when a process waiting for either an external event or the expiry of a preset time interval reaches the end of the time interval before the external event has been detected. If, for example, the process has sent a message and no *acknowledgment has been detected at the end of the preset time period, then the process may take appropriate action, such as retransmitting the message.

timer *See* counter.

time sharing A technique whereby the time of a computer can be shared among several jobs, a brief period being allocated (by the *operating system) to each job in turn. During such a period – known as a *time slice* – the job is permitted to use the resources of the computer, i.e. the processor, main store, etc. A *multiaccess system relies on time sharing.

time slice *See* time sharing.

TLU *Abbrev. for* table look-up. *See* table.

token *See* lexical analysis.

top-down design An approach to the design of a program, or a computer system, that starts with a statement of what is required of the program or system. This is broken down into a succession of different levels that are progressively more detailed. At each level more basic elements are introduced to describe exactly what is required. These elements are then defined in the next stage by introducing even more basic elements. The process stops when there is sufficient detail for the elements to be written in the chosen programming language or to be brought together to form the desired system.

touchpad *See* touch-sensitive device.

touch-sensitive device A flat rectangular device that responds to the touch of, say, a finger by transmitting the coordinates of the touched point (i.e. its position) to a computer. The touch-sensitive area may be the *VDU screen itself, in which case it is called a *touch-sensitive screen*; alternatively it may be part of the keyboard or a separate unit that can be placed on a desk. In the first case the computer user can, for example, make a selection from a number of options displayed on the screen by touching one of them; in the latter two cases movement of the finger across the so-called *touchpad* can cause the *cursor to move around the screen. *See also* light pen; mouse.

trace A report of the sequence of actions carried out during the execution of a program. It is produced by a *trace program*. A trace program records – or *traces* – the sequence in which the statements in the program are executed, and usually the results of executing the statements. It is thus possible to follow changes in data values at each stage of the program. There may be additional options offered by a trace program, for example it may trace changes to the value of a specific variable in the program. The trace information is stored in a *trace table*. A trace program can be used in *debugging a program.

trace program, trace table *See* trace.

track 1. The portion of a magnetic storage medium along

which data is stored. In *magnetic disks the tracks are concentric circles along which data is recorded as a stream of bits. There are several hundred tracks on a hard disk and in the region of a hundred on a floppy disk. The tracks are subdivided into *sectors for the purposes of reading and writing items of data. In *magnetic tape the tracks run parallel to the edges, present-day tapes usually having nine tracks. Individual characters are encoded across the width of the tape. Data is written to and read from tape in *blocks – the equivalent of sectors on disks.

2. One of several (usually eight) regions running parallel to the edges of *paper tape and along which holes can be punched.

trackerball A device for generating signals that can cause the *cursor or some other symbol to be moved about on a display. It consists of a ball supported on bearings so that it is free to rotate in any direction. The ball is held in a socket with less than half its surface exposed, and can be rotated by the operator's fingers. The direction of rotation produces a corresponding movement of the cursor.

tractor feed A technique for advancing *continuous stationery through a *printer. The mechanism used to achieve this is called a *tractor* or *forms tractor*, and consists of a pair of loops that can be rotated in steps by the printer. The continuous stationery has a row of regularly spaced holes down each side, which engage with pegs or pintles on the loops and allow the paper to be accurately registered and advanced. *See also* cut sheet feed; friction feed.

trailer label *See* tape label.

train printer *See* line printer.

transaction A single message fed into a system. The message could have been submitted in one go or could have been assembled by means of a dialogue. It could be a request for information from a *file or *database or could involve the updating of a particular piece of information, or both. The actual updating or retrieval process initiated by a transaction is also referred to as a transaction.

transaction file A collection of *transactions assembled prior to the updating of a *master file. Transaction files are used only in *batch processing. *See also* file updating.

transaction processing A method of organizing a *data processing system in which *transactions are processed to completion as they arise, rather than being collected together for subsequent processing as occurs in *batch processing. An *on-line computer is therefore required. Transaction processing is used, for example, in travel agents to check the availability of airline seats, accommodation, etc.: if acceptable a booking can be made and the booking record updated on the spot.

transfer To send data from one point to another point. The process is known as a *transfer* or *data transfer*, and more specifically may be a *file transfer. The word transfer is used to describe the movement of data within a computer system – i.e. between storage *locations – or over a long-distance *transmission line.

transfer rate *See* data transfer rate.

transistor An electronic device constructed from semiconductor material and used for amplification and switching purposes. Various types can be produced with different characteristics. In computer hardware, transistors are used for their switching properties, especially in *logic circuits and *semiconductor memory. Invented in 1948, the transistor was used at first in discrete form. Compared with the electronic valve it was much smaller, consumed very little power, and was both cheap and reliable. From about 1959 it could be fabricated as part of an *integrated circuit. In both forms it has made a great impact on computer development (*see* second, third, fourth generation computers).

translation table A table of information that is stored within a processor or a peripheral device and is used to convert encoded information into another form of code with the same meaning. There are a wide variety of codes used in computing, and sometimes more than one code may be used within a single computer system. For output devices such as printers the *ASCII code is widely used, but the code used in the processor may be *EBCDIC. An appropriate translation table would then be used to make the required conversion.

translator A program that converts a program written in one language into the equivalent program in another language. *Compilers and *assemblers are examples: a compiler translates a program written in a high-level language, such as Pascal, into machine code; an assembler translates a program written in assembly language into machine code.

transmission The sending of data from one place for reception elsewhere. The data is said to have been *transmitted.* The data may be analog or digital measurements, encoded characters, or information in general, and is carried as an encoded signal. The words transmission and transmit are usually restricted to use in telecommunications, describing the movement of data over, say, a telephone line.

transmission channel *Another name for* communication channel.

transmission line (communication line) Any physical medium used to carry information between different locations. It may, for example, be a telephone line, an electric cable, an optical fibre, a radio beam, or a laser beam. *Compare* data link.

transmit *See* transmission.

tree One form in which a collection of data items can be held in computer memory. It is a nonlinear structure, similar in form to a family tree (see diagram). The set of locations at which data items are stored are called

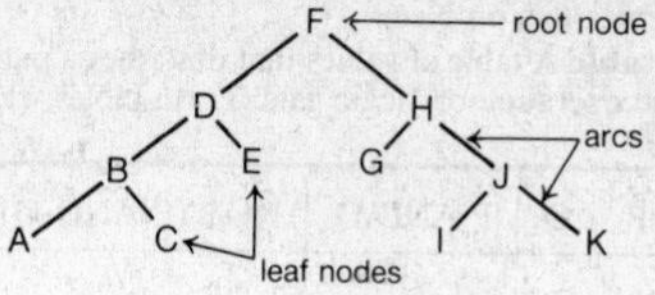

Binary tree

nodes. One particular item of data (at the *root node*) has *links to one or more other items, which in turn may possibly have links to one or more other items, and so on. There is thus a unique path from the root node in a tree to any other node. For instance, the data item C in the diagram can be accessed from the root node F via D and B.

The diagram shows an example of a *binary tree*. This is a tree in which each node has links, or arcs, to no more than two other nodes. Each node therefore consists of a data item and two links, left and right. The *leaf nodes* at the bottom of the diagram have empty links. Note that trees are drawn upside down with the root at the top and the leaves at the bottom.

truncation The process applied to a number whereby all digits after a specified number of significant digits are ignored. For example, truncation of the number 3.257 69 to 4 or to 5 digits yields 3.257 or 3.2576 respectively. In computing, truncation is usually required because the *registers in a computer can hold only a fixed number of binary digits (bits). When the result of an arithmetic operation requires more than this fixed number of bits, either truncation or *rounding will take place. The truncated value is an approximation to the true value of the number, and leads to a *truncation error*. Repeated truncation can cause a build-up of such errors and the programmer should try to minimize this problem.

truth table A table of values that describes a particular *logic operation or *logic gate. Truth tables were first

P	Q	P AND Q	NOT (P AND Q)
0	0	0	1
0	1	0	1
1	0	0	1
1	1	1	0

P	Q	P OR Q	NOT (P OR Q)
0	0	0	1
0	1	1	0
1	0	1	0
1	1	1	0

Truth tables for AND, OR, and NOT operations

used in connection with statements in logic that could be assigned one of two truth values – *true* or *false*. They can be used in computing to describe the logic operations, such as AND, OR, and NOT, that are performed for example in the *arithmetic and logic unit of a central processor. The truth table of a particular operation lists all possible combinations of the two truth values of the quantities on which the operation is to be performed (the operands), together with the truth value of the outcome of each of the possible combinations. If there are 2 operands, P and Q, there are 2^2, i.e. 4 possible outcomes. Truth tables for AND, OR, and NOT operations are shown in the table. The truth values are represented as 1 (for the value *true*) and 0 (for the value *false*).

Truth tables are also used to describe or determine the function of a logic gate. The truth table of a particular gate lists the output obtained for all the possible combinations of inputs. With 2 inputs, each of which can be at one of two voltages, there are 4 possible output voltages. With 3 inputs there are 8 possible outputs. The truth tables for *AND and *OR gates with two inputs are identical to those shown in the table for P AND Q and P OR Q. The truth table for a *NOT gate (which always has one input) is identical to that for NOT P.

truth value Either of two values, *true* or *false*, that can be assigned to a logical expression or conclusion in *Boolean algebra. The values are symbolized by T and F. When used in computing these so-called *logical values* can be represented by and stored as a single bit (usually 1 for *true* and 0 for *false*). Larger units such as a byte or word are also used to store logical values since this is simpler and quicker, although less efficient in storage space. *See also* truth table.

TTL *Abbrev. for* transistor-transistor logic. A family of *logic circuits that are all fabricated with a similar structure by the same *integrated-circuit techniques. The circuits are bipolar in nature and are all characterized by fairly high *switching speeds. *Schottky TTL* has higher switching speeds and lower power requirements than the standard TTL. Both versions have a lower *packing density than *CMOS. *See also* ECL.

turnaround document A document, such as a gas bill or a bank cheque, that after being prepared in *OCR or *MICR by a computer is 'turned around' by a person receiving it and returned to the system to complete a transaction.

turnaround time 1. The time that elapses between the submission of a job to a computer facility and the return of the results. This is the only time that really matters to someone using a computer in this way.

2. The time taken to reverse the direction of transmission on a one-way (*simplex) or a *half-duplex communication channel.

turnkey operation The delivery and installation of a complete computer system plus applications programs so that the system can be placed into immediate operational use. This operational system is called a *turnkey system.*

turtle graphics A method by which information from a computer can be turned into pictures or patterns. The original drawing device was a simple pen-plotter known as a *turtle*, a small motorized carriage carrying one or more pens and connected to the computer by a flexible cable. The carriage wheels can be precisely controlled, enabling the turtle to be steered in any direction across a floor or other flat surface covered in paper or similar material; the pens can be raised or lowered by control signals to produce the drawing.

The action of the turtle can now be simulated by graphics on the display of a small computer: the *screen turtle* is usually a triangular arrow that may or may not produce a line as it is made to move across the screen. *See also* Logo.

TV monitor *See* monitor.

twisted pair An electric cable consisting of two similar wires that are each electrically insulated by a plastic sheath and are twisted around one another to improve the transmission of signals. Bundles of tens or hundreds of twisted pairs are commonly encased in an outer protective sheath to make large cables.

two's complement *See* complement.

type *See* data type.

typewriter terminal *See* teletypewriter.

U

ULA *Abbrev. for* uncommitted logic array.

unary minus The arithmetic operation that takes only one *operand (hence the word 'unary') and that makes a positive operand negative and a negative operand positive. The *operator for unary minus is the minus sign, –. It is usually highest in the *order of precedence.

unary operator (monadic operator) *See* operator.

unbundling The separation of *systems software charges from hardware charges in the marketing of computer systems. Originally systems software was included in the purchase without additional charges since it was minimal and thus represented a small part of the total cost of the system. Unbundling has been brought about by hardware becoming less expensive while systems software became a larger proportion of the total cost. Many microcomputer systems, however, include a number of programs such as *word processors or *spreadsheets in the purchase price as an incentive to buy. This can be attractive since the computer manufacturer buys many copies of the software at a large discount and passes much of the saving on to the customer.

uncommitted logic array (ULA) A semiconductor *chip on which sets of *logic gates have been fabricated in a standard form but are not yet connected. The interconnections are made after manufacture so that a required circuit pattern can be achieved.

unconditional jump (unconditional branch) *See* jump.

underflow The condition arising when the result of an arithmetic operation in a computer is too small to be stored in the location allocated to it. For example, a fraction represented by eight leading 0s before the significant bits could not be stored in an 8-bit word. If there were no means to detect underflow, results would be unreliable and might be incorrect. Facilities are therefore provided to detect underflow. It can then be corrected. Normally the offending number is replaced by 0. *See also* overflow.

UNIVAC *Short for* universal automatic computer. *See* first generation computers.

UNIX *Trademark* An *operating system introduced by Bell Laboratories in 1971 for use on Digital Equipment's PDP 11 minicomputers. The aims of UNIX were to provide a simple uniform environment in which a relatively small number of users, with a considerable degree of cooperation, could collaborate on a single computer system. UNIX has proved extremely popular and there are now versions available for a large number of 16-bit minicomputers. UNIX has also appeared in versions for much larger machines, and for single-user microcomputer systems.

unpack *See* pack.

upward compatible *See* compatibility.

user-friendly Denoting a piece of hardware or software that a user should find easy to use, convenient, or helpful, i.e. that a user should not find confusing or intimidating.

user interface The means of communication between a person and a computer system, referring in particular to the use of input/output devices with supporting software.

user port An electrical socket in a microcomputer that with associated circuitry allows the computer user to connect additional peripheral devices. The individual pins of the port may be set or tested from a user's program. The port can be used to control or acquire data from external devices.

user program Usually, a program written by a user of a computer system. *See also* applications program.

utility program Any of a collection of programs that forms part of every computer system and provides a variety of generally useful functions. Examples of utility programs are *loaders, *text editors, *link editors, programs for copying *files from one storage device to another, for file deletion and *file maintenance, for *searching and *sorting, and for *debugging of programs.

V

validation The checking of data for correctness, or for compliance with the restrictions imposed on it. The checks are known as *validity checks*. They are done by computer, and an error message will be produced if an error is detected. For example, a validity check is performed after the input of data to ensure that the value of each item of data lies within the acceptable range, that the item is of the right type, etc. If the values are meant to lie between, say, 0 and 500, the validity check would detect any number exceeding 500 or any negative number. It would also detect that a letter had been input when a digit was intended. A validity check ought to be written into a program by the programmer. *See also* data cleaning.

validity check *See* validation.

variable A *character or group of characters that is used to denote some value stored in computer memory and that can be changed during the execution of a program. Each variable used in a program is associated with a particular *location or group of locations in memory.

The variable can take any value from a set of specified values of the same kind. The values may, for example, be *integers from the set 0 to 99 say, they may be the *real numbers that a computer is able to handle, they may be the logical values *true* or *false*, or they may even be colours from the set *red*, *green*, *blue*. The particular value taken by the variable can be changed by means of an *assignment statement. The *name selected by the programmer to identify the variable, together with the *scope of the variable and the type of data involved (e.g. integers, reals, etc.), is stated in the program in a *declaration.

variance *See* standard deviation.

VDU *Abbrev. for* visual display unit. A device that can display computer output temporarily on a screen. The information can be composed of letters, numbers, or other characters, or can be in the form of pictures, graphs, or charts. The information can be changed or erased under the control of a computer; this computer may be at a remote site or may be a microcomputer of which the VDU forms a part. The VDU is usually paired with a *keyboard, by which information can be fed into the computer. A VDU plus keyboard is now the most commonly used computer *terminal.

The screen can normally display 80 characters on each of 24 lines, but these numbers vary from one machine to another. Each character can be chosen from 96 standard letters, numbers, punctuation marks, brackets, etc., plus a number of other symbols. A screen with graphics capability can draw pictures, graphs, etc. Instead of being divided into rows and columns, the graphics screen is divided into a much larger number of tiny rectangular areas called *pixels* (short for *picture elements*). Each pixel can be any one of a number of shades (e.g. of grey) or any of a number of colours if it is a colour display.

Most VDUs have a selection of display attributes that can be used to emphasize or differentiate items. For instance a character can be made to blink; its intensity can be dim or bright; it can be underlined; it can be displayed in *reverse video (e.g. bright characters on a dark background rather than vice versa); the colour of foreground and background can be set.

vector A one-dimensional *array.

vector graphics A method of producing pictorial images in which each line of the image is produced by a continuous movement of the spot on a VDU screen or the pen of a plotter. *Compare* raster graphics.

verification The checking of the accuracy of data after it has been transcribed. It is done most commonly when data has been encoded by an operator at a keyboard reading from a document. The document is subsequently rekeyed by another operator, and the two sets of input data compared by machine. Any differences are indicated and suitable action is taken. Corrections can be made if the encoded data is recorded on magnetic tape or disk. The verification process may be performed on a machine dedicated to the task, and called a *verifier*. When data is recorded on magnetic media, as is generally the case, the same equipment (keyboard and display connected to the recording system) can be used for the entry of the data and its verification.

verifier *See* verification.

videotex A computer-based system providing information to users via telephone links. Both text and primitive graphics can be transmitted. Special videotex terminals are available for professional use, at a travel agent, for example, and include a colour *monitor, a *keyboard, and a *modem (for connection to the telephone network). A microcomputer with special software and a modem or *acoustic coupler can be used in a home or school. The user selects information by typing in numbers, and the information is transmitted as a coded telephone signal and displayed on the screen, one 'page' at a time. Videotex provides *interactive access to one or more sources of information; dialogue between the user and the videotex computers is conducted by means of the keyboard. Videotex is used at present mainly by businesses. Systems available in the UK include British Telecom's public *Prestel* service and many private systems. *See also* teletext.

viewdata An early generic name for *videotex and for the UK's Prestel service.

virtual storage A means of effectively extending the amount of storage space available in the *main store of a (usually large) computer. In virtual storage systems, programs can be written requiring more main store than is physically present in the computer (or more than the *operating system is prepared to allow them). The programs can address areas of main store that do not in fact exist, and during execution parts of the program not currently needed remain on *backing store.

Data and instructions are divided by the operating system into blocks of fixed length; these blocks are called *pages*. When a reference to a storage location is made, the system hardware detects whether or not the required location is physically present in main store. If it is not, an *interrupt is generated and the page containing the required location is transferred, by the operating system, from backing store to main store. A page is thus the unit of interchange between backing store and main store. When a page held in main store is no longer required by the processor, it may be transferred back to backing store. The backing-store device is known as a *swapping device*.

visual display unit *See* VDU.

VLSI *Abbrev. for* very large scale integration. *See* integrated circuit.

voice input device A device in which speech is used to feed data or system commands directly into a computer system. Such equipment involves the use of *speech recognition processes, and can replace or supplement other input devices. Some voice input devices can recognize spoken words from a predefined vocabulary; other devices have to be trained for a particular speaker.

volatile memory A type of memory whose contents are lost as soon as the power supply to the memory is switched off. *Compare* nonvolatile memory.

volume label *See* tape label.

W

WAN *Abbrev. for* wide area network.

wand A hand-held penlike device that is connected to a computer and is used to read printed *bar codes or *OCR characters. It is moved steadily over the surface of the printing, and an audible and/or visual signal is produced if the data has been sensed satisfactorily.

warm start *See* restart.

while loop (while do loop) *See* loop.

wide area network (WAN) A computer *network that is distinguished from a *local area network because of its longer-distance communications. The network may cover, say, a whole country or may include the sites of a large multinational organization. The communications are usually provided by one or more national or international governmental entities such as British Telecom. The facilities offered by such bodies include data communications over telephone lines or over dedicated lines – special high-quality lines reserved for the purpose; the link-up is made by means of *modems. More recently national and international *packet switching services have been provided. The term wide area network is often used to mean the public packet switching service of a particular country or region.

Winchester disk (Winchester) The hard magnetic disk used in a *Winchester disk drive.

Winchester disk drive A highly advanced *disk drive introduced by IBM in the early 1970s. It has been adopted by many manufacturers and is now used in large and small computers. It uses one or more hard *magnetic disks – known as *Winchester disks* – that are mounted inside a hermetically sealed container together with the read/write heads and their supporting mechanism. Originally this module was removable from the disk drive. Recent Winchester drives tend to have the disks plus heads permanently attached and sealed within the disk drive. The design of the heads and the disks has increased the recording *density by increasing the number of tracks per inch and the number of bits per inch of track. The storage *capacity of the disks ranges from a few megabytes in the case of microcomputers to over a thousand megabytes for mainframes.

window A rectangular area on a display screen inside which a portion of a stored image or file can be displayed. The window can be of any size up to that of the screen; more than one window can usually be displayed at once. The process of obtaining the portion of the image or file visible through the window is called *windowing*. The visible window formed by the process can be moved to allow examination of the different portions making up the entire stored image or file.

word (machine word; computer word) A collection of bits that is treated as a single unit by the hardware of a computer. The number of bits in a word is called the *word length*. The word length is fixed in most computers, and in present-day machines is usually 32 bits or 16 bits. *Main store is divided into either words or *bytes. In the former case, each storage location holds one word, and the word is thus the smallest addressable unit, i.e. the smallest unit to be identified by an *address.

What the contents of a word signify is determined entirely by its context. A given bit sequence could represent a *machine instruction in one part of main store, while in another part it might represent an *integer number, a *real (i.e. fractional) number, or perhaps one or more *characters, depending on word length. A 16-bit word, for example, could hold integers between −32 768 and +32 767, or two characters, or a machine instruction. 16 bits is not really enough to store *floating-point numbers to any useful *precision, so a number of consecutive words are used.

word length *See* word.

word processing (wp, WP; text processing) A computer facility that enables users to compose letters, reports, and other documents and to edit, reformat, store, and print them. It may be a *stand-alone word-processing system consisting of a keyboard with extra keys to perform wp functions, a screen, a printer, and a floppy or hard disk as *backing store. Alternatively it may be a general-purpose microcomputer system that has a wp program as part of its repertoire. These two systems are currently converging: stand-alone machines are becoming more flexible and able to perform tasks other than wp, while the quality of wp programs available for general-purpose micros is improving so that it is effectively as good as that of the stand-alone systems.

The document is automatically displayed on the screen of the system as it is typed on the keyboard, and words can be corrected, inserted, and deleted. The system allows the user to specify left and right margins between which text is automatically justified (if desired) as it is typed in, and sometimes hyphenated. It is usually possible to reposition blocks of text in the document, to search for and replace strings of text in the document, to add text from other files, to have boldface and underlined text, and to include spaces for tables, figures, etc. Spelling can sometimes be checked.

The document can be stored for future use and/or printed any number of times, generally in a choice of formats and paper sizes. Variable information such as names, addresses, or prices can be substituted when printing the document for easy production of form letters, contracts, etc.

word processor (wp, WP) A computer system designed specifically for *word processing.

work file A *file held very briefly on backing store and used to overcome space limitations in main store or to carry information between one job and the next.

working space (workspace; working store; working area; scratchpad) A portion of *main store that is used for the temporary storage of data during processing, including intermediate results needed during a calculation. The contents of the working space will not be preserved after the program has finished. It is the responsibility of the programmer to ensure that the working space does not overlap the program code, although in some high-level languages and operating systems this is made difficult or impossible.

workspace *Another name for* working space.

workstation A position in, say, an office, data processing room, or factory where an operator has access to all the facilities required to perform a particular task that involves a computer in some way. The electronic equipment would normally include at least a *keyboard and a *VDU, and possibly a *printer, *disk drive, *mouse, and *communication line.

wp or **WP** *Abbrev. for* word processing or word processor.

wrap-around A feature of a VDU or printer, allowing it to output lines of text that would otherwise be too long to be displayed or printed in their entirety. The line appears as two or more successive lines on the screen or paper.

write To record data in some form of storage, usually either in a *magnetic medium such as disk or tape or in semiconductor *RAM.

write head *See* tape unit.

write instruction A *machine instruction that causes

an item of data to be recorded on some form of storage.

write-permit ring (write ring) *See* tape unit.

X,Y,Z

XON/XOFF *See* flow control.

XOR gate *Short for* exclusive-OR gate. *See* nonequivalence gate.